Landmarks in English Literature

Landmarks in English Literature

Philip Gaskell

Edinburgh University Press

© Philip Gaskell, 1998
Edinburgh University Press
22 George Square, Edinburgh

Typeset in Ehrhardt and Futura by
Norman Tilley Graphics, Northampton,
and printed and bound in Great Britain by
the Cromwell Press Ltd,

A CIP record for this book is available
from the British Library

ISBN 0 7486 1060 X

Contents

Preface   vii
Acknowledgements   viii
A Note on Texts   ix

1   The Literary Canon   1
General principles – Chronological charts – Cultural
evolution – Canonical authors – The canon and modern
critical theory – The instability of the canon – The canonical
list: medieval, renaissance, neoclassical, romantic, modernist

2   Fiction   31
The nature of fiction – Structure – Plot and suspense –
Author and narrator – Point of view – Setting – Character –
Dialogue and monologue – Symbolism and allegory –
Intertextuality and metafiction – Seven novels

3   Poetry   70
The nature of poetry – Metre – Sound – Language –
Seven poems

4   Drama   104
The nature of drama – Techniques and constraints –
Origins and early development – Later development

Appendix: Creative Writing – Creative Reading   141
Creative writing and the study of literature – The writer's
materials – Planning and research for fiction – Revision –
Equipment for writing – Publication – Copyright

Annotated Bibliography   154
Language – Literature – Creative writing

Index   165

Someone said: "The dead writers are remote
from us because we *know* so much more
than they did." Precisely, and
they are that which we know.
(T. S. Eliot, 1919)

Preface

This book aims to make English Literature[1] available to general readers and students who want to find out more about the major authors and their work. It attempts to enable people to appreciate and enjoy works of literature by seeing them in context, both past and present, and by finding out how they work technically. It is in fact a sort of instruction book that sets out to help people to see where the books they read belong in the history and development of literature, to place them in the context of their times, to understand how they have been made by their authors; and in this way to appreciate them more effectively. Its aim is not so much to tell people how to respond aesthetically or what to think, but to provide them with the means to respond and think for themselves, with an approach that is more appreciative, historical and technical than theoretical or critical.

The book begins with an annotated "canonical" list of those authors that anyone wanting to place and understand a work of literature has to be aware of, together with notes on a supplementary list of secondary but still important authors. Then it describes and considers in turn the nature, history, and techniques of the three main literary modes, fiction, poetry, and drama, with substantial examples. Lastly there is an appendix on creative writing as a method of learning about literature; and an annotated bibliography of reference books and texts.

---

[1] The term "English Literature" refers here not to the literature of England alone but to that of the British Isles, including Ireland; it does not include the whole of literature in English.

Acknowledgements

I am very grateful for advice and assistance given to me by Mary Hocking, John Hurst, Jackie Jones, Jo Pye, Dr Gillian Rogers, Alison Sproston, and Dr Ella Westland.

The publisher wishes to thank the following for permission to use material in copyright: Faber and Faber Ltd for excerpts from: 'Tradition and the Individual Talent', and 'The Love Song of J. Alfred Prufrock' in *Collected Poems 1909–1962*, by T. S. Eliot; 'O Where are you going?' from *Collected Poems* by W. H. Auden; Letter to Harriet Monroe from *Letters of Ezra Pound*; and *Rosencrantz and Guildenstern are Dead* by Tom Stoppard. Kingsley Amis from *Memoirs*, copyright © Kingsley Amis 1991, reprinted by kind permission of Jonathan Clowes Ltd, London, on behalf of the Literary Estate of Kingsley Amis. From *Don Quixote* by Cervantes, translated by J. M. Cohen (Penguin Classics 1950), copyright © J. M. Cohen 1950; from *The Canterbury Tales* by Geoffrey Chaucer, translated by Nevill Coghill (Penguin Classics 1951, 4th edn 1977), copyright © 1951 by Nevill Coghill, copyright © Nevill Coghill 1958, 1960, 1975, 1977; from *Fairy Tales* by Charles Perrault, translated by Geoffrey Brereton (Penguin Classics 1957), copyright © Geoffrey Brereton 1957, reproduced by permission of the Author's Estate. Extracts from *Ulysses* by James Joyce, copyright © the Estate of James Joyce. Extract from 'The Ruined Cottage', reprinted from William Wordsworth, *The Ruined Cottage and the Pedlar*, edited by James A. Butler, copyright © 1978 by Cornell University, used by permission of the publisher, Cornell University Press. The Society of Authors on behalf of the Bernard Shaw Estate for extracts from *Androcles and the Lion* and *Saint Joan* by Bernard Shaw. From 'Oedipus the King' from *Theban Plays* by Sophocles, reproduced by kind permission of W. W. Norton & Company and Penguin. From the *Shepherds' Play* and from *Everyman*, reproduced by kind permission of W. W. Norton & Company. Every effort has been made to trace copyright holders; if any have been inadvertently overlooked, the publisher will be pleased to make the necessary arrangement at the first opportunity.

A Note on Texts

As far as possible, quotations from literary texts are taken from the first editions, with modernisation of spellings and so on. Recommended paperback texts are listed in the Annotated Bibliography at the end.

Chapter 1

The Literary Canon

General Principles

The immediate need, when approaching an unfamiliar work of literature with the aim of understanding and appreciating it, is to see where it belongs in the literary landscape. This means, first, having a general historical picture – political, economic, and cultural – of as much of the past as possible over the whole period of English literature from the mid-fourteenth to the mid-twentieth century; and secondly knowing something at first hand about the relatively small number of authors whose work has been central to the development of our literary culture, and whose influence has been particularly strong on their successors.

The first requirement can best be met by a background of a broad education and good general knowledge; though making a chronological chart will help to organise the material and fill in any gaps.

The second requirement will probably need some hard reading, but provided we can be sensible about working on a list of "canonical" authors and their most important works, there should be no great difficulty here either. I say that good sense is needed at this point because lists of "great authors", "100 best books" and so on are liable to attract ribald comment in professional academic circles (though it is on just such lists that university literature courses are in fact based). But, although any well-educated person will certainly have heard of all the names on my list of primary canonical authors, it is most unlikely that he or she will have had first-hand experience of reading all of them. If we are frank about it, this applies to nearly everybody; even the graduate in English who has actually read a substantial amount of the writings of every one of the eighteen authors on my list[1] – not just snippets, or books about them – is a rarity.

---

[1] This does not even include all the twenty-six authors considered by Harold Bloom to make up the Western Canon since Dante; or the thirty-six authors on my supplementary list. For all these lists, see pp. 8–9 below.

Chronological Charts

Putting authors into their historical contexts requires some sort of chronological scaffolding to which they can be attached. The simplest form of such scaffolding is a series of home-made charts, consisting of several sheets for each century, which are written out with dates marked down the margins, and five or six factual columns across the page. The headings for the columns might be: year; world history; British history; technology; painting, music; literature; year.[2] See specimen chronological chart on pages 4–7.

Cultural Evolution

What we must do next is to identify the influential authors, and get a sense of how literature has developed at their hands. Evolution is a familiar concept. We are aware that virtually everything around us develops over time, from the lifeless rocks of the lithosphere, through the living organisms of the botanical and zoological kingdoms, to the incorporeal cultures of our own species; all are continuously evolving into new and usually more complex – though not necessarily "better" – forms. Each of these changed forms, we see, is based on the development that immediately preceded it, so that most of the characteristics of the predecessor are preserved and reappear in the next version; thus the development before the last is not lost, merely changed slightly; likewise with the development before that, and so on. It follows that "new" forms do not normally appear without incorporating some "old" characteristics. (Eventually, of course, the form of the final version may differ markedly from that of its original progenitors, but with enough information the steps of the development can be traced.)

So it is with the arts. In a picture gallery it is plain to see how successive "schools" of painting derive from each other. Similarly with music, it is equally plain that even the most remarkable innovators knew and were influenced by the work of their predecessors. Not surprisingly, the same process may be traced in literature. Every novelist, every poet, every dramatist – however great or small – writes to some extent under the influence of all that his or her predecessors have written in the same modes. This is not to say that he himself will have read everything that they have written, or that he is consciously copying his predecessors' work; but simply that their work will have come to him as an unavoidable influence through the medium of whatever he *has* read.

---

[2] Many encyclopaedias include chronological charts of this sort, which can be used for starting to fill in home-made ones.

Literary influences may be seen both in the general output of successive cultures – for example, the Latin literature of Augustan Rome is obviously derived from the Greek literature of earlier periods – and in the work of particular major writers. Some literary influences are much stronger than others. It is hard to see how any eighteenth-, nineteenth- or twentieth-century writer – whether novelist, poet, or dramatist – in Europe or America can have avoided being influenced to some degree by Shakespeare; on the other hand the influence of a minor poet writing in a little-known language will have been very slight.

Canonical Authors

A way of reducing the manifold possibilities of literary achievement and influence to a manageable form is to attempt the construction of a literary canon – a list of generally acknowledged important authors – that recognises not only the high quality and innovative power of the writers included in it, but also the strength of their influence on those who followed them. To do this in a thoroughgoing way would mean trying to identify all the great writers from Homer onwards who have had a major influence on the course of western literature, including many writing in languages other than English. Harold Bloom's *The Western Canon* (1994) attempted to do this – but only from Dante onwards – with a list of twenty-six "canonical" western writers: Dante, Chaucer, Montaigne, Shakespeare, Cervantes, Milton, Molière, Johnson, Goethe, Wordsworth, Jane Austen, Dickens, Whitman, George Eliot, Tolstoy, Ibsen, Emily Dickinson, Freud, Proust, Joyce, Virginia Woolf, Kafka, Pessoa, Borges, Neruda, and Beckett.[3]

We shall be less ambitious here with a shorter list dealing only with writers in English, and again looking for the best, the most innovative, and the most influential authors (though of course the "best", the "most innovative", and the "most influential" authors are commonly the same): Chaucer, Spenser, Shakespeare, Donne, Milton, Dryden, Pope, Johnson, Blake, Wordsworth, Jane Austen, Byron, Tennyson, Dickens, George Eliot, Conrad, Joyce, and T. S. Eliot. Both here and in subsequent chapters we shall not be looking at writers later than the modernists of the early 1920s; the canon is continuously developing, and we cannot yet identify those mid- and late twentieth-century writers who will eventually be recognised as canonical.

[3] Bloom's list is given here in chronological order according to dates of birth; he arranges them slightly differently. The names will be familiar, except perhaps for those of the Portuguese poet Fernando Pessoa and the Chilean poet Pablo Neruda; he does not include major classical influences on later western literature, such as Virgil, Horace, and Ovid.

Specimen chronological chart, covering the last third of the nineteenth century

	World history	British history	Technology
1867	N. German Confederation and Austro-Hungarian Empire founded	2nd Reform Bill	dynamite Faraday d.
1868		1st TUC Gladstone PM	typewriter
1869	Suez Canal opened Gandhi b.		margarine
1870	Franco-Prussian War (to 1871) Lenin b.	Education Act	celluloid
1871	German Empire founded		
1872		secret ballot	
1873			
1874		Winston Churchill b. Disraeli PM	
1875			
1876			telephone
1877	US Reconstruction ends Russo-Turkish War (to 1878)	Queen Victoria Empress of India	frozen meat
1878			
1879	Stalin b. Trotsky b.		electric light
1880		1st Boer War (to 1881) Gladstone PM	
1881	Tsar Alexander II assassinated	Disraeli d.	anthrax vaccine
1882	F. D. Roosevelt b.		petrol engine
1883	Karl Marx d. Mussolini b.		skyscraper
1884			Maxim machine gun; Linotype

Painting, music	Literature	
	Trollope, *Last Chronicle of Barset*; Ibsen, *Peer Gynt*; Marx, *Das Kapital I*; Baudelaire d.	1867
	Browning, *The Ring and the Book* Morris, *The Earthly Paradise* (to 1879)	1868
	Trollope, *Phineas Finn* Gide b.	1869
	D. G. Rossetti, *Poems* Dickens d.	1870
	G. Eliot, *Middlemarch*; L. Carroll, *Through the Looking Glass*; Proust b.	1871
	Tennyson, 1st *Collected Poems*; Hardy, *Under the Greenwood Tree*; Butler, *Erewhon*	1872
	Rimbaud, *Un Saison en Enfer* Tolstoy, *Anna Karenina* (to 1876)	1873
1st Impressionist Exhibition	Hardy, *Far from the Madding Crowd*; Trollope, *Phineas Redux*; Thomson, *The City of Dreadful Night*	1874
Gilbert and Sullivan, *Trial by Jury*; Bizet, *Carmen*	Trollope, *The Way We Live Now*	1875
Brahms, 1st Symphony; Wagner, *Ring* cycle	Trollope, *The Prime Minister*; James, *Roderick Hudson*; G. Eliot, *Daniel Deronda*; Twain, *Tom Sawyer*	1876
Tchaikovsky, *Swan Lake*	James, *The American* Ibsen, *Pillars of Society*	1877
	Hardy, *The Return of the Native* Masefield b.; Edward Thomas b.	1878
	James, *The Europeans*; Meredith, *The Egoist*; Ibsen, *A Doll's House*; E. M. Forster b.	1879
	Trollope, *The Duke's Children*; Dostoievsky, *The Brother Karamazov*; Ouida, *Moths*; George Eliot d.; Flaubert d.	1880
Picasso b. Bartók b.	James, *The Portrait of a Lady* Ibsen, *Ghosts*; Dostoievsky d.	1881
Manet, *Bar at the Folies Bergères*; Stravinsky b.	Stevenson, *Treasure Island*; Ibsen, *Enemy of the People*; D. G. Rossetti d.; Trollope d.; Joyce b.; Virginia Woolf b.	1882
Wagner d.	Trollope, *Autobiography*; Nietzsche, *Also sprach Zarathustra*; Turgenev d.	1883
	Ibsen, *The Wild Duck*; Twain, *Huckleberry Finn*; OED begins; RV of the *Old Testament*	1884

Specimen chronological chart, covering the last third of the nineteenth century *continued*

	World history	British history	Technology
1885		Salisbury PM	steam turbine safety bicycle
1886		1st Home Rule Bill Gladstone PM Salisbury PM	
1887		Queen Victoria Golden Jubilee	
1888	Wilhelm II Kaiser		Kodak box camera
1889	Hitler b. Nehru b.		petrol-powered car; Eiffel Tower
1890	Bismarck falls		1st English power station
1891	Trans-Siberian Railway (to 1904)	Parnell d.	
1892		Gladstone PM	thermos flask diesel engine
1893	Goering b.	2nd Home Rule Bill ILP founded	zip fastener
1894	Dreyfus affair (to 1906) Nicholas II Tsar	Rosebery PM	
1895	Kiel Canal opens	Salisbury PM	cine film X-rays
1896	Herzl founds Zionism; Nobel prizes; 1st modern Olympiad		radioactivity of uranium
1897			wireless messages aspirin
1898	Spanish-American War Zola, *J'accuse*	Gladstone d.	submarine radium
1899		2nd Boer War (to 1902)	
1900		Labour Party founded	zeppelin quantum theory

Painting, music	Literature	
	Haggard, *King Solomon's Mines*; Zola, *Germinal*; DNB begins; Pater, *Marius the Epicurean*; D. H. Lawrence b.; Ezra Pound b.	1885
	Stevenson, *Dr Jekyll and Mr Hyde*, *Kidnapped*; Hardy, *The Mayor of Casterbridge*; S. Sassoon b.	1886
Borodin, *Prince Igor*	Hardy, *The Woodlanders*; Doyle, *A Study in Scarlet*; R. Brooke b.	1887
	Kipling, *Plain Tales from the Hills*; Strindberg, *Miss Julie*; T. S. Eliot b.	1888
	Tolstoy, *The Kreutzer Sonata*; R. Browning d.; G. M. Hopkins d.	1889
Mascagni, *Cavalleria Rusticana*; Van Gogh d.	E. Dickinson, *Poems*; Wilde, *The Picture of Dorian Gray*; Frazer, *The Golden Bough*; Ibsen, *Hedda Gabler*; Morris, *News from Nowhere*	1890
	Gissing, *New Grub Street*; Hardy, *Tess of the d'Urbervilles*; Rimbaud d.	1891
Dvořák, *New World Symphony*	Shaw, *Widowers' Houses*; Yeats, *Countess Kathleen*; Tennyson d.	1892
	Thompson, *The Hound of Heaven*; Kipling, *Many Inventions*; Maupassant d.	1893
Toulouse-Lautrec, *Moulin Rouge*	Moore, *Esther Waters*; Grossmith, *Diary of a Nobody*; Kipling, *The Jungle Book*; Du Maurier, *Trilby*; Stevenson d.	1894
	Yeats, *Poems*; Hardy, *Jude the Obscure*; Conrad, *Almayer's Folly*; Wilde, *The Importance of Being Earnest*	1895
Puccini, *La Bohème*	Housman, *A Shropshire Lad*; Chekhov, *The Seagull*; W. Morris d.	1896
Brahms d.	Wells, *The Invisible Man*; Conrad, *The Nigger of the "Narcissus"*	1897
	James, *The Turn of the Screw*; Shaw, *Plays Pleasant and Unpleasant*; Wells, *The War of the Worlds*; Hemingway b.; Fontane d.	1898
Monet, *Water Lilies* Joplin, *Maple Leaf Rag*	Kipling, *Stalky & Co.*; Tolstoy, *Resurrection*; Freud, *The Interpretation of Dreams*	1899
Puccini, *Tosca*	Conrad, *Lord Jim*; Shaw, *Three Plays for Puritans*; Chekhov, *Uncle Vanya*; Wilde d.; Nietzsche d.	1900

These are the eighteen central figures about whom we must make it our business to learn something at first hand. If a serious effort is made to read the works proposed on this list, readers will find that they soon have a clear idea of their importance and position relative to each other, and that it will be possible to fit any *other* author or work that is to be read into its place in the major pattern. To make this easier, brief notes on thirty-six other important authors are intercalated with the primary canonical group of eighteen.

The whole list, in chronological order of date of birth, is as follows (the eighteen major canonical authors are given in **bold type**; authors who also figure in Chapter 2 on Fiction are marked F, in Chapter 3 on Poetry P, and in Chapter 4 on Drama D):

Medieval
William Langland, poet, c.1330–c.1400
Geoffrey Chaucer, poet, c.1343–1400   P
John Skelton, poet, c.1460–1529

Renaissance
Sir Thomas Wyatt, poet, c.1503–1542
Henry Howard Earl of Surrey, poet, c.1517–1547
Edmund Spenser, poet, c.1552–1599
Christopher Marlowe, dramatist and poet, 1564–93   D
William Shakespeare, dramatist and poet, 1564–1616   D
Ben Jonson, dramatist and poet, 1573–1637   D
John Donne, poet, c.1572–1631   P
John Webster, dramatist, c.1580–c.1625   D
George Herbert, poet, 1593–1633
John Milton, poet, 1608–74   P
Andrew Marvell, poet, 1621–78

Neoclassical
John Dryden, poet and dramatist, 1631–1700   D
Daniel Defoe, journalist and novelist, c.1661–1731
Jonathan Swift, satirist and poet, 1667–1745
Alexander Pope, poet, 1688–1744   P
Samuel Richardson, novelist, 1689–1761   F
Henry Fielding, novelist, 1707–54
Samuel Johnson, critic and essayist, 1709–84
Laurence Sterne, novelist, 1713–68
Thomas Gray, poet, 1716–71
Oliver Goldsmith, poet, dramatist and novelist, c.1730–1774 D

Romantic
William Blake, poet, 1757–1827
Robert Burns, poet, 1759–96
William Wordsworth, poet, 1770–1850   P
Sir Walter Scott, novelist and poet, 1771–1832
Samuel Taylor Coleridge, poet and critic, 1772–1834
Jane Austen, novelist, 1775–1817   F
George Gordon, Lord Byron, poet, 1788–1824
Percy Bysshe Shelley, poet, 1792–1822
John Keats, poet, 1795–1821
Alfred, Lord Tennyson, poet, 1809–92   P
Elizabeth Gaskell, novelist and biographer, 1810–65
William Makepeace Thackeray, novelist, 1811–63
Robert Browning, poet, 1812–89
Charles Dickens, novelist, 1812–70   F
Anthony Trollope, novelist, 1815–82
Emily Brontë, poet and novelist, 1818–48
George Eliot, novelist, 1819–80   F
Matthew Arnold, poet and critic, 1822–88
Thomas Hardy, novelist and poet, 1840–1928
Gerard Manley Hopkins, poet, 1844–89
Oscar Wilde, dramatist and poet, 1854–1900

Modernist
George Bernard Shaw, dramatist and critic, 1856–1950   D
Joseph Conrad, novelist, 1857–1924   F
Rudyard Kipling, short-story writer and poet, 1865–1936
William Butler Yeats, poet, 1865–1939
Edward Morgan Forster, novelist, 1879–1970
James Joyce, novelist, 1882–1941   F
Virginia Woolf, novelist, 1882–1941
David Herbert Lawrence, novelist, 1885–1930
Thomas Stearns Eliot, poet and dramatist, 1888–1965   P

The Canon and Modern Critical Theory

Some relatively recent schools of literary criticism have argued on theoretical grounds against the idea of working from a list of generally acknowledged important authors; but, since my approach to literature will be more appreciative, historical, and technical than critical and theoretical, I do not propose to enter these debates here. There are good introductory accounts of literary criticism and dictionaries of literary terms which cover the development of criticism from Aristotle onwards, and which explain the essentials of modern critical theory.[4]

A further objection to the canonical approach is that it is likely to be based on the work of "Dead White Males". In the list of prominent authors given above, all are Dead, all are White, and 90 per cent are Male. This is difficult to avoid because there are relatively few women writers – and scarcely any Living Black Female writers – of sufficient artistic quality to put in place of the Dead White Males in any general account of English literature.

The Instability of the Canon

The canon proposed here is of course essentially personal; it is my choice, and other critics might choose other writers. It represents, moreover, a single point in a continuously evolving process of identifying and appreciating major writers.

There can be no satisfying every taste with any one list. Some names are omitted which others will think should be included, and some included which others will say should be omitted. There is also an obvious lack of foreign influences: Dante certainly influenced the development of English literature, as did the major ancient Greek and Latin authors. There were also writers who exercised a great influence on their contemporaries and immediate successors, but who do not now seem quite eligible for the first team: Scott and Thackeray (who are included in the supplementary list) are obvious examples.

A case will be made for the inclusion of each of the authors on our canonical list; but it is certain that someone writing in 1900 would have produced a different list, and that someone else writing 100 years hence will produce a different one again. The evolution of the canon results both from the appearance of new talents and new ways of writing, and from changes that take place from one period to the next of critical sensibility, of literary points of view, and of developments in literary scholarship.

The Canonical List

The list is given in five sections – medieval, renaissance, neoclassical, romantic, modernist – with notes to explain why each author is included,

---

[4] The modern critical theories referred to include, among others, the New Criticism, Structuralism, Deconstruction, Feminism, and the New Historicism; see the Annotated Bibliography, p. 157 below.

and warning of any particular difficulties that may be encountered. The sections headed "What to read" are obviously not all-inclusive. The major, essential, works are proposed; and, in addition to this, for the poets, Helen Gardner's *New Oxford Book of English Verse* (*NOBEV*) is referred to for usually shorter but still important works. The shorter notes on the additional authors follow a similar pattern.

Medieval

The change from Old to Middle English – from a Germanic dialect to the earliest form of our language, which added an extensive French vocabulary and evolved a simplified grammar – was completed by the end of the thirteenth century. Soon afterwards, two fourteenth-century poets, contemporaries of each other, each wrote major works in the new language. The style of one, William Langland, looked back to the Old English form in which alliteration and caesura[5] stops dominated the verse of *Piers Ploughman*; while that of the other, Geoffrey Chaucer, looked forward to the stressed and rhymed verses of renaissance Europe. Langland had few followers; Chaucer set the course of poetry in English.

Chaucer (Geoffrey Chaucer, c.1343–1400). Chaucer was a prolific author in both verse and prose, but the work that has most influenced his successors is *The Canterbury Tales*; indeed it is in this exuberant, many-coloured collection of stories that the future of English poetry was contained. Unfortunately, Middle English can put up a subtler and more misleading barrier between writer and modern reader than does a good translation of a work in a foreign language, because the meanings of many apparently familiar words then differed more or less from what we mean by them now. One solution, not altogether satisfactory, is to use the Penguin "translation" into modern English verse by Nevill Coghill; but it is probably better to work through the original, old spelling and all, with a glossary. Apart from the problem of the language, Chaucer's tales – many of them traditional – are relatively easy to understand, having a timeless quality that does not date.

What to read: Canterbury tales: the General Prologue; the Miller's tale; the Wife of Bath's prologue and tale (precise dates unknown, but probably written c.1387–1400).[6] See also *NOBEV*, "The Complaint of Troilus" and "Love Unfeigned" from *Troilus and Criseyde* (c.1385–90).

---

[5] These technical terms, and others such as blank verse, heroic couplets, metaphysical, sonnet, and stress, are explained in Chapter 3 on Poetry, below.

[6] See pp. 81–5 below.

Chaucer's contemporary **William Langland** (c.1330–c.1400) was a cleric in minor orders, whose vivid religious allegory of *The Vision of Piers the Ploughman* tells how the poet, asleep on the Malvern Hills, sees in a dream a panorama of mankind laid out in front of him – a fair field full of folk – in all its variety and imperfection; and how he is led on to seek redemption by trying to live a good Christian life in spite of the difficulties in his way, Piers himself figuring both as everyman and as redeemer. Langland's west-country dialect, and his old-fashioned alliterative verse, can be daunting to non-specialists, and unfortunately there is only a brief (modernised) extract in *NOBEV*; but there is a good recent translation of *Piers Ploughman* in the Oxford World's Classics.

John Skelton (c.1460–1529), although he was a successful court poet of the early Tudor period, can also be seen as England's last medieval poet. His breathless, semi-metrical "Skeltonics" – rhymed lines of two and three stresses tumbling over each other – have a Chaucerian vitality that is still irresistible; they have influenced twentieth-century poets such as Robert Graves. There is an excellent selection of his work in *NOBEV*.

Renaissance

By the early sixteenth century, Middle English had become early Modern English, old-fashioned to our ears but perfectly comprehensible, especially if we are familiar with the language of the King James Bible. The strongest outside influence on English literature for the next 100 years was that of the poets and storytellers of Italy and France; but there was, besides, a new interest in classical learning and literature; a huge influx of new vocabulary; and a time of excited, unrestrained experiment in literary style that lasted until the Restoration.

Sir Thomas Wyatt (c.1503–1542) and **the Earl of Surrey** (c.1517–1547) were among the first to use continental styles of poetry in English verse. Wyatt was a diplomat who, inspired by Petrarch, was the first to write intelligent and moving Italianate verse in English; but his command of stressed metre was uncertain, and his verses do not always scan as smoothly as they might.

It was not easy for prominent men to avoid being accused of treason in the second quarter of the sixteenth century; Wyatt was imprisoned for a time in the Tower of London, and his younger contemporary Surrey was executed. Following Wyatt, Surrey turned to Italian poetic models, although his approach was closer than Wyatt's to Latin originals; his pleasing – and metrically smooth – sonnets were written with a rhyme-scheme of his own invention.[7]

Both poets are well represented in *NOBEV*.

Spenser (Edmund Spenser, c.1552–99). Spenser's poetry, although written in early Modern English and Italian-influenced verse-forms, is deliberately backward-looking in its language, composed in a simulation of Chaucerian English with an antique spelling, to present themes of religion, patriotism, and chivalry. His greatest work, *The Faerie Queene*, exhibits the knightly virtues in a romantic epic of magical adventures. Both the chivalric content of his verse and its technical brilliance had an effect on the development of English poetry; Milton greatly admired his work, and in the nineteenth century alone his influence may be seen in poems by Shelley, Keats, Byron, and Tennyson.

What to read: Here we come upon a difficulty which will recur, and which had better be faced squarely: Spenser is an author who some (but not all) modern readers find boring. *This is perfectly all right*: readers, as well as writers, differ from each other, and it would be unreasonable to expect anyone to take with equal fervour to every one of the "great" authors.[8] But even those who find Spenser hard work should still make the effort to read, say, part of the first Canto of *The Faerie Queene* (published 1590), preferably in an annotated edition that retains the deliberate archaism of Spenser's spelling; and, in *NOBEV*, the great wedding hymn *Epithalamion* (1594).

Shakespeare (William Shakespeare, 1564–1616). Bloom places Shakespeare at the central node of the canon, in whom all previous literary influences – classical, medieval, and renaissance – are drawn together; and from whom radiates by far the most powerful and widespread influence on all subsequent western literature.[9] This may seem exaggerated, but if so it is not by much; certainly it is not possible to make a serious study of western literature without knowing something about Shakespeare (to ignore him would be like trying to study the development of western music while ignoring Beethoven).

The textual situation is complicated; there is no manuscript of any

[7] Known later as the "English" sonnet, and used by Shakespeare and others; see pp. 77–8 below.

[8] As an undergraduate reading English at Oxford, Philip Larkin – himself to become a considerable poet – wrote in his college library copy of Spenser the following comment: "First I thought Troilus and Criseyde [by Chaucer] was the most *boring* poem in English. Then I thought Beowulf was. Now I *know* that The Faerie Queene is the dullest thing out." (Kingsley Amis, *Memoirs*, 1991, p. 54.)

[9] Harold Bloom, *The Western Canon*, ch. 2.

complete play of Shakespeare's, and the early printed editions are both imperfect and at variance with each other; so we rely on the textual studies of nineteenth- and twentieth-century Shakespeare scholars, in which the convention has been firmly established that modern spelling is substituted for the erratic and unauthoritative spelling of the early printed texts.

What to read: It is not easy to recommend particular plays – everyone has their own favourites, and it is perfectly possible to read *all* the plays, one after the other – but a best ten might include *The Merchant of Venice, Henry IV Part I, Hamlet, Twelfth Night, Measure for Measure, Othello, King Lear, Macbeth, Antony and Cleopatra*, and *The Tempest* (written probably in this order in the period c.1597–1611).[10] In *NOBEV*, "Songs" from various plays; selected *Sonnets* (1590s); and "The Phoenix and the Turtle" (by 1601).

The most convenient way to read Shakespeare is in such annotated editions of individual plays as the *New Cambridge* and *New Arden Shakespeares*; best of all – it can be even more illuminating than going to the theatre – is to read a play while listening to an audio tape of a good production, so that the written word is illuminated by the spoken word and vice versa. If this is done, difficulties of interpretation are miraculously overcome.

Shakespeare's exact contemporary **Christopher Marlowe** (1564–93), and his successors **Ben Jonson** (c.1573–1637) and **John Webster** (c.1580–c.1625), are all discussed, with examples of their work, in Chapter 4 on Drama below.

Donne (John Donne, c.1572–1631). Donne, along with Chaucer, Dryden, Wordsworth, and T. S. Eliot (all included in this list), was one of the great revolutionaries of English poetry. He found versification regular and sweet; he left it fractured and sour. Rejecting mellifluous word-music, and replacing conventional similes with contemporary references, he wrote love songs, religious poems, and verse satires in a style that was harsh and uncompromising, and which had a strong effect on English poetry during the first half of the seventeenth century.[11] A cradle Catholic who became an Anglican divine, Donne also preached soul-wrenching sermons which (unlike his poems) were published during his lifetime, and which were a landmark in the development of English prose.

Donne's importance as the author of religious poetry and prose is a

---

[10] See p. 120 below.

[11] Donne and others influenced by his contemporary metaphors were later called "Metaphysical" poets, but this was not a term they used themselves.

reminder that the work of some of our canonical authors contains overt elements of spirituality, being either directly religious (Donne, Milton, Blake, T. S. Eliot), or having an underlying but still noticeable religious content (Spenser, Shakespeare, Wordsworth, George Eliot); and that the others all show signs of the inherent spirituality that appears to be a fundamental constituent of great art.[12]

What to read: The *Songs and Sonnets*[13] and the *Holy Sonnets*; "Seek True Religion!" from *Satire III* in *NOBEV*. Donne's poems (published posthumously in 1633, but impossible to date with certainty; some of the poems were probably written in the 1590s) are best read in an annotated edition.[14]

George Herbert (1593–1633), born of a cultured and aristocratic family, was a fellow of Trinity College, Cambridge, and later a member of Parliament, who gave up his public career to dedicate his life to God as a country parson and author of religious poetry and prose. His moving, deeply-felt religious poems were influenced by the prevailing "metaphysical" fashion, but unlike Donne's poems they were generally simple and graceful in language and style; they were, he said, "a picture of the many spiritual conflicts that have passed betwixt God and my soul". There is a good selection in *NOBEV*.

Milton (John Milton, 1608–74). Like Chaucer, Milton was an immensely prolific writer, both as a technically brilliant poet and as a libertarian political pamphleteer. His most lastingly influential works were his two great blank-verse epics, *Paradise Lost* and *Paradise Regained*, which tell the stories respectively of the fall of man and of his redemption. Both poems are huge, resonant structures in blank verse, sharply visualised although written after Milton had become blind, and markedly dramatic in their handling of character; no special knowledge is needed for reading them other than recognition of the (non-biblical) story of the rebellion of Satan in Heaven, of the account in *Genesis* of the temptation and fall of Adam and Eve, and of the Gospel story of Christ's resistance to temptation in the wilderness.

What to read: *Paradise Lost* Books 1–2 (1667);[15] and in *NOBEV* "Hymn on the Morning of Christ's Nativity" (1629); extracts from *Comus* (1637); *Lycidas* (1637); three "Sonnets"; and extracts from *Samson Agonistes* (1671).

[12] By "spiritual" I mean "concerned with sacred or religious things; holy; divine; inspired" (*COD*).
[13] See pp. 85–8 below.
[14] See the Annotated Bibliography.
[15] See pp. 89–92 below.

From now on, the texts of canonical authors writing in English are well established and easy to obtain in both annotated and unannotated editions.

Andrew Marvell (1621–78) was another Cambridge man who, after a career as a tutor, became an MP and a traveller on political business. As a public and political man, his loyalties were inconspicuously divided between republicanism and restoration; while, as a poet, he was a transitional figure between the renaissance and neoclassical periods. In his own time he was known as a satirist; and his witty, delicate lyrics, long neglected, were generally recognised for the masterpieces they are only in the early twentieth century; in particular the *tour de force* "To His Coy Mistress" is widely known and appreciated. Again, there is a good selection in *NOBEV*.

Neoclassical

Although the renaissance was sparked by a renewed interest in classical culture, its literary expression tended towards exuberance rather than control. From about 1660 until the late eighteenth century, veneration for classical models became paramount; and with this came a belief that written language should be governed by traditional, formal rules. (There were parallel movements in graphic art and architecture.) Regularity, order, and proportion were valued in form; as were, in content, emotional restraint, elegance, and wit. These values dominated art until the end of the eighteenth century.

Dryden (John Dryden, 1631–1700). The least personal, most objective of English poets, Dryden reflected in his poems, plays,[16] and critical writings all the central issues of his age, religious, political, artistic, and philosophical. He was the outstanding literary figure of the last four decades of the seventeenth century; and it was his skill in versification and his sharp intelligence that did most to steer literature into the new classicism. Other poets before him – Donne for one – had written satires in five-stress rhymed couplets, but it was Dryden who first lifted the form – to be known as "heroic couplets"[17] – to a new level of polished elegance. Dryden also made a fine verse translation of the *Aeneid*, which is still an agreeable way of approaching Virgil.

What to read: The key poems are *Absalom and Achitophel* (1681), in which Dryden used a biblical parallel to satirise the politics of the Stuart succession; and *Mac Flecknoe* (1682), which devastated the reputation of

---

[16] See pp. 128–30 below.
[17] The term "heroic couplet" derives from the use of this form in heroic tragedies and translations of classical epics in the late seventeenth and eighteenth centuries.

the minor poet Thomas Shadwell. See also in *NOBEV*, "Vox Populi" from *The Medal* (1682); "Confessio Fidei" from *The Hind and the Panther* (1687); and *Alexander's Feast* (1697).

Daniel Defoe (c. 1661–1731) – businessman, traveller, secret agent, journalist, pamphleteer – produced, among some 560 books, pamphlets, and journals, a handful of works of fiction which were in the main line of the development of the English novel. Best known are *Robinson Crusoe* (1719); *Captain Singleton* (1720); *Moll Flanders*, *A Journal of the Plague Year*, *Colonel Jack* (1722); and *Roxana* (1724): engaging first-person narratives that purported to be authentic memoirs. Dashed off when Defoe was about 60, these novels were episodic (made up of a series of incidents connected by the main character); most of them were picaresque (concerning rogues and scoundrels); they were all immediately popular; and they still attract more readers than any other eighteenth-century fiction.

Jonathan Swift (1667–1745) was an Anglo-Irishman who was born in Dublin, and was, from 1713, Dean of St Patrick's (Church of Ireland) Cathedral in that city. Like Defoe, he was a prolific political pamphleteer, especially as a darkly cynical satirist in verse and prose; in *A Modest Proposal* (1729) he suggested that the solution to the problem of an over-populated and famine-ridden Ireland was to encourage the poor to eat their babies. He is best known now as the author of the novel-length satirical allegories *The Tale of a Tub* (1704) and *Gulliver's Travels* (1726). His very funny "Verses on the Death of Doctor Swift" is included in *NOBEV*; ironically his last years were clouded by a form of dementia.

Pope (Alexander Pope, 1688–1744). Pope did not invent a poetic mode but, like Shakespeare and Tennyson, he brought an already existing mode to the highest pitch of perfection. In his case, it was the heroic couplet pioneered by Dryden of which he made himself consummate master; and all neoclassical English verse has to be judged in relation to Pope's brilliant achievement. Because he was a Roman Catholic and therefore excluded from the universities, the Church, and all official posts, he had perforce to support himself, and he was the first major poet to do so solely by writing. Although he was pre-eminently a satirist, his best-selling works were his stirring verse translations of Homer's epics, the *Iliad* and the *Odyssey*.

What to read: Start with the early *An Essay on Criticism* (1711), which lays out the canons of taste in the Augustan Age;[18] go on to the *Epistle to Dr*

---

[18] "Augustan" because the early eighteenth-century neoclassicists saw themselves as the literary heirs of Augustan Rome, and especially of Virgil and Horace.

Arbuthnot (1735),[19] Pope's great satire in defence of his own work; and the last Book of *The Dunciad* (1743), a spoof heroic poem in praise of dullness with "notes variorum". These poems require annotation if the allusions in them are to be understood;[20] but they can be enjoyed without annotation for the perfection of their style, wit and high spirits. In *NOBEV*, see two extracts from *The Rape of the Lock* (1712); and "Elegy to the Memory of an Unfortunate Lady" (1717).

The work of **Samuel Richardson** (1689–1761) is discussed in Chapter 2 on Fiction, below. His most distinguished successors among eighteenth-century novelists were **Henry Fielding** (1707–54) and **Laurence Sterne** (1713–68). The well-born Fielding, after a moderately successful career as a dramatist (which gave him a firm grasp of idiomatic dialogue), was provoked by the appearance in 1740 of Richardson's *Pamela* to become a novelist himself; and for the rest of his short life he combined a second career as a reforming London magistrate with writing fiction and journalism. *Joseph Andrews* (1742) and *Tom Jones* (1749) were the first, highly original, modern novels in English, written in prose with third-person narrators; their influence led on to the work of Scott, Dickens, and Thackeray, and so eventually to the novels of our own time.

Sterne was an eccentric Yorkshire parson, a pluralist and something of a womaniser. *Tristram Shandy*, his comic masterpiece, which appeared in nine volumes over a period of eight years (1759–67), combined techniques of metafiction[21] and stream of consciousness that were unparalleled until the twentieth century, in a slight and disordered narrative interrupted by wild digressions, instead of the traditional linear modes of epic and prose fiction. Sterne's other major work, *A Sentimental Journey through France and Italy* (1768), was also experimental, being a playful mixture of travel book, autobiography, and novel of sensibility.

Johnson (Samuel Johnson, 1709–84). Johnson wrote a pretty good poem (*The Vanity of Human Wishes*, 1749), a fairly good novel (*Rasselas*, 1759), and a not very good play (*Irene*, 1749); he compiled the first dictionary of the English language on historical principles; and he was the subject of Boswell's incomparable biography (1791). Nevertheless, it is as the preeminent neoclassical moralist, literary critic, essayist, and prose stylist that he is included here. His criticism encompassed the earliest edition of

[19] See pp. 92–5 below.
[20] There is a convenient one-volume annotated edition of the Twickenham Pope (see the Annotated Bibliography below).
[21] For metafiction, see pp. 43–4 below; for stream of consciousness, see pp. 41–2.

Shakespeare to be based on sound textual principles, and an unparalleled series of biographical prefaces to the English poets. His widely influential prose style was balanced, Latinate, and orotund.

What to read: Some of Johnson's most interesting work is scattered through his periodicals *The Rambler* (1750–2) and *The Idler* (1758); but his critical genius is most easily approached through the *Prefaces* to his *Dictionary* (1755) and his *Shakespeare* (1765), and through the prefaces to – usually known as the *Lives* of – the poets Cowley, Milton, Savage, and Pope (most of the prefaces were written and revised 1779–83, but the life of Savage dates from 1744).

Thomas Gray (1716–71), who spent most of his quiet life as a don at Cambridge, was almost, but not quite, a romantic poet. He sometimes wrote in a simple language relatively unencumbered by poetic diction (especially in the famous "Elegy Written in a Country Churchyard", 1751), and he was attracted by the obscure, the melancholy, the sub-lime – a quality of awesome grandeur, especially in nature – and the picturesque; yet he was never entirely free of a neoclassical fondness for order and emotional control. There is a good selection of his work in *NOBEV*.

The career of **Oliver Goldsmith** (c.1730–1774) as a dramatist is discussed in Chapter 4 on Drama, below. He also wrote two notable semi-autobiographical poems, *The Traveller* (1764) and *The Deserted Village* (1770, of which there is a brief extract in *NOBEV*); and an influential novel of "sensibility", *The Vicar of Wakefield* (1766).

Romantic

At the end of the eighteenth century, there was a reaction against the formal rules and emotional restraint of neoclassicism in literature. (Again there were parallel reactions in architecture – the gothic revival; in music – Beethoven; and in painting – Goya and Friedrich.) In poetry, there had been eighteenth-century forerunners to the romantic movement, as for instance in the supposed medieval poems attributed to "Ossian" and "Thomas Rowley",[22] and in the work of the neglected William Blake (see the next entry); but the central figures were Wordsworth and Coleridge, whose *Lyrical Ballads* (1798) set off a thoroughgoing revolution in English poetry. Where neoclassicism favoured universals, formality of language, and adherence to rules, the romantic poets led by Wordsworth turned to the speech of ordinary men for personal, subjective accounts of individual experience. The first flowering of the romantic revival had come to an

---

[22] These were actually by James Macpherson and Thomas Chatterton respectively.

end by about 1825, but its subjective, individualistic approach proved a liberating force in English literature for the rest of the nineteenth century.

Blake (William Blake, 1757–1827). Blake, a graphic artist as well as a poet, was a religious mystic quite out of tune with the sensibility of the eighteenth century. Most of his contemporaries thought him mad – which by their formal standards he undoubtedly was – and they could not understand his symbolic commentaries on what he saw as the destruction of the individual spirit of man by generalising, neoclassical enlightenment. Despite this lack of influence on the art of his own time, Blake's assault on neoclassicism was increasingly influential during the nineteenth century, and his central position in the development of romantic art is now generally recognised.

What to read: Blake's long mystical poems are difficult to understand – they are indeed still subject to differing interpretations – and they are best approached through an annotated anthology of extracts such as that in the second volume of *The Norton Anthology of English Literature* (6th edition). The lyrics in *Songs of Innocence and of Experience* (1789–84) on the other hand are readily accessible, and imply the essence of what Blake had to say.

Robert Burns (1759–96), the "Heaven-taught ploughman", eventually escaped from the drudgery of farming a smallholding to literary success and lasting fame as Scotland's national poet. His beguiling *Poems, chiefly in the Scottish Dialect* (1786) were rooted in the oral traditions of Scottish song, and were only slightly affected by the modes of contemporary literature (though he could write in "correct" eighteenth-century English when he wanted to). His last major poem was "Tam o' Shanter" (1791), not included in the selection of his lyrics in *NOBEV*.

Wordsworth (William Wordsworth, 1770–1850). Wordsworth, with his collaborator S. T. Coleridge, saw as clearly as Blake did what he disliked in late eighteenth-century poetry – the artificiality of its language, and its remoteness from individual, subjective experience – and he determined to publish work which would demonstrate and explain an alternative approach. This he did with *Lyrical Ballads* in 1798,[23] and in effect turned English poetry into a new direction, writing in "the real language of men" about the joys and sorrows of ordinary people. The period during which he produced his greatest and most influential work lasted a mere ten years (from 1797), although he continued to write copiously until his death more than forty years later.

---

[23] *Lyrical Ballads* was very largely by Wordsworth; Coleridge's chief contribution was the long and important "The Rime of the Ancient Mariner".

What to read: "Lines Composed a Few Miles above Tintern Abbey" (1798); "The Ruined Cottage" (1799);[24] "The Old Cumberland Beggar" (1800), "Michael" (1800), "Resolution and Independence" (1802); "Ode: Intimations of Immortality" (1802–4); plus the "Preface" to *Lyrical Ballads* (1798, enlarged 1800); and substantial portions of Wordsworth's magnificent autobiographical blank-verse poem *The Prelude* (1805, 1850),[25] one of the great journeys in literature in which the author arrives where he started and knows the place for the first time.[26]

Samuel Taylor Coleridge (1772–1834) began his literary career before he met Wordsworth in 1797, but it was their intense collaboration as friends and literary partners over the next fourteen years (1797–1811) that led to his finest work as a poet. *Lyrical Ballads* (1798) has already been mentioned; its "Rime of the Ancient Mariner" is given whole in *NOBEV*, along with "Frost at Midnight" (1798), "Dejection: an Ode" (1802), and "Kubla Khan" (1816). Later, Coleridge concentrated increasingly on writing literary criticism.

Jane Austen (1775–1817). Jane Austen belonged chronologically to the romantic revival, but she was still chiefly influenced by neoclassical forms in her own approach to fiction. Her life was notable both for its narrow frame and for its almost complete lack of incident; she lived with her family, never married, never travelled far from home, and died a maiden aunt at 41. Yet it was within these very limitations that she developed the psychological novel of manners, producing six masterpieces in a period of about fifteen years. The ironical subtlety of her observation and her dry, perfectly adapted style set the standard for the classic nineteenth-century novel.

What to read: There are only six major novels, and none of them is bad, but some are more immediately appealing than others. Start with *Pride and Prejudice* (published 1813, though begun much earlier);[27] then try *Emma* (1816) and *Persuasion* (published posthumously in 1818). The other three novels are *Sense and Sensibility* (1811), *Mansfield Park* (1814), and *Northanger Abbey* (published with *Persuasion*, 1818).

Sir Walter Scott (1771–1832) was the first great pan-European novelist and poet, his works being "the daily food, not only of his

---

[24] See pp. 95–7 below.

[25] Wordsworth began *The Prelude* in 1799, but continued to add to and tinker with it for the rest of his life. There are parallel-text editions of the main 1805 and 1850 versions.

[26] T. S. Eliot, *Little Gidding*, lines 241–2.

[27] See pp. 50–2 below.

countrymen, but of all educated Europe";[28] and he was a major influence
on the development of the novel – especially the historical novel – in the
nineteenth century. By profession a lawyer, he wrote copiously, made a
fortune, lost it, and virtually worked himself to death paying off his
debts. The great series of Waverley novels (1814–31) is a *tour de force*,
the most accessible of them being, perhaps, *The Heart of Midlothian*
(1818). *NOBEV* includes "Young Lochinvar" from *Marmion* (1808), and
some later lyrics.

Byron (George Gordon, Lord Byron, 1788–1824). Intensely English
though he was, Byron has always been appreciated more as a European
writer than as a British one, being taken as the incarnation of a fundamental
type of romanticism in the myth of the "Byronic hero", as described for
instance in his dramatic poem *Manfred* (1817): the myth of the passionate,
moody, guilt-ridden but unrepentant wanderer, superior to the common
run of mankind but doomed to conflict and defeat by the hypocrisy of the
ordinary; the individualist myth that pervaded much of nineteenth-
century thought and culminated in Nietzsche's Superman standing outside society's criteria of good and evil.[29] Paradoxically for such an arch-
romantic, Byron's poetic style was descended from neoclassical models
(especially Pope) rather from the earlier romantic poets; which perhaps
accounts in part for the relatively low esteem in which his work has been
held in his own country.

What to read: Byron's last, unfinished epic *Don Juan*[30] is certainly his
masterpiece, as both Shelley and Byron himself recognised at the time,
excelling in fluent versification and wit, yet tempered with an underlying
astringency. Start with the first canto (1819); it is difficult not to go on.
In *NOBEV*, see "She Walks in Beauty" (1814); "The Eve of Waterloo"
and "The Dying Gladiator" from *Childe Harold* III and IV (1816-18);
Prometheus (1816); and "So, We'll go no more a-roving" (1817).

Byron's friend and fellow-exile **Percy Bysshe Shelley** (1792–
1822) – atheist, political utopian, and disciple of William Godwin –
produced his finest work towards the end of his short life (he was
drowned in a boating accident in Italy at the age of 30). His masterpiece
was the verse drama *Prometheus Unbound* (1820); there is an extract in
NOBEV, together with his better-known odes to the west wind and a
skylark, the sonnet "Ozymandias", and other lyrics.

The life of **John Keats** (1795–1821), apothecary's apprentice, was

---

[28] Lockhart's *Life of Scott* (1839), p. 316.
[29] In *Thus spake Zarathustra* (1883–92) and *Beyond Good and Evil* (1886).
[30] Pronounced "Don Djú-an", not "Don Whán".

even shorter, ending with his death from consumption, which makes the power and opulence of the poems written in his early twenties the more remarkable. *NOBEV* includes all five of the great odes (to a nightingale, on a Grecian urn, to Psyche, on melancholy, and to autumn), "La Belle Dame Sans Merci", and the sonnet "On First Looking into Chapman's Homer".

Tennyson (Alfred, Lord Tennyson, 1809–92). Tennyson produced a large body of work over a long lifetime without any serious depreciation of his astonishing technical and aesthetic virtuosity; he had, as T. S. Eliot said, "the finest ear of any English poet since Milton".[31] He was not a great originator either of style or of thought, but no poet of the romantic period had a greater command of the emotional charge, the magic, and the sheer beauty of the English language, together with unrivalled metrical mastery; and he left an unavoidable mark on the poetry of his successors. He rose to great heights of popularity in the middle years of his career, though his reputation began to wane towards its end. There remains a feeling, perhaps, that a poet so fluent and so popular in his own time cannot have been all that good; but an open-minded rereading of his masterpieces will show it to be mistaken.

What to read: "Mariana" (1830); "The Lady of Shalott" (1832, rev. 1842); "Oenone" (1832, rev. 1842); "The Lotos Eaters" (1832, rev. 1842);[32] "Ulysses" (1842); "Tears, Idle Tears" and "Now Sleeps the Crimson Petal" (from *The Princess*, 1847); "Tithonus" (1860); "The Passing of Arthur" (from *Idylls of the King*, 1869, incorporating "Morte d'Arthur", 1842); and "Crossing the Bar" (1889); plus the extracts in *NOBEV* from *In Memoriam* (1850).

Robert Browning (1812–89). If Tennyson was master of the emotional music of language, Browning displayed equally astonishing skill in handling the spoken word of everyday speech, moulding it into a series of metrical monologues and dialogues. For the most part he used five-stress lines, usually blank but occasionally rhymed, and his metrical control in this form was unrivalled: his characters really do "talk poetry", notably in his powerful verse "mystery novel" *The Ring and the Book* (1868).[33] *NOBEV* includes only one of the five-stress monologues –

---

[31] From the Introduction to *Poems of Tennyson*, 1936, a notable essay on Tennyson's art by a fellow-master.

[32] See pp. 97–100 below.

[33] Browning's wife Elizabeth Barrett Browning (1806–61) had already written a novel in verse, *Aurora Leigh* (1857), which, though occasionally rough in its versification, was a notable feminist tract.

the rhymed "My Last Duchess" – together with a number of poems in other metres, including the magical "Home Thoughts from Abroad".

Dickens (Charles Dickens, 1812–70). Dickens's output of fiction was prodigious; no other writer, perhaps, in any language has produced so much and such a variety of work of the highest quality. It ranges from the sparky jokes and good-humoured caricature of the early works (from *Pickwick*, 1837, to *Martin Chuzzlewit*, 1843), via the sentimental but powerful Christmas books of 1843–8, to the sombre complexity of his later novels (from *Dombey and Son*, 1848, to *Our Mutual Friend*, 1865). Nor, indeed, has any writer (even Tennyson, even Tolstoy) had such universal success and acclaim in his own lifetime. His influence on western culture was huge and international – it is hard to imagine the mid-nineteenth century without Dickens bestriding it – yet, not surprisingly, his influence on contemporary literature was not immediate: he was *sui generis*, and no-one tried to match him in his own style.

What to read: Although Dickens is always recognisably himself, his novels did not repeat themselves, and it is virtually impossible to choose a manageable few that are truly representative; but, to take a chance, try *Oliver Twist* (1838), *A Christmas Carol* (1843), and *David Copperfield* (1850);[34] then, if still going strong, add *Martin Chuzzlewit* (1843), *Hard Times* (1854), and *Little Dorrit* (1857). Enthusiastic Dickensians will insist on recommending others.

The mid-nineteenth century was the great age of the substantial, bourgeois English novel: there were not only Dickens and George Eliot, but also Thackeray, the Brontës, Mrs Gaskell, and Trollope, all of whom are still read, enjoyed, and admired.

William Makepeace Thackeray (1811–63) began to make his name as a writer in the 1840s – he had scraped his living until then as a journalist – and his first (and perhaps best) major novel, *Vanity Fair*, appeared in 1847. This was followed by *Pendennis* (1848–50), *Henry Esmond* (1852), *The Newcomes* (1853–5), and other, less successful works of fiction. Thackeray satirised the society and morals of his time with a keen eye for their absurdities; and, while his work attracted more admiration in his own day than it generally does in ours, he was a central figure in the development of his art.

Wuthering Heights, the only novel of **Emily Brontë** (1818–48), was not much liked when it was published in 1847, but it has come to be appreciated for its complex and violent plot, and for the intensity of its

---

[34] See pp. 52–7 below.

evocation of place and character – the intensity of an author who was also a poet of great accomplishment (there is a good selection in *NOBEV*). Emily's elder sister Charlotte Brontë (1816–55), whose gripping *Jane Eyre* also appeared in 1847, was immediately and lastingly successful; but her most notable heroines (Jane Eyre, and Lucy Snowe, in *Villette*, 1853), were essentially fantasised versions of herself as she would have liked to be, and not everyone finds their bold, priggish, and improbably successful characters entirely convincing.

Elizabeth Gaskell (1810–65) was the wife of a Unitarian minister in industrial Manchester, who somehow found time and space, while helping her husband in his ministry, running a busy household, and bringing up her children, to write half a dozen novels of exceptional quality, as varied in their approach as they were skilful in their execution. *Mary Barton* (1848) and *North and South* (1855) are two uncompromising but different approaches to the disturbing facts of industrialisation in the city that Engels took as the primary source for his *Condition of the Working Classes in England* (1845). *Cranford* (1853) anatomises the social comedy of small-town rural England; *Sylvia's Lovers* (1863) is a historical novel set among the whalers and press-gangs of Whitby; and *Wives and Daughters* (1866, not quite completed at the time of the author's death) is an unhurried but keenly perceptive study of family life. All of them are well crafted, and are peopled with characters of recognisable authenticity.

The legendary industry of **Anthony Trollope** (1815–82) produced no fewer than forty-seven novels (1847–81), the first twenty of them written when he was still a full-time official in the Post Office on whose behalf he travelled the world, and when he hunted as often as three times a week in the season. The astonishing thing is that, with a few exceptions, they are extraordinarily good, investigating the society of his time with a keen and sympathetic insight. Recognition came to him late – he was already 40 when *The Warden* (1855), his first popular success, was published – but from then on his audience was assured. The two great series of six Barsetshire novels (1855–67) and six political novels (1864–80) are unparalleled in English literature for their range and perception.

George Eliot (pseudonym of Mary Ann – later Marian – Evans, 1819–80). At her best, George Eliot wrote the essential Victorian novel: works that were long, morally aware but a gripping read, both emotionally frank and intellectually rigorous, and presented in a style of controlled elegance. Where Dickens's genius for understanding people was unconstrained by cerebral analysis or stylistic convention, George Eliot was a learned intellectual who could nevertheless empathise with people's emotions and feelings, and discuss them with clarity; and where Dickens was high-spirited, she was serious – but seldom deadly serious, for her characters come alive, and our interest in them is enhanced by her penetrating analyses of their emotional and moral problems. She is the only English author who can be compared in this respect with Tolstoy.[35]

What to read: There is considerable variety in George Eliot's eight major works of fiction, and not all are wholly successful; but *Middlemarch* (1872),[36] her longest and finest novel, is almost flawless, and is the inevitable first choice. After that try *Silas Marner* (1861), a much shorter work which encapsulates both George Eliot's high seriousness and her emotional sympathy in a tale that has the compelling readability of a moral fable; and *The Mill on the Floss* (1860), the most autobiographical of her mature works.

The later nineteenth century was a time of uneasy literary stirring, similar to that preceding the romantic revolution at the end of the eighteenth century, when it was felt that change should come – was coming – but no-one quite knew how. It was sensed by the poet and critic Matthew Arnold, the poet and novelist Thomas Hardy, the poet Gerard Manley Hopkins, and the dramatist and poet Oscar Wilde; four very different writers, but all contributors to what was to become modernism.

Matthew Arnold (1822–88), poet, critic, and inspector of schools, suggested satirically in *Culture and Anarchy* (1869) that English society was divided into three classes: a barbarian aristocracy, a philistine bourgeoisie, and an ill-educated populace, which were in barren mutual opposition, and which lacked a refined culture that could lead to a more tolerant and productive civilisation. In all his work, first in verse and later in prose, major themes were regret for the fading certainties of art and religion, and opposition to the rising tide of lowbrow vulgarity. In *NOBEV*, see the marvellous "Dover Beach" (from *New Poems*, 1867).

Thomas Hardy (1840–1928) was a country architect who became a ground-breaking novelist and poet. His fifteen major novels, which appeared from 1871 to 1895, concerned man's battle in life and love with the always indifferent forces of nature and the frequently cruel constraints of social convention; his last (and perhaps best) novel, *Jude the Obscure* (1895), was widely condemned for its pessimism and supposed

---

[35] George Eliot did not read Tolstoy, though Tolstoy read, and was influenced by, George Eliot.

[36] See pp. 57–60 below.

indecency. The many poems which followed in his old age from 1898 to 1928 expressed a personal melancholy in simple language, but were not widely appreciated until after his death. There is an adequate selection of his spare, short-lined verse in *NOBEV*.

Gerard Manley Hopkins (1844–89) achieved a technical revolution in the form of his verse. A Roman Catholic convert and Jesuit priest who wrote religious poetry, Hopkins was effectively cut off from the mainstream of English culture, and was prevented from publishing his startling poems by his Jesuit superiors, who neither liked them nor found them suitable to his calling. The poems survived in manuscript, however, and were eventually published nearly thirty years after his death, in 1918. Hopkins's powerful poems, one-pointedly centred on God, used astonishing innovations of rhythm – strong stresses tolling beneath hurrying, tumbling unstressed syllables, which he called "sprung rhythm" – and of sound, with rich patterns of rhyme and assonance within the lines. *NOBEV* has a good selection of his sonnets.

Oscar Wilde (1854–1900), the flamboyant Irish star of the aesthetic movement of the 1880s and 1890s, is as often remembered for the tragic rise and fall of his life as for the provocative brilliance of the work that grew out of it; yet the melodramatic wit of his gothic novel *The Picture of Dorian Gray* (1890) and the comic perfection of his dramatic masterpiece *The Importance of Being Earnest* (1895) both demanded a reconsideration of nineteenth-century values which had a lasting effect on the development of modernism (and *Earnest* in particular is as dazzlingly alive today as it was a century ago). See also the moving extracts from *The Ballad of Reading Gaol* (1898) in *NOBEV*.

Another expatriate Irish wit, **George Bernard Shaw** (1856–1950), is discussed, with an extract from his work, in Chapter 4 on Drama, below.

Modernist

Just as the end of the eighteenth century saw the romantic reaction against neoclassicism, so the end of the nineteenth saw the beginnings of the modernist revolution which transformed literature, painting (the post-impressionists), architecture (skyscrapers, the Bauhaus), music and dance (Debussy, Stravinsky, the Ballet Russe, jazz), science (relativity, quantum theory), war (machine guns, artillery barrages), transport (motor cars, aeroplanes), communications (telephones, cinema, radio), social standards (feminism, free love, Freudian psychology), and politics (Communism, Fascism). The moral individualism of the romantics gave way to a period of social promise and threat, shared in about equal quantities.

Conrad (Joseph Conrad, the anglicised name of Teodor Josef Konrad

Korzeniowski, 1857–1924). Not the least extraordinary thing about
Conrad was the fact that English was not just the second but was actually
the *third* language of this great English novelist (the first two being Polish
and French). After twenty years at sea as an officer in the British merchant
marine, he began in the 1890s (by now a naturalised British citizen) to write
his complex, internal psychodramas, many of them presented as exciting
sailors' yarns; modernist works that were a startling departure from the
classical Victorian novel, and which effectively put a stop to its further
development.[37]

What to read: Conrad's full-length novels tended to grow from what had
started as short stories or novellas, the form in which he was outstandingly
successful. The novellas *The Nigger of the "Narcissus"* (1897), *Heart of
Darkness* (1902), *Typhoon* (1903), and *The Shadow Line* (1917), and the
short stories "Youth" (1902) and "The Secret Sharer" (1910), are as good
as anything he ever wrote. Of the full-length novels, *Lord Jim* (1900,
Conrad's own favourite),[38] and *Under Western Eyes* (1911), are excellent;
Nostromo (1904) is perhaps somewhat overrated.

Rudyard Kipling (1865–1936) was as skilful a short-story writer as
Conrad, though favouring tales in a more condensed form, and a poet of
daunting fluency. For much of the twentieth century, Kipling has been
out of fashion, disregarded as a jingoistic imperialist, but the range and
subtlety as well as the vitality of his best work – and its quality seldom
fell off – is astonishing. All the eight collections of his adult stories, from
Plain Tales from the Hills (1888) to *A Diversity of Creatures* (1917), contain wonderfully varied examples of short-story writing; and his best
novel, *Kim* (1901), is a delicate and loving account of the India that
existed, unseen by most Anglo-Indians, beneath the skin of the British
Raj. The selection of his verse in *NOBEV* includes the very different
"Danny Deever" and "The Way through the Woods".

Kipling's exact contemporary, the Irishman **William Butler Yeats**
(1865–1939), who was influenced first by the aesthetic movement and
later by the French Symbolists, brought a passionate Celtic mysticism
to an intensely sensual poetic vision. Early poems of fairyland were
succeeded by engagement with the occult and with the struggle for Irish
independence; the selection in *NOBEV* gives some indication of Yeats's
range.

---

[37] The only parallel is with the mature works of Dostoievsky, which Conrad read – and
disliked – after he had settled into his own mode.

[38] See pp. 60–3 below.

Joyce (James Joyce, 1882–1941). If Conrad, a Pole, was the first modernist novelist in English, it was Joyce, an Irishman, who wrote *Ulysses*, the definitive modernist novel. From the beginning, Joyce, under the influence of Ibsen and of the French Symbolists, was writing in a mode that was uncompromisingly new, and he remained an innovator throughout his life. After a slow start in the first decade of the twentieth century, his originality and power were recognised, and he was able to follow his own very clear idea of where he wanted to go. His influence was widespread throughout western literature – he lived abroad in continental Europe for most of his life – but, like Dickens, his own style was so individual that he had few direct imitators.

What to read: Start with the short stories in *Dubliners* (1914), and the autobiographical novel *A Portrait of the Artist as a Young Man* (1916); but it is then essential to go on to *Ulysses* (1922),[39] which is not nearly as difficult as it looks, provided that a crib such as Harry Blamires's *The New Bloomsday Book* (1988) is used for the first reading. Most of *Finnegans Wake* (1939) is too obscure for non-specialists, though some idea of its quality may be had by listening to the gramophone record of Joyce reading from the "Anna Livia Plurabelle" section, while consulting the transcript and notes in *The Norton Anthology of English Literature*, 6th edition, II, pp. 2,076–80.

Edward Morgan Forster (1879–1970), most of whose novels were published in 1905–10 before Joyce's work began to appear, was an essentially Edwardian novelist, examining with cool irony the culture and class system of his well-educated contemporaries; outstanding are *The Longest Journey* (1907) and *Howard's End* (1910). He drafted a homosexual novel, *Maurice*, in 1913–14, but it was not published until 1971; and his last work, *A Passage to India* (1924), was followed by a silence of forty-six years.

Forster was a member of the "Bloomsbury" group,[40] as was his fellow-novelist **Virginia Woolf** (1882–1941), who started writing shortly before Forster stopped, and who was influenced by Joyce in her use of interior monologue.[41] In her feminist novels, from the relatively conventional *The Voyage Out* (1915) to her last completed work, *Between*

---

[39] See pp. 63–8 below.

[40] The most important members of the group were, in order of seniority, Roger Fry, Desmond McCarthy, E. M. Forster, Vanessa Bell (née Stephen), Leonard Woolf, Lytton Strachey, Clive Bell, Virginia Woolf (Vanessa's sister, married to Leonard), Maynard Keynes, Duncan Grant, and David Garnett.

[41] See pp. 41–2, 67–8 below.

the Acts (1941), Virginia Woolf allows her characters to fragment into ephemeral states of mind within well-controlled fictional forms.

David Herbert Lawrence (1885–1930), herald of new freedoms in literature and sexuality, would have nothing to do with either Bloomsbury or Joyce. His early, and perhaps best, novels (*Sons and Lovers*, 1913, *The Rainbow*, 1915, and *Women in Love*, 1920) stress the contrasts between nature and machine-civilisation, between the freedom of instinct and the control of will; it is not always easy to take their self-conscious freedoms of style and content seriously. Lawrence was also a fine short-story writer, and one of the few successful poets to use free verse; see especially "Snake" in *NOBEV*.

T. S. Eliot (Thomas Stearns Eliot, 1888–1965). English poetry was tired at the beginning of the twentieth century. Innovations had been attempted – notably by Gerard Manley Hopkins (1844–89), though nearly all his work remained unknown until 1918 – but even the "Georgian" poets (writing in the reign of George V, which began in 1910)[42] favoured a poetical style that was still largely derived from the later romantics. Now an American who was turning himself into an Englishman stopped romantic verse dead in its tracks in 1917 with the publication of *Prufrock*.[43] Here at last was modernist verse: Symbolist, obscure, internalised, learned, witty and colloquial in style, it was poetry in a new and contemporary form. Eliot, a keen and perceptive literary critic as well as a poet, followed this up in 1922 – the year of *Ulysses* – with his epoch-making *The Waste Land*, which, despite esoteric references that need annotation,[44] confirmed his position as England's leading poet. His work continued to develop thereafter, culminating in the great *Four Quartets* (1935–42, his last major work as a poet).

What to read: "The Love Song of J. Alfred Prufrock" (1917);[45] "Gerontion" (1920); *The Waste Land* (1922); *The Hollow Men* (1925); *Ash Wednesday* (1930); *Murder in the Cathedral* (play, 1935); *Four Quartets* ("Burnt Norton", 1935; "East Coker", 1940; "The Dry Salvages", 1941; "Little Gidding", 1942).

---

[42] *Georgian Poetry* was a series of five volumes of verse (1912–22), which began with poems by Rupert Brooke, W. H. Davies, John Masefield, and others.

[43] "Prufrock" had first appeared in an American periodical in 1915; but it was its English publication in book form in 1917 that made Eliot's reputation.

[44] Annotation, that is, beyond the spoof notes provided by Eliot himself.

[45] See pp. 100–3 below.

Chapter 2

Fiction

The Nature of Fiction

Telling stories must have begun very early in human history – in fact stories may be as old as language itself – and storytelling was perhaps mankind's first literary activity, preceding even the word-music that became poetry and the imitations and dancing that became drama. (Soon, of course, these three fundamental literary modes mingled with each other, as stories were told and sung in verse, and verse-stories were performed dramatically, mixtures which have persisted into our own times.)

Sometimes the stories were "true", but more often they were not; and we have come to use the term "fiction" – an invented or imaginary thing – for stories which are made up for the entertainment, instruction, and aesthetic pleasure of their audience. Over the past four centuries, the mainstream of literature has come increasingly to consist of invented stories, long or short, written out in prose, and reproduced for a variety of readers: the novels, the novellas, and the short stories which are the dominant literary form of our own time.

Not only is fiction something invented, but its form and its constituents are also an artificial representation of things said and done, just as much as the two-dimensional, coloured canvas of a painting is an artificial representation of something seen. In a novel, plot, point of view, setting, character, dialogue and all are selected and moulded by the author into a neat, coherent form that is not much like the untidy incoherence of everyday life, but which gives the experienced reader the illusion of reality. The reader in effect learns to collaborate with the author by suppressing his or her awareness of the contrived nature of the artifact and, by becoming immersed in the story, accepting the work as a sufficient simulacrum of real life.

It is worth emphasising that fiction, if it is any good, is entertaining. Some novels may require more effort of the reader than others; but if the book does not please by having such qualities as being gripping, amusing, beautiful, or attractively instructive, it will be put aside, and the author's attempt to communicate will have failed. Some of the most enduring stories are traditional fairy tales, which do have these qualities, and we shall look at how the best known of them, *Cinderella*,[1] is made, and see how its parts compare with those of a widely popular nineteenth-century novel, Charlotte Brontë's *Jane Eyre* (1847),[2] which tells an analogous tale at greater length.

Structure

The structure of a story – its "plot" – is usually divisible into three parts. There is first an original situation in which the chief characters are placed; there are secondly actions or events which alter the position or understanding of these characters; and there is finally the resolution, a new situation for the characters resulting from this alteration. Thus the story has a beginning, a middle, and an end.

At its most basic, in all its many versions, *Cinderella* is the tale of a young girl who is misprized, who is then recognised, and who is finally given her due; in most versions, her enemies include two unattractive sisters, and in many she marries the man who recognises her. *Cinderella* is plainly divided into the usual three parts. Perrault begins by setting out the original situation:

> Once there was a nobleman who took as his second wife the proudest and haughtiest woman imaginable. She had two daughters of the same character, who took after their mother in everything. On his side, the husband had a daughter who was sweetness itself; she inherited this from her mother, who had been the most kindly of women.
>
> No sooner was the wedding over than the stepmother showed her ill-nature. She could not bear the good qualities of the young girl, for they made her own daughters seem even less likeable. She gave her the roughest work of the house to do. ...

and so on. Having explained how Cinderella got her nickname (from sitting

---

[1] The version we shall use is the one written out in French by Charles Perrault in the 1690s, in the Penguin translation by Geoffrey Brereton (Charles Perrault, *Fairy Tales*, Penguin Classics 1957, "Cinderella"). This is the most familiar, to English-speaking readers, of the several hundred versions of the story found all over the world, which include aspects of *King Lear*, and the earliest recorded version from ninth-century China (see I. and P. Opie, *The Classic Fairy Tales*, 1974, "Cinderella").

[2] The Penguin Classics *Jane Eyre* has an interesting introduction by Q. D. Leavis. The best biography of Charlotte Brontë is by Winifred Gérin, Oxford 1967; see also Tom Winnifrith, *Charlotte and Emily Brontë: A Literary Life*, London 1989.

in the cinders in the chimney corner), Perrault proceeds to the second, active division of the tale:

> One day the King's son gave a ball, to which everyone of good family was invited. Our two young ladies received invitations, for they cut quite a figure in the country. So there they were, both feeling very pleased and very busy choosing the clothes and the hair-styles which would suit them best. ...

Cinderella, of course, is not invited, but has instead to help her stepsisters to beautify themselves. Left behind at home on the first night of the ball, she is visited by her fairy godmother, who by magic provides her with the means to attend it, stipulating only that Cinderella must return home by midnight. All goes well on the first night – Cinderella is unrecognised but admired by all, especially the Prince – but on the second night of the ball she forgets the time and rushes home on the stroke of twelve, leaving behind one of her glass slippers.[3] The Prince, determined to find her, announces that he will marry the girl whose foot exactly fits the slipper. The stepsisters try to force their feet into the unyielding glass slipper but fail; whereupon Cinderella puts it on without difficulty. It fits her perfectly, and she is recognised as the beautiful girl the Prince is looking for, proving it by producing the other slipper of the pair. The story can then move into its final phase of resolution, setting out the new situation:

> Then the two sisters recognised her as the lovely princess whom they had met at the ball. They flung themselves at her feet and begged her forgiveness for all the unkind things which they had done to her. Cinderella raised them up and kissed them, saying that she forgave them with all her heart and asking them to love her always. She was taken to the young Prince in the fine clothes which she was wearing. He thought her more beautiful than ever and a few days later he married her. Cinderella, who was as kind as she was beautiful, invited her two sisters to live in the palace and married them, on the same day, to two great noblemen of the Court.

Now this three-part arrangement, situation/action/resolution, forms the basis of the plots of nearly all fiction, although it may not always be as obvious as it is here. The story of *Cinderella*, for instance, could have been told in the first person by Cinderella herself, in the frame of a tale re-counted long afterwards to her own children; she could have started with her happy childhood, the sad death of her mother, her father's second marriage, and his neglect of her; then she could have gone on to the ball and the miraculous intervention of her fairy godmother; and finally she

---

[3] Perrault insists that the slipper is made of glass – the subtitle of the story is *La petite pantoufle de verre* – both because it cannot be stretched to fit the wrong foot and because the beauty of the foot the Prince seeks is visible inside it.

could have explained how their father, now the King, had cleverly recognised her, and had helped her to deal with her problem family so that everyone could live happily ever after. Alternatively the tale could have been told from somebody else's point of view, in the first or third person; from that of the stepmother or one of the stepsisters, for instance, or of Cinderella's father, or of the Prince; or from several different points of view. Yet another scheme might be to present the story as a series of documents, such as Cinderella's journal, and letters between Cinderella and her best friend (people did write a lot of letters in those days), in which the best friend's story of her own life could be introduced as counterpoint to Cinderella's tale. In any of these variants, moreover, the story could be told in an order that departs from a plain chronological sequence, flashing backwards and forwards to indicate parallels and shift emphasis. All this is possible without fundamentally altering the original tale or its three-part structure.

Turning to *Jane Eyre*, we find that it shares with *Cinderella* the basic story of a young girl who, having lost her natural parents, suffers persecution at the hands of the family of relatives (including a wicked aunt and two unpleasant sisters) to which she is consigned; who is then by chance brought into contact with a man far above her in station with whom she falls in love; and who, overcoming great difficulties, is finally recognised and married by him. But within this basic framework Jane experiences a much longer and more complex series of adventures than does Cinderella. She is sent, aged 10, from her foster home to a boarding school for poor orphans, where she is presented as a liar by the cruel evangelical clergyman who oversees it; but her truthfulness is recognised by the senior mistress and Jane is a success at the school, eventually joining the staff. Feeling the need to move on at the age of 18, she advertises for a post as a governess, and obtains one to look after a little French girl, the illegitimate daughter (it seems) of Mr Rochester of Thornfield Hall. Jane, although poor and plain, fascinates her moody, masterful employer with her charm and intelligence; they fall in love; and Mr Rochester, although he has a mad wife hidden in the house, attempts to marry her. The ceremony is interrupted at the very last moment, Jane refuses to be Mr Rochester's mistress, and she runs away without means of support. After nearly dying of exposure, she is taken in at Moor House, the home of St John Rivers and his two sisters, who turn out by miraculous chance to be her cousins and with whom she shares an unexpected inheritance of £20,000. St John, another clergyman who conceals the need to control people in the guise of Christian charity, tries to persuade Jane to marry him and go with him to India as a missionary's wife, but she is again prevented at the last moment from making an injudicious marriage, this time by a telepathic call for help from Mr Rochester. Heeding it, she returns to look for him at Thornfield Hall, where she finds the house burned down and learns that Mr Rochester is living in retirement, blinded and maimed by the fire that has killed his mad wife. She goes to him; and the Byronic hero, tamed by his blindness and no longer in full control of her, is fit at last to become her husband.[4]

Here again we have the three-part structure – situation/action/resolution – presented in the form of the life history of a friendless orphan who eventually marries a rich man; a plot that may be described as a "wish-fulfilment story" (see the next section), deriving from the kind of fantasies which we have all experienced at one time or another.[5] In *Jane Eyre*, the story turns on four crises in Jane's life, each one being a three-part story in itself, and each one being precipitated by a man over whom Jane wins a moral victory (John Reed, the bully of the foster family; the hypocritical Mr Brocklehurst the school superintendent; and her two suitors, the masterful Mr Rochester and the coercive St John Rivers). By and large, Jane's eventual success is the result of her own efforts and strong character, but she does have some supernatural aid – the equivalent of a fairy godmother – in the form of the gross coincidence of her collapsing, destitute, at the house of the people who can best help her, and of Mr Rochester's telepathic call for help.

The analysis of the structure of these two stories suggests a number of further questions about how fiction is made – questions concerning plot, narrator, point of view, character, dialogue, and so on – which must be dealt with separately.

Plot and Suspense

Although it is possible for a novelist to invent a new plot within the three-part structure, it is in fact rarely done because most of the best plots have been used in many ways already. Here is a selection of popular ones:

Wish-fulfilment story I: an ordinary person becomes such a notable success in the world that he or she is generally recognised to be an extraordinary person.

Wish-fulfilment story II: a child is orphaned or abandoned by his or her parents, is brought up by unsympathetic foster parents, but succeeds in the world despite these drawbacks.

[4] Elizabeth Barrett Browning, in her verse-novel *Aurora Leigh* (1857), similarly blinds Romney Leigh to fit him for marriage with Aurora.

[5] In *Villette* (1853), Charlotte Brontë's other major novel, the same character, a few years older, is analysed with greater self-knowledge in the guise of Lucy Snowe.

Wish-fulfilment story III: some disaster brings a person down from his or her position in life; by strength of character he or she regains it.

Love story I: boy meets girl, they fall in love, circumstances oppose their union, and *either* they overcome all difficulties and end happily, *or* they don't and end unhappily.

Love story II: a girl is wooed or seduced by a man who is far above her in station, and *either* the man is persuaded by her goodness to love and marry her in spite of her humble origins, *or* he isn't and she is ruined.

Love story III: a girl is loved by two (or more) men, and has to choose between them; *either* she chooses the right one, *or* she doesn't.

Jealousy story: a husband suspects his wife of deceiving him (or, more rarely, vice versa); she is innocent, but they both suffer as a result of his unreasonable jealousy.

Adultery story: a wife deceives her husband and leaves him for another man; the new liaison falters, and *either* she comes to grief, *or* she is reunited with her husband.

Revenge story: the hero discovers some great wrong done to him or his kin, and sets out to seek revenge.

Hubris story: a proud man overreaches himself (or a man aspiring to be honourable fails to be so), and comes to grief as a result of his own actions.

Quest story: the hero sets out to seek some prize or treasure, over-coming various obstacles, helped perhaps by clues along the way.

There are of course other possible plots; and it will be seen that more than one plot can be combined in a single story. It will also be seen that in every one of these plots the author has the opportunity to introduce the element of suspense, the ingredient that keeps the reader turning the pages to find out what happens next. In *Cinderella* we have suspense right from the start (how is Cinderella going to escape from her wretched situation when even her father won't help her?), and it is kept up all through the story (how will the fairy godmother get her to the ball? will she remember to leave by midnight? will she be allowed to try on the slipper? will she be the only one it fits?). Similarly with *Jane Eyre*: how is Jane going to cope with each crisis as it occurs? And above all, will her love for Mr Rochester be reciprocated, and will it result in their marriage? We may guess that it will, but we are kept guessing until the very end.

Conflict, and action deriving from it, usually produces suspense; so does the introduction of the supernatural, of unrecognised love, of mysterious clues, and of dramatic irony (that is, when the reader is allowed to know something that the characters in the story don't).

Author and Narrator

There is obviously no telling who originally invented the tale of *Cinderella* (a combination of Wish-fulfilment story I and Love story I), so in practice we begin with an "author", who is Charles Perrault. This author, a real person writing away in his study, is in fact not writing the story in his own person – for how can this real person have experienced at first hand everything that is to be told? – but is using the device of a "narrator", an invented narrative voice. The narrator can see and tell us about simultaneous but separated events, can describe the thoughts of one or more of the participants in these events, and can comment objectively on the characters and their actions, in ways that would be unavailable to the real author. The narrator usually uses the flexible third person, as Perrault does here, saying "he or "she" did this or that. Alternatively the narrator can speak with the "I" of the first person, as the narrator of *Jane Eyre* does, usually because the author is seeking to present the main character in depth, and perhaps because it makes the telling of the story more lifelike.

The narrator can have more than one posture. He can be made to stand back, like Perrault's narrator, and appear to be telling the "truth" as far as possible, even if selectively, from a position of knowing everything; he is a "reliable" narrator. If on the other hand he is a participant in the story speaking in the first person, he can be made to tell his own version of the "truth" as an "unreliable" narrator. In either case the narrator will have no more reality than any character in the story, but will be the product of the author's imagination.

Point of View

The narrator necessarily speaks from a point of view. If his point of view is that of absolute omniscience, in which no character or event is more important than another, the story tends to lack focus; and it is therefore usual for the narrator to have limited knowledge, so that each part of the story is brought into focus by being told, even in the third person, from the point of view of one character at a time with whom the reader can identify, or occasionally two; in practice this means that the third-person narrative describes and comments on what this particular character sees and thinks but not – or only marginally – what any other characters are seeing and thinking until the point of view is changed. In *Cinderella*, the point of view is very largely that of Cinderella herself; it is mostly her knowledge of the stepsisters, the fairy godmother, and the Prince that is described or implied by the narrator, and we can only guess from her point of view what these peripheral characters might be thinking, or might be doing when she is not there.

First-person narration, as used in *Jane Eyre*, although it can have great immediacy, is more limiting, because the narrator can never see beyond the one character he or she speaks for, while being prevented from commenting objectively on this character's own experience; and, besides, the sheer improbability of extended first-person narration can actually seem more obvious than the different artificiality of third-person narrative skilfully handled.

Setting

The structure and plot of a novel is set in a particular environment. This is very often a contemporary environment that is familiar to author and reader; but novels can be set in a fantastic parody of the present, or in the past, or in the future, or in another galaxy, without necessarily preventing the reader from accepting and enjoying the artifice. Similarly, a novel written a century or two ago, and therefore dealing with a world outside the reader's experience, can be enjoyed as if it were a historical novel written today. Perrault evidently expects his readers to accept a world which includes a faceless Prince who falls instantly in love and wants to marry a complete stranger, and a fairy godmother with magical powers that literally drive a coach and horses through everyday reality; and they do so without difficulty. Charlotte Brontë, on the other hand, evidently expects her readers to accept Jane's experiences as taking place in a possible reality that parallels her readers' lives, even to the extent of believing in the Byronic Mr Rochester, who improbably combines the ultimates of masculine tenderness and masculine strength.[6]

Character

Convincing characters are at the heart of a good story; no other feature of a novel is more important. Not only must the main characters seem to be people that the reader can believe in and so identify with, but they should also react to and learn from experience in the way that people normally do; in short, the author must be able to bring them to life. Credible characters in novels are usually composites, made up partly of bits of the author himself and partly of bits of other people, remade into something original by the author's creative imagination. As a result, each author's characters tend

---

[6] On the Byronic hero, see p. 22 above.

to have a "family likeness", not so much within individual novels as in different novels by the same author.

In fiction of the past, both the appearance and the nature of the characters in a novel were often directly and minutely described; nowadays the novelist is more likely to display characters obliquely through what they say and do, and through what other characters in the book report of them. But in either case the reader should be able to experience the characters in a novel in the same way as our living acquaintances are revealed to us, by the progressive removal of the veils behind which they seek to conceal themselves.

All this applies to the main characters in a novel, and there can only be so many of them; minor characters will have to be created as well. There is no need for them to be as lifelike as the main characters – indeed it would interfere with the balance of the story if space were given to making them so – and they will inevitably be relatively one-dimensional. In fact they are like the people we meet only once, at a party or on a journey; whereas the main characters are more like our family and close friends.

Fairy-tale characters like Perrault's are essentially representative of single characteristics; they do not develop or come to life. Thus Cinderella is always as kind as she is beautiful, the stepsisters are proud and haughty (their repentance at the end of the story is unconvincing), the fairy god-mother is a benevolent magician, and Prince is – a Prince. Jane Eyre, on the other hand, being the reflection of Charlotte Brontë herself and having her author's hopes and fears, can be explored in detail from the inside: everything is seen through the medium of a consciousness which is recognisably real, and with which the reader can identify; the other characters in the story do not live in the same way, but exist only as parts of Jane's imaginative experience.

Dialogue and Monologue

Conversation, dialogue, is the means whereby people naturally communicate with each other. But here we meet a paradox, because the natural-sounding dialogue written by a good novelist is not really natural at all, but is actually highly artificial. If an ordinary conversation between two or more people is critically observed, it will be seen that it is full of hesitations, repetitions, sentences that stop before they are finished, sentences that never seem to end, interruptions, two people speaking at once, abrupt jumps from one subject to another, and so on; and furthermore that meaning is sometimes conveyed not only by grammatical construction and word order, but also by gesture, tone of voice, speed of utterance, slight

variations of vocal pitch or emphasis, and so on. Obviously a verbatim transcript of such a normal conversation would not do in a novel, however
experimental: it would not only be intolerably tiresome to read, but it
would often misrepresent what was actually intended to be conveyed.

So what has been developed for the novel is a form of dialogue which
seems natural but which is actually not natural at all. Dialogue is written
so that each speech *sounds* exactly right when it is read, either silently or
aloud; but most of the tedious and inconsequential repetitions, hesitations,
non sequiturs, and so on, are left out; and as far as possible the grammar and
word order carry the meanings that might in reality be expressed by tone
of voice, emphasis, and so on. This does not mean that characters in a novel
never repeat themselves, hesitate, or lose track of what they are saying, or
that their gestures and tones of voice are not indicated when this would
be helpful; obviously there will be occasions when, in natural-seeming
dialogue, such things will be recorded; but they will be recorded for a
purpose other than that of merely reproducing the inelegances of real
conversation.

Well-written dialogue will be vital, expressive and individual; and it will
not only reveal something about the characters who are speaking it, but
will also indicate their differences from each other, even when they are
supposed to have the same cultural background. But writing satisfactory
dialogue in one or more of the hundreds of the regional dialects of British
and American English not native to the author, or in the dialects of those
whose first language is not English, is remarkably difficult to achieve; it is
a special skill, akin to being a good mimic, which not all authors have.

Perrault's dialogue in *Cinderella* is well handled for its period; it is light
and amusing, though inevitably revealing little about character:

> Her Godmother, seeing Cinderella all in tears, asked what was the matter.
> "If only I could ... If only I could ..." She was weeping so much that she could
> not go on.
> Her godmother, who was a fairy, said to her: "If only you could go to the ball,
> is that it?"
> "Alas, yes," said Cinderella with a sigh.
> "Well," said the godmother, "be a good girl and I'll get you there."

The treatment of the dialogue in *Jane Eyre* varies considerably with its
context. Jane herself, though capable of improbably long disquisitions,
prefers to speak briefly and to the point; she is sometimes submissive (when
her remarks are usually at odds with her thoughts) and sometimes sharp,
and it seems likely that this was Charlotte Brontë's own way of talking. Also
largely realistic is the dialogue given to children and to servants and common folk, some of it in northern dialect. But realism is frequently absent

from the speeches of Mr Brocklehurst, Mr Rochester, and St John Rivers, the men with whom Jane does battle, for they are liable to argue (each in his own style) in lengthy, complex sentences that are comprehensible on the page but which would be not be easy either to construct or to understand in actual conversation. Here is a dialogue in which St John Rivers attempts to control Jane by means of dishonest argument:

> "I am ready to go to India, if I may go free."
>
> "Your answer requires a commentary," he said; "it is not clear."
>
> "You have hitherto been my adopted brother – I, your adopted sister: let us continue as such; you and I had better not marry."
>
> He shook his head. "Adopted fraternity will not do in this case. If you were my real sister it would be different: I should take you, and seek no wife. But as it is, either our union must be consecrated and sealed by marriage, or it cannot exist: practical obstacles oppose themselves to any other plan." ...
>
> "St John," I returned, "I regard you as a brother – you, me as a sister: so let us continue."
>
> "We cannot – we cannot," he answered with short sharp determination: "it would not do. You have said you will go with me to India: remember – you have said that."
>
> "Conditionally."
>
> "Well – well. To the main point – the departure with me from England, the co-operation with me in my future labours – you do not object. Your have already as good as put your hand to the plough: you are too consistent to withdraw it. You have but one end to keep in view – how the work you have undertaken can best be done. Simplify your complicated interests, feelings, thoughts, wishes, aims; merge all considerations in one purpose: that of fulfilling with effect – with power – the mission of your great Master. To do so, you must have a coadjutor: not a brother – that is a loose tie – but a husband. I, too, do not want a sister: a sister might any day be taken from me. I want a wife: the sole helpmeet I can influence efficiently in life, and retain absolutely till death." (*Jane Eyre*, ch. 34)

A method of recording what goes on in a character's head, in addition to what results in speech, was developed by a few authors early in the twentieth century, notably James Joyce, Virginia Woolf, and William Faulkner, and it is now part of the technical equipment of most novelists. Known as "stream of consciousness" or "interior monologue",[7] this method can be wonderfully convincing in skilled hands – Joyce's *Ulysses* contains some of the best examples[8] – but a moment's reflection will show that it is just as artificial as a novelist's ordinary dialogue. While the verbalisation of thought undoubtedly does go on in our heads much of the time, it goes on

---

[7] "Stream of consciousness" (a term coined by the philosopher William James in 1890) originally meant the whole waking process of continuous thought, whether in words or not. "Interior monologue" properly refers to the verbalisation of this process, or of part of it.

[8] See pp. 67–8 below.

as only one part of a continuous, comprehensive mental process involving not only words but also insights, ideas and sense impressions that are not verbalised; so that even the best "interior monologue" in a novel has to be supplied with artificial clues, and can give no more than a limited impression of actual mental processes.

Symbolism[9] and Allegory

A symbol in a novel is comparable to an extended simile, describing something which is in some way parallel to the main subject, and which enhances and enriches it. For instance, the blizzard that is raging when Anna Karenina's night train stops at a station between Moscow and Petersburg, and she is accosted by Vronsky, symbolises the storm of passion that is overwhelming them both. Again, later in the same novel, the mare Froufrou, broken in a steeplechase by Vronsky, symbolises both Anna, whom Vronsky is selfishly ruining, and women generally who are ridden by men for the sake of excitement and pleasure, regardless of the consequences.

Allegory, on the other hand, is a special form of extended symbolism, in which the implicit intention is that the set of characters, situations, and events that is described in the fiction actually represents and clarifies another and entirely different set of characters, situations, and events. Well-known allegories of this sort are Bunyan's *The Pilgrim's Progress*, Swift's *Gulliver's Travels*, Butler's *Erewhon*, and Orwell's *Animal Farm*. (Also, in our literary canon, Spenser's *The Faerie Queene* and Dryden's *Absalom and Achitophel* are cast in allegorical form.)

Fairy tales such as *Cinderella* are often symbolic – her lovely glass slipper could suggest the fragility of a young woman's beauty – and sometimes allegorical. The tale of the serial killer Bluebeard, who murders his wives after they enter a forbidden room and are found out, seems to be an allegory of the relationship of marriage in a society dominated by vengeful, authoritarian men, while the villain's blue beard may be a symbol of his excessive masculinity.

Symbolism is openly used in *Jane Eyre*, as when the great "irongarthed" chestnut tree at Thornfield Hall is struck and split by lightning

[9] "Symbolism" was a also movement in French literature that flourished especially in the period 1880–95, and was a reaction against realist and naturalist tendencies in art generally. The Symbolists sought to elicit a private, even spiritual, mood by describing "not the thing itself but the effect that it produces" (Mallarmé), emphasising suggestion rather than direct description, and evoking affinities between the material and the spiritual worlds. The Symbolist movement had some effect on the work of James Joyce, Virginia Woolf, and T. S. Eliot, and through them on their successors.

in a storm, forecasting the ruin and maiming of Mr Rochester; who says, after the event: "I am no better than the old lightning-struck chestnut-tree in Thornfield orchard".[10]

Intertextuality and Metafiction

Intertextuality means referring to, or using, some earlier work in the book that is presently being written.[11] References to previous works of art are commonplace: in architecture, in painting, and in music, as well as in literature. This is natural enough – even inevitable – when the fact of evolution in art is taken into account; each new work of art carries within it the art of its predecessors, and the artist may sometimes choose to make his debt to the past more than usually plain.

In fiction, the reference may be an oblique one, as when William Golding writes *The Lord of the Flies* as a sour parallel to R. M. Ballantyne's optimistic *The Coral Island*; or it may be central to the new work, as when Joyce explicitly builds the episodes of his *Ulysses* on the scaffolding of Homer's *Odyssey*.

Metafiction is also intertextual, in that it is fiction not just about other fiction, but fiction about itself. In its most obvious form, the author dismisses the narrator and steps out of the frame to discuss the novel he is writing. Storytellers have always allowed themselves to address their readers directly (especially in fairy tales: "And now, reader, let us return to Grandma's cottage ..."), but such formulae do not always indicate whether it is the author or the narrator who is speaking. (In *Jane Eyre*, however, the narrator addresses the reader directly on many occasions, and it is clear that it is Jane who is doing so, not Charlotte Brontë.)

A form of metafiction is also found in movies, where film-makers delight in making films about making films; François Truffaut's *Day for Night* (1973) does it very well, and there are numerous American examples from *What Price Hollywood?* (George Cukor, 1932) to *The Player* (Robert Altman, 1992, which starts by being about making films, and ends by proposing itself as the next film to be made).

True metafiction in literature, however, began with *Tristram Shandy* (1760–6), where Sterne kept interrupting the story and saying in effect, "Look at me, I'm writing this silly novel, isn't it fun! What's going to come next?" But there was little more to be done along these lines, and

---

[10] *Jane Eyre*, ch. 37.
[11] "Intertextuality" is also a technical term in critical theory, where it is proposed that every text is an *intertext* in a succession of texts already existing or yet to be written.

metafiction became uncommon except in occasional asides until quite recently, when some twentieth-century novelists, uncomfortably conscious of the artificiality of their medium, have attempted to overcome the problem by breaking the mould.[12]

Seven Novels

Having used *Cinderella* and *Jane Eyre* to illustrate the basic techniques of fiction, we look now at the use and development of these techniques in seven exemplary novels: *Don Quixote*, 1605–15; *Pamela*, 1740; *Pride and Prejudice*, 1813; *David Copperfield*, 1850; *Middlemarch*, 1871; *Lord Jim*, 1900; and *Ulysses*, 1922.[13]

1. **Cervantes** (Miguel de Cervantes Saavedra, 1547–1615)
   Don Quixote de la Mancha, 1605, 1616

Author: Cervantes was an impecunious old soldier who attempted to support himself by writing first a pastoral novel, *La Galatea* (1585), which was unsuccessful, and then *Don Quixote* (1605, 1615), which was an immediate hit; he had also written poems and plays; a collection of short stories which was published in 1613; and another tale of adventure, *Persiles y Sigismunda*, which appeared posthumously in 1617. Despite the great success of *Don Quixote*, his masterpiece, he died poor.

Text: The first part of *Don Quixote* appeared in 1605, the second ten years later in 1615. It was immediately translated into English (by Thomas Shelton, 1616), but the earlier translations are patchy, and it is best to use J. M. Cohen's Penguin translation into modern English (1950). *Don Quixote* was written by fits and starts, being frequently laid aside in favour of other work, and Cervantes did not bother to go back and revise the resulting blemishes and inconsistencies.

Length (in the English translation): Part I, c.197,000 words; Part II, c.212,000 words; total c.409,000 words.

Story and structure: The story of *Don Quixote* is the tale of a crazed knight, who is deluded by the romances he has read into thinking that he is following in the footsteps of the knights errant of the age of chivalry; assisted by his shrewd rustic squire, he lurches incompetently from one absurd adventure to another, mistaking windmills for giants and inns for

[12] See, for instance, ch. 13 of John Fowles, *The French Lieutenant's Woman* (1969); Kurt Vonnegut, *Slaughterhouse Five* (1969); Margaret Drabble, *The Realms of Gold* (1975); and David Lodge, *Changing Places* (1975).

[13] The one novel that was not written in English, *Don Quixote*, heads the list because it is the ancestor of all the others.

castles. Beyond this there is no plot or structure, for the episodes follow each other without much connection between them, and are interrupted with digressions and separate tales not involving Don Quixote. It is a loose, "episodic" form of fiction, which continued to be popular until late in the eighteenth century. The appeal of the great original lay in the story's engaging characters, the absurdity of its tales, its racy style, and its ironical humour; indeed it is still a wonderfully good read, despite its considerable length, provided that the *longueurs* – mostly the digressions and separate tales – are skipped, and that the reader is not put off by the numerous inconsistencies of detail.

Characters: The strength of *Don Quixote* lies – as it must in any successful novel – in its main characters: Don Quixote himself, who develops from being the butt of everyone's jokes into a lovable idealist whose dreams, however ludicrous, have dignity and influence; and his counterpart, the squire Sancho Panza, a peasant realist, fixer, and wit, whose hard eye for the main chance is softened by his genuine admiration and affection for his master. Their contrasting characters are shown and developed both by what they say and do, and by the author's commentary.

Narrative method: It is never quite clear who is telling the story. Sometimes it is simply "I"; sometimes it is "I" repeating a tale he has heard from "Cide Hamete Benengeli, a very exact historian and very precise in all his details" (Part I, chapter xvi); but most of the time we are in the presence a third-person omniscient narrator, who keeps generally to the points of view of Don Quixote and Sancho Panza. It is this familiar narrative technique, along with plain, unsophisticated dialogue in direct speech, that makes *Don Quixote* – now nearly 400 years old – still so easy to read. This can be seen from the famous adventure of the windmills:

> At that moment they caught sight of some thirty or forty windmills, which stand on that plain, and as soon as Don Quixote saw them he said to his squire: "Fortune is guiding our affairs better than we could have wished. Look over there, friend Sancho Panza, where more than thirty monstrous giants appear. I intend to do battle with them and take all their lives. With their spoils we will begin to get rich, for this is a fair war, and it is a great service to God to wipe such a wicked brood from the face of the earth."
>
> "What giants?" asked Sancho Panza.
>
> "Those you see there," replied his master, "with their long arms. Some giants have them about six miles long."
>
> "Take care, your worship," said Sancho; "those things over there are not giants but windmills, and what seem to be their arms are the sails, which are whirled round in the wind and make the millstone turn."
>
> "It is quite clear," replied Don Quixote, "that you are not experienced in this matter of adventures. They are giants, and if you are afraid, go away and

say your prayers, while I advance and engage them in fierce and unequal battle."

As he spoke, he dug his spurs into his steed Rocinante, paying no attention to his squire's shouted warning that beyond all doubt they were windmills and no giants he was advancing to attack. But he went on, so positive that they were giants that he neither listened to Sancho's cries nor noticed what they were, even when he got near them. Instead he went on shouting in a loud voice: "Do not fly, cowards, vile creatures, for it is one knight alone who assails you."

At that moment a slight wind arose, and the great sails began to move. At the sight of which Don Quixote shouted: "Though you wield more arms than the giant Briareus, you shall pay for it!" Saying this, he commended himself with all his soul to his lady Dulcinea, beseeching her aid in his great peril. Then, covering himself with his shield and putting his lance in the rest, he urged Rocinante forward at a full gallop and attacked the nearest windmill, thrusting his lance into the sail. But the wind turned it with such violence that it shivered his weapon in pieces, dragging the horse and his rider with it, and sent the knight rolling badly injured across the plain. Sancho Panza rushed to his assistance as fast as his ass could trot, but when he came up he found that the knight could not stir. Such a shock had Rocinante given him in their fall.

"O my goodness!" cried Sancho. "Didn't I tell your worship to look what you were doing, for they were only windmills? Nobody could mistake them, unless he had windmills on the brain."

"Silence, friend Sancho", replied Don Quixote. "Matters of war are more subject than most to continual change. What is more, I think – and that is the truth – that the same sage Friston who robbed me of my room and my books has turned those giants into windmills, to cheat me of the glory of conquering them. Such is the enmity he bears me; but in the very end his black arts shall avail him little against the goodness of my sword."

"God send it as He will," replied Sancho Panza, helping the knight to get up and remount Rocinante, whose shoulders were half dislocated. (*Don Quixote*, pt I, ch. viii)

2. Richardson (Samuel Richardson, 1689–1761)
Pamela; or, Virtue Rewarded, 1740–1.

Author: Richardson was a successful printer and publisher in London who at the age of 50 was inspired to write – in only two months – this first novel in two volumes about a resourceful servant-girl. It was a huge success, and he went on to write a continuation (*Pamela* Part II, volumes 3 and 4, 1741) and two more novels, *Clarissa* (1748) and *Sir Charles Grandison* (1754). Richardson, one of the founders of the modern novel, influenced many writers both at home and abroad, most immediately Fielding (one of the authors whom Richardson published), and later in the century Diderot and Rousseau.

Text: Being his own printer and publisher, Richardson was in a position to revise the text of *Pamela* each time it was reset for a new edition, which he did in each of the eight further editions that appeared during his lifetime. But even that was not the end of it, for he virtually rewrote the book in his artistic maturity, leaving behind a final text that was published in 1801. There are thus three main versions of volumes 1 and 2 of *Pamela* which are very different from each other: (1) the original text of 1740, in which Pamela's language and behaviour are spontaneous and plebeian; (2) the last of the emended editions that appeared in Richardson's lifetime (the "8th" edition, dated 1762 but published in 1761), where Pamela's manners have been progressively elevated and dignified; and (3) the final, largely rewritten version published in 1801, in which Richardson not only continued to refine the tone of his novel and the behaviour of his chief characters, but also and more fundamentally attempted to shift its moral balance. Of these three versions, the first and the last are the most rewarding (the second being neither one thing nor the other). Here is a real choice: is it better to read the last, 1801, version, which represents Richardson's final intentions for the novel; or the first, 1740, less sophisticated but livelier version, which represented Richardson's intentions at the time it was first published?

The nature and extent of Richardson's revisions can be seen in transcripts of the same extract from one of Pamela's letters in its first and last versions (both extracts are given on p. 48 in their original spelling and punctuation). In the final version published in 1801, the very conviction carried by the original, 1740, picture of Pamela had become something of an embarrassment: it was the picture of a lively and likeable but also common and self-seeking servant-girl, whose reward for the technical preservation of her "virtue" was marriage to the libertine who had taken advantage of his position to molest her. If Pamela's virtue was to be worth preserving, and if marriage to Mr B. was to be its proper reward, then both characters had to be cleared of their grosser imperfections; Pamela would have to be presented as one of nature's ladies, and Mr B. would have to have some of the standards of behaviour, as well as the position, of a gentleman. So, in the final version, the sprightly, flirtatious Pamela is given a serious, moral character, and Mr B. a less disgraceful one. In the original version of this extract, Pamela roundly calls Mr B. a rake whose vice has taken him from bad to worse. In the revision, while Pamela still remarks that vicious people may easily go from bad to worse, the observation no longer applies to Mr B. He is not called a rake; indeed, she says, he is not really wicked at all, only foolish – though of course he is not unusually foolish, seeming so now only because of his natural contempt for her position. Mr B. no longer keeps company with the grossly immoral Squire Martin; and Pamela's

First version, 1740

Well, said he, I will set this down by itself, as the first Time that ever what I advis'd had any Weight with you. And I hope, said I, as the first Advice you have given me of late, that was fit to be followed! – I wish, said he, (I'm almost asham'd to write it, impudent Gentleman as he is! I wish) I had thee as quick another Way, as thou art in thy Repartees – And he laugh'd, and I tripp'd away as fast as I could. Ah! thinks I, marry'd! I'm sure 'tis time you was marry'd, or at this Rate no honest Maiden will live with you.

Why, dear Father and Mother, to be sure he grows quite a Rake! Well, you see, how easy it is to go from bad to worse, when once People give way to Vice!

How would my poor Lady, had she liv'd, have griev'd to see it! But may-be he would have been better then! – Tho', it seems, he told Mrs. *Jervis*, he had an Eye upon me in his Mother's Life-time; and he intended to let me know as much by the Bye, he told her! Here's Shamelessness for you! – Sure the World must be near an End! for all the Gentlemen about are as bad as he almost, as far as I can hear! – And see the Fruits of such bad Example: There is 'Squire *Martin* in the Grove, has had three Lyings-in, it seems, in his House, in three Months past, one by himself; and one by his Coachman; and one by his Woodman; and yet he has turn'd none of them away. Indeed, how can he, when they but follow his own vile Example. There is he, and two or three more such as he, within ten Miles of us; who keep Company and hunt with our fine Master, truly; and I suppose he's never the better for their Examples. But, God bless me, say I, and send me out of this wicked House! (*Pamela*, 1740, i: 84–5)

Last version, 1801

I will set this down by itself, replied he, as the first time that ever what I advised had any weight with you. – And I will add, returned I, as the first advice you have given me of late, that was fit to be followed!

He laugh'd, and I snatch'd my hand from him, and hurried away as fast as I could. Ah! thought I, marry'd! I'm sure 'tis time you were marry'd, or at this rate no honest maiden ought to live with you.

How easy it is to go from bad to worse, when once people give way to vice! – But do you think, my dear father, that my master shew'd any great matter of wit in this conversation with his poor servant? But I am now convinc'd that *wickedness* is *folly* with a witness. Since, if I may presume to judge, I think he has shewn a great deal of foolishness, as well in his sentiments and speeches, as in his actions to me; and yet passes not for a silly man, on other occasions, but the very contrary. Perhaps, however, he despises me too much to behave otherwise than he does to such a poor girl.

How would my poor lady, had she liv'd, have griev'd to see him sunk so low! But perhaps, in that case, he would have been better. Tho' he told Mrs. Jervis he had an eye upon me, in his mother's lifetime; and that he intended to let me know as much by-the-bye! Here's shamelessness! Sure the world must be near at an end; for all the gentlemen about are almost as bad as he! – And see the fruits of such examples! There is 'Squire Martin in the Grove has had three lyings-in in his house, in three months past; one by himself, and one by his coachman, and one by his woodman; and yet he has turn'd neither of them away. Indeed, how can he, when they but follow his own vile example? (*Pamela*, 1801, i: 82–3) appeal to be sent out of "this wicked House" – the house of which she herself is to become mistress – is deleted.

Length: Volumes 1 and 2, 1740: c.256,000 words; 1801, c.209,000 words.

Story and structure: As we have seen in considering the text of *Pamela*, the story is of a servant-girl whose employer, Mr B., makes a series of attempts on her virtue, and eventually, all else failing, marries her. It is also plain that Richardson was increasingly concerned to make a *moral* point with his story, to persuade his readers of the importance of following the dictates of virtue and religion. Beyond this there is not much plot, and the structure is simple and linear; Mr B.'s mother, Pamela's employer, dies, leaving her at the mercy of Mr B., who separates Pamela from her friends, imprisons her in his country house, offers to make her his mistress, tries to rape her, and eventually, all else having failed, offers to marry her; at first she refuses but eventually agrees, and becomes a model wife. Virtue *is* rewarded, but at a price that may seem to us excessive.[14]

Characters: The only character of any depth is that of Pamela herself (concerning whom see *Text* above); and it is Pamela alone who comes fully alive and fascinates the reader. Mr B., and all the lesser characters, are seen through Pamela's eyes, and her descriptions of them tell us more about her than she reveals about them. Because Richardson's underlying concern throughout his career as a novelist was to promote morality, the more his subsidiary characters were made to convey a moral message, the less lifelike they became. Here it is only Pamela herself who is – at least in the first version of 1740 – free of this constraint, and is brought to exuberant life by the power of Richardson's creative imagination.

Narrative method: *Pamela*, though not quite the first, is the first great epistolary novel, that is a novel presented entirely in documentary form, chiefly as letters and journals. Richardson, lightly disguised as the "editor" of the Pamela papers, believed that he had hit upon "a new Species of writing", but in fact there had been predecessors. The point of view is largely Pamela's, the writer of the journal and most of the letters; but there are five other correspondents, each with his or her own style and point of view. Dialogue is reported both in direct and in indirect speech. This method, though in truth no more realistic than that of the omniscient narrator or of the first-person narrative, gives a great sense of immediacy, and certainly contributed at the time to the book's success.

---

[14] What we may consider to be the dubious morality of Richardson's novel parallels the sexual morality presented in *Don Quixote*, in which honour is preserved so long as even the most barbarous seduction is legitimised by marriage.

3. Jane Austen (1775–1817)
Pride and Prejudice, 1813

Author: Jane Austen[15] wrote six major novels, of which *Pride and Prejudice*, begun as a youthful work called *First Impressions* and later rewritten and published in 1813, was the second to appear, after *Sense and Sensibility* (1811). It was followed by *Mansfield Park* (1814), *Emma* (1816), and the early *Northanger Abbey*, published posthumously together with her last completed novel *Persuasion* in 1818. Her work was appreciated by discriminating readers in her own lifetime, but her reputation as a novelist of the first importance was established only after her death.

Text: No manuscript either of *First Impressions* or of *Pride and Prejudice* has survived, so we are dependent entirely on the text of the first edition, which was probably corrected in proof by the author. The second and third editions that appeared in Jane Austen's lifetime have no independent authority.

Length: c.151,000 words.

Story and structure: Jane Austen worked in fine detail on a small canvas, delicately delineating in comedies of manners aspects of the only life that she knew from personal experience: the social interactions of middle- and upper-middle-class families and individuals, set in a few locations in southern England during the Napoleonic wars (which get hardly a mention). Within these limits, all six major novels have a basic story in common: that of a heroine (or in the case of *Sense and Sensibility* two heroines) whose main preoccupation is with courtship and whose prime ambition, eventually achieved despite social obstacles, is marriage. The several versions of this story, which vary considerably in their characters, situations, and solutions, are worked out with an amused irony (sometimes funny, sometimes wickedly satirical) in a style of scintillating brilliance. The structure of *Pride and Prejudice* is rather more complex than most, involving, besides the heroine and her parents and sisters and aunt and uncle, their relative Mr Collins; his patroness, Lady Catherine de Bourgh and her daughter; Mr Darcy and his sister; Wickham, the villain; and the Bingley and Lucas families – some two dozen persons (besides several minor figures) engaged in a complicated social dance in which their relative positions and mutual attitudes are constantly changing.

Characters: Most of Jane Austen's heroines are slightly flawed; Elizabeth Bennet and Emma Woodhouse, for instance, tend to excesses of self-confidence, while Fanny Price and Anne Eliot suffer from the lack of it; and these flaws they manage to overcome, rather than alter, during the course

---

[15] See p. 21 above.

of their stories. This accords with what we observe, that people, while they may learn from experience, seldom change fundamentally in personality. Thus the majority of the characters in *Pride and Prejudice*, including that of the heroine Elizabeth Bennet, though thoroughly probed at a social level, and brilliantly represented both by their own speech and actions and by the comments of others, do not develop much in the course of the novel; what changes is the way in which they perceive, and are perceived by, the other characters. Thus Elizabeth's opinion of Mr Darcy changes radically; but at the end of the book she remains a wiser version of the Elizabeth of the early chapters, while Mr Darcy is seen, both by her and by the reader, in a fairer and pleasanter light.

Narrative method: Jane Austen uses the omniscient third-person narrator, largely but not exclusively attached to the point of view of the heroine. For instance, the narrator can be describing a situation or conversation in which Elizabeth Bennet and her thoughts are prominent, and then, when she leaves the room, will switch immediately to describing what goes on behind her back (as in vol. I, ch. 8). Letters between the characters are also used to describe and explain events that happen off-stage.

Conversation, which is the central means of telling the story, is mostly given in direct speech; and true metafictional asides are uncommon.[16] The effect is more recognisably modern than is that of the work of the major eighteenth-century novelists by whom Jane Austen was influenced (Richardson, Fielding, Sterne, and Fanny Burney), as the following extract shows; it describes the beginning of the hostile encounter between Elizabeth and Lady Catherine de Bourgh – a formidable precursor of Lady Bracknell – where they go at each other like two ships of the line exchanging broadsides:

"You can be at no loss, Miss Bennet, to understand the reason of my journey hither. Your own heart, your own conscience, must tell you why I come."

Elizabeth looked with unaffected astonishment.

"Indeed, you are mistaken, Madam. I have not been at all able to account for the honour of seeing you here."

"Miss Bennet," replied her ladyship, in an angry tone, "you ought to know, that I am not to be trifled with. But however insincere *you* may choose to be, you shall not find *me* so. My character has ever been celebrated for its sincerity and frankness,

---

[16] But see the metafictional aside in the last chapter of Jane Austen's early novel *Northanger Abbey*: "The anxiety, which in this state of their attachment must be the portion of Henry and Catherine [the heroine], and of all who loved either, as to its final event, can hardly extend, I fear, to the bosom of my readers, who will see in the tell-tale compression of the pages before them, that we are all hastening together to perfect felicity".

and in a cause of such moment as this, I shall certainly not depart from it. A report of a most alarming nature, reached me two days ago. I was told, that not only your sister was on the point of being most advantageously married, but that *you*, that Miss Elizabeth Bennet, would, in all likelihood, be soon afterwards united to my nephew, my own nephew, Mr. Darcy. Though *I know* it must be a scandalous falsehood; though I would not injure him so much as to suppose the truth of it possible, I instantly resolved on setting off for this place, that I might make my sentiments known to you."

"If you believed in impossible to be true," said Elizabeth, colouring with astonishment and disdain, "I wonder you took the trouble of coming so far. What could your ladyship propose by it?"

"At once to insist upon having such a report universally contradicted."

"Your coming to Longbourn, to see me and my family," said Elizabeth, coolly, "will be rather a confirmation of it; if, indeed, such a report is in existence."

"If! do you then pretend to be ignorant of it? Has it not been industriously circulated by yourselves? Do you not know that such a report is spread abroad?"

"I never heard that it was."

"And can you likewise declare, that there is no *foundation* for it?"

"I do not pretend to possess equal frankness with your ladyship. *You* may ask questions, which *I* shall not choose to answer."

"This is not to be borne. Miss Bennet, I insist on being satisfied. Has he, has my nephew, made you an offer of marriage?"

"Your ladyship has declared it to be impossible."

"It ought to be so; it must be so, while he retains the use of his reason. But *your* arts and allurements may, in a moment of infatuation, have made him forget what he owes to himself and to all his family. You may have drawn him in."

"If I have, I shall be the last person to confess it."

"Miss Bennet, do you know who I am? I have not been accustomed to such language as this. I am almost the nearest relation he has in the world, and am entitled to know all his dearest concerns."

"But you are not entitled to know *mine*; nor will such behaviour as this, ever induce me to be explicit."

"Let me be rightly understood. This match, to which you have the presumption to aspire, can never take place. No, never. Mr. Darcy is engaged to *my daughter*. Now what have you to say?"

"Only this; that if he is so, you can have no reason to suppose he will make an offer to me." (*Pride and Prejudice*, vol. III, ch. 14)

4. **Dickens** (Charles Dickens, 1821–70)
The Personal History of David Copperfield, 1849–50

Author: Dickens[17] wrote fourteen major novels, beginning with *Pickwick* in 1836–7 and ending with his last completed novel *Our Mutual Friend* in 1864–5. *David Copperfield*, the eighth, came at the mid-point both of his career, and of his immense popularity, in 1849–50.

[17] See p. 24.

Text: Most of Dickens's novels were published in shilling Numbers on the last day of each month. *David Copperfield* was typical in consisting of eighteen monthly parts of thirty-two octavo pages, each totalling just under 20,000 words, plus a final "Double" Number of forty-eight pages. There were also two plates of illustrations by "Phiz" (Hablôt K. Browne) in each part – Dickens considered the illustrations to his novels important adjuncts to the text – and, in addition, a frontispiece and engraved title-page in the Double Number for those who wanted to bind up their collections of parts.

Dickens wrote the book part by part, and was seldom more than a week or two ahead of the mid-month deadline. This meant both that the beginning of the story could not be reconsidered in the light of its ending, and that publication might be interrupted at any time by illness or accident. Yet for Dickens these disadvantages were outweighed by the value of the mutual relationship that developed between him and his readers as each part appeared, whereby their reactions influenced and encouraged him as the tale unfolded.

A man of extreme energy, Dickens wrote with astonishing ease. He started to write each Number with a bare summary, the "Number plan", which was followed by a single manuscript draft of the text, lightly revised and corrected (both these documents survive); this manuscript was then set by the printers straight into pages, and author's proofs (which also survive), probably accompanied by the manuscript copy, were sent to Dickens for correction, though the actual revisions he made were few.[18] The corrected type pages were stereotyped straight away, and stereo plates were used for printing both the individual parts and the single-volume issues that appeared from 1850.

Length: c.370,000 words.

Story and structure: The story is essentially a very simple one, being presented as David Copperfield's autobiography, from rejected orphan to famous author; its first chapter is headed "I Am Born", and its final one "A Last Retrospect". It is of course a version of the story of Dickens's own life, the most obviously autobiographical features being Dickens's self-image as a rejected child,[19] his experiences as a drudge in a blacking factory and as the son of a convicted debtor, and his hopeless love as a young man for Maria Beadnell. The story is told, moreover, chronologically in the first person, its chief complication being the introduction of a large cast of

[18] Strictly speaking, "correction" means putting right an error (usually of transcription), and "revision" means improving what is already correctly transcribed; but in practice the term "proof correction" is often used to mean both the correction and the revision of proofs.

[19] Others of Dickens's rejected children were Oliver Twist, Little Nell, Florence Dombey, and Pip.

additional characters whose lives engage and re-engage with Copperfield's: chief among them the Murdstones, the Peggottys and Little Em'ly, Steerforth and his mother and Rosa Dartle, the Micawbers, Betsy Trotwood and Mr Dick, Agnes Wickfield and Dora Spenlow, Uriah Heep, and Traddles. The novel divides naturally into three main parts, comprising Copperfield's childhood, told from the child's point of view; his youth and early manhood; and his maturity. It is a measure both of Dickens's genius, and of his personal engagement in the tale as he reviews his own life from the middle of it, that he can make out of these plain ingredients a convincing novel that touches so many readers' deepest feelings – despite occasional episodes of melodrama and sentimentality – and that grips them without letting go from end to end.

Characters: Although David Copperfield is as much the main character of his own story as Pamela was of hers, Dickens brings his subsidiary characters to life in a way that Richardson does not. It is not so much that they are described in the round – they are, after all, seen from only one point of view, and tend towards caricature – as that their chief features are so vividly and memorably drawn: once known, it is impossible to forget Wilkins Micawber or Betsy Trotwood or Uriah Heep. Copperfield himself is another matter. We follow him as he grows from childhood to manhood, and his development is plain to see both in the way he tells his story and in the maturing of his outlook, as he learns and recognises the central importance to him as a human being of self-knowledge and generosity; while his capacity to love changes along with his understanding of worldly affairs.

Narrative method: Dickens's narrator is of course David Copperfield himself, speaking in the first person; and he is inevitably both an implausible and an unreliable narrator. The implausibility associated with a first-person narrative is unlikely to trouble the reader, for it is possible, however improbable, that an intelligent writer like Copperfield could write an autobiography in this form, with all its verbatim reports of conversations and its skilful interweaving of character and story. As for its unreliability, it is plain that both a real autobiography and Copperfield's narrative must be highly selective in what they choose to say, however much their authors seem to want to be telling the truth; it is the nature of such documents to tell the truth as the author wants it to be received, with all the particular emphasis and omission that this approach requires, not as it might be seen by someone else such as an independent biographer or a third-person narrator.

Dickens's method of drawing the all-important minor characters is to fasten on to particular characteristics of their appearance, attitudes, and

turns of phrase, and to stay with these features, not developing them much
further, but using the resulting caricatures – illustrated and emphasised by
the brilliantly drawn caricatures in Phiz's plates – both as entertainment in
themselves and as throwing more light on Copperfield's character by showing his reactions to them.

The variety and skill of Dickens's narrative techniques can be illustrated
by extracts from the three main parts of the book, dealing respectively with
Copperfield's childhood, youth, and maturity:

[*Childhood*: David Copperfield, aged about 8, and exiled to an appalling
boarding school, has just been told of the death of his beloved mother]
… I cried, and wore myself to sleep, and awoke and cried again. When I
could cry no more, I began to think; and then the oppression on my
breast was heaviest, and my grief a dull pain that there was no ease for.

And yet my thoughts were idle; not intent upon the calamity that
weighed upon my heart, but idly loitering near it. I thought of our house
shut up and hushed. I thought of the little baby, who, Mrs Creakle said,
had been pining away for some time, and who, they believed, would die
too. I thought of my father's grave in the churchyard, by our house, and
of my mother lying there beneath the tree I knew so well. I stood upon
a chair when I was left alone, and looked into the glass to see how red my
eyes were, and how sorrowful my face. I considered, after some hours
were gone, if my tears were really hard to flow now, as they seemed to
be, what, in connexion with my loss, it would affect me most to think of
when I drew near home – for I was going home to the funeral. I am
sensible of having felt that a dignity attached to me among the rest of the
boys, and that I was important in my affliction.

If ever child were stricken with sincere grief, I was. But I remember
that this importance was a kind of satisfaction to me, when I walked in
the playground that afternoon while the boys were in school. When I saw
them glancing at me out of the windows, as they went up to their classes,
I felt distinguished, and looked more melancholy, and walked slower.
When school was over, and they came out and spoke to me, I felt rather
good in myself not to be proud to any of them, and to take exactly the
same notice of them all, as before.

(*David Copperfield*, part III, ch. 9)

[*Youth*: David, in his late teens, gets drunk during a dinner given in his
lodgings to the attractive but untrustworthy Steerforth and his dubious
friends Grainger and Markham]
Somebody was smoking. We were all smoking. *I* was smoking, and

trying to suppress a rising tendency to shudder. Steerforth had made a speech about me, in the course of which I had been affected almost to tears. I returned thanks, and hoped the present company would dine with me tomorrow, and the day after – each day at five o'clock, that we might enjoy the pleasures of conversation and society through a long evening. I felt called upon to propose an individual. I would give them my aunt. Miss Betsey Trotwood, the best of her sex!

Somebody was leaning out of my bedroom window, refreshing his forehead against the cool stone of the parapet, and feeling the air upon his face. It was myself. I was addressing myself as "Copperfield", and saying, "Why did you try to smoke? You might have known you couldn't do it." Now, somebody was unsteadily contemplating his features in the looking-glass. That was I too. I was very pale in the looking-glass; my eyes had a vacant appearance; and my hair – only my hair, nothing else – looked drunk.

Somebody said to me, "Let us go to the theatre, Copperfield!" There was no bedroom before me, but again the jingling table covered with glasses; the lamp; Grainger on my right hand, Markham on my left, and Steerforth opposite – all sitting in a mist, and a long way off. The theatre? To be sure. The very thing. Come along! But they must excuse me if I saw everybody out first, and turned the lamp off – in case of fire.

Owing to some confusion in the dark, the door was gone. I was feeling for it in the window-curtains, when Steerforth, laughing, took me by the arm and led me out.

(*David Copperfield*, part VIII, ch. 24)

[*Maturity*: David, now a famous author, looks at the end of his autobiography at what has happened to some of those who have peopled it; and here at the former friend of his late "child-wife" Dora]

What ship comes sailing home from India, and what English lady is this, married to a growling old Scotch Croesus with great flaps of ears? Can this be Julia Mills?

Indeed it is Julia Mills, peevish and fine, with a black man to carry cards and letters to her on a golden salver, and a copper-coloured woman in linen, with a bright handkerchief round her head, to serve her Tiffin in her dressing-room. But Julia keeps no diary in these days; never sings Affection's Dirge; eternally quarrels with the old Scotch Croesus, who is a sort of yellow bear with a tanned hide. Julia is steeped in money to the throat, and talks and thinks of nothing else. I liked her better in the Desert of Sahara.

Or perhaps this *is* the Desert of Sahara! For, though Julia has a stately house, and mighty company, and sumptuous dinners every day, I see no green growth near her; nothing that can ever come to fruit or flower. What Julia calls "society", I see; among it Mr Jack Maldon, from his Patent Place, sneering at the hand that gave it him, and speaking to me of the Doctor as "so charmingly antique". But when society is the name for such hollow gentlemen and ladies, Julia, and when its breeding is professed indifference to everything that can advance or can retard mankind, I think we must have lost ourselves in that same Desert of Sahara, and had better find the way out.

(*David Copperfield*, parts XIX and XX, ch. 64)

5. **George Eliot** (Mary Ann – later Marian – Evans, 1819–80)
    Middlemarch: a Study of Provincial Life, 1871–2

Author: George Eliot[20] wrote eight major works of fiction from *Scenes of Clerical Life* (1858) to *Daniel Deronda* (1876), of which *Middlemarch*, appearing in 1871–2, was the last but one; by this time, with Dickens recently dead, George Eliot was widely recognised as the country's greatest novelist.

Text: Early in 1869 George Eliot began to write a story about a provincial town, but eventually got stuck, and in November 1870 she began instead to write a new story called "Miss Brooke". This went much better, and she soon realised that the two stories could be combined in a single comprehensive study of provincial life. Part-publication (see below) began in December 1871, but George Eliot did not finish writing the novel until September of the following year; and publication of the Parts continued until December 1872.

The manuscript and proofs of *Middlemarch* survive, from which it can be seen that thousands of minor changes were made to George Eliot's text to bring it into line with the "house style" of the publisher, William Blackwood.[21] This always had been (and still is) a normal procedure; and because this printed text of a novel is the one that a professional author expected, and usually accepted in proof without demur, it is the one that is followed by most later editors, even in preference to the text of an author's

---

[20] See pp. 25–6 above.

[21] A printer's or publisher's "house style" chiefly involves orthography, punctuation, and the handling of abbreviations. Printers and publishers have always considered it their duty to ensure that these details should accord at least with the standards and conventions of their own time, and usually with those of their particular firm. Differences of spelling and contraction make little difference to the meaning of a text, but differences of punctuation can affect the meaning; nevertheless, few authors until comparatively recent times have actively objected to the house styling of their punctuation, and many have even welcomed it.

manuscript where it survives (though of course a manuscript reading will be preferred where it appears that the printer has made a mistake).

The publication of *Middlemarch* in eight large Parts (called "Books") from December 1871 to December 1872 was an innovation proposed by George Eliot's consort G. H. Lewes;[22] and a four-volume book edition was published at the same time as the last Part. Another impression followed in 1873; and a one-volume Cheap edition, significantly revised by the author, came out in 1874. It is this Cheap edition, the last one to be corrected by George Eliot herself, that would normally be chosen as "copy text" for a modern edition, with reference back to the earlier texts in order to spot and correct any errors, large or small, that had crept in.[23]

Length: c.340,000 words.

Story and structure: Perhaps surprisingly, there is a bond between *Middlemarch* and *Pamela*, which is that their authors were both consciously trying to extend the bounds of society's moral awareness and understanding. More than this, George Eliot sought to increase our ability to make sense of the world by probing the relationship between the individual and the community. She does this by taking several parallel plots, or experiences, and weaving them together into a fabric that enables us better to compare and understand their meaning. In doing so, she not only uses the traditional structure of situation/action/resolution – for her individual stories of Dorothea–Casaubon–Ladislaw, Lydgate–Rosamond–Ladislaw, Fred Vincy–Bulstrode–Raffles, Fred Vincy–Mary Garth–old Featherstone, all have features that may be seen as beginnings, middles, and ends – but she also abandons it by interlacing the stories with each other in such a way that they are seen to be part of a living continuum without accountable beginning and without foreseeable end.

It is surely no accident that *Middlemarch* and the other great tapestry-novel with which it may fairly be compared – *War and Peace* – are both *historical* novels, set in a past with a background of important public events that were still just within living memory, but were yet sufficiently distant to be looked at objectively and used as settings for those who experienced them. Tolstoy covered a wider range of settings; but against the narrower

---

[22] G. H. Lewes felt that publishing *Middlemarch* in large Parts would suit the structure of the book; and he also hoped that publishing the book in serial parts that could be bought for five shillings each would work against the restrictive trade practice of publishing three-volume novels at the prohibitive price of 10s 6d per volume for the benefit of the lending libraries.

[23] A "copy text" is the text, including its spelling, punctuation, and so on, on which a later edition is based. Any probable or certain textual errors that are identified in it will be corrected by its editor; and if this edited version has been skilfully done, it should be an improvement on all previous texts.

background of the life of a provincial town at the time of the First Reform Bill, George Eliot was equally successful in using history to illuminate the relationships between people and their community.

Characters: Just as important as the compelling structure of *Middlemarch* are the skill and profundity with which George Eliot drew its characters. Not only does Dorothea Brooke appear in three living dimensions, her hopes and fears being as real to us as those of members of our own families, but the chief subsidiary characters are now probed to a depth hitherto unparalleled in English fiction. Brilliant as Dickens was in drawing – and caricaturing – his chief subsidiary characters, he never quite equalled the psychological insight shown by George Eliot in her descriptions of Mr Casaubon or Lydgate or Rosamond Vincy.[24] There was indeed a limit to the possibilities of psychological perception in the 1870s, and a limit too to what could be achieved with the host of minor characters, however acutely described, that people *Middlemarch*; but George Eliot successfully took both the structure and the characterisation of the classic nineteenth-century novel as far as it could go.

Narrative method: Finally, George Eliot also took the device of the omniscient third-person narrator about as far as it could go. The narrator's commentary is an integral part of *Middlemarch*, his (or her?) attitudes and changing perspectives being every bit as important as the novel's other major features. The narrator ensures that we are always aware of the immense difficulty of reconciling the needs of the individual with those of society, and aware of the incomplete, patchy connections that exist between separate individuals, and between individuals and the people around them.

In 1873, Henry James wrote that *Middlemarch* "sets a limit, we think, to the development of the old-fashioned English novel".[25] It seems that he was right; but it is difficult to find a representative passage that is short enough to quote. Here are Dorothea and Mr Casaubon in Rome on their wedding journey, which is not proving altogether satisfactory as a honeymoon:

> [Mr Casaubon] had not found marriage a rapturous state, but he had no idea of being anything else than an irreproachable husband, who would make a charming young woman as happy as she deserved to be.
>
> "I hope you are thoroughly satisfied with our stay – I mean, with the result so far as your studies are concerned," said Dorothea, trying to keep her mind fixed on what most affected her husband.
>
> "Yes," said Mr Casaubon, with that peculiar pitch of voice which makes the

---

[24] Her ablest predecessor in this respect was perhaps Elizabeth Gaskell, especially in *Wives and Daughters* (1866).

[25] *Galaxy*, 15 (1873), 428.

word half a negative. "I have been led further than I had foreseen, and various subjects for annotation have presented themselves which, though I have no direct need of them, I could not pretermit. The task, notwithstanding the assistance of my amanuensis, has been a somewhat laborious one, but your society has happily prevented me from that too continuous prosecution of thought beyond the hours of study which has been the snare of my solitary life."

"I am very glad that my presence has made any difference to you," said Dorothea, who had a vivid memory of evenings in which she had supposed that Mr Casaubon's mind had gone too deep during the day to be able to get to the surface again. I fear there was a little temper in her reply. "I hope that when we get to Lowick, I shall be more useful to you, and be able to enter a little more into what interests you."

"Doubtless, my dear," said Mr Casaubon, with a slight bow. "The notes I have here made will want sifting, and you can, if you please, extract them under my direction."

"And all your notes," said Dorothea, whose heart had already burned within her on this subject, so that now she could not help speaking with her tongue. "All those rows of volumes – will you not now do what you used to speak of? – will you not make up your mind what part of them you will use, and begin to write the book which will make your vast knowledge useful to the world? I will write to your dictation, or I will copy and extract what you tell me: I can be of no other use." Dorotheà, in a most unaccountable, darkly-feminine manner, ended with a slight sob and eyes full of tears.

The excessive feeling manifested would alone have been highly disturbing to Mr Casaubon, but there were other reasons why Dorothea's words were among the most cutting and irritating to him that she could have been impelled to use. She was as blind to his inward troubles as he to hers ... (*Middlemarch*, Book II, ch. xx)

6. Conrad (Joseph Conrad, 1857–1924)
Lord Jim: a Tale, 1899–1900

Author: Conrad[26] wrote thirteen full-length novels, one of them in collaboration, and nine volumes of novellas and tales; the first novel was *Almayer's Folly* (1895) and the last *Suspense* (an incomplete historical novel published posthumously in 1925); but Conrad's work was a minority taste until 1914, when his novel *Chance* made it more generally popular. *Lord Jim* (1900, his own favourite) followed two earlier novels, a novella, and a collection of tales.

Text: *Lord Jim*, which Conrad first tried writing as a short story, and then started again as a full-length novel, was published in thirteen instalments in *Blackwood's Magazine*, 1899–1900, with serial publication beginning

[26] See pp. 27–8 above.

before the writing was finished.[27] Conrad then tightened up the story by cutting and altering parts of it for book publication in 1900. The last edition which he approved was that of 1921, but this edition included many extra commas and so on, which were not necessarily Conrad's; and there is a good case for using the 1900 version as copy text for a modern edition, with corrections and revisions from the surviving manuscripts and later printed editions.

Length: c.134,000 words.

Story and structure: *Lord Jim* is a psychological study of one man, the hero Jim (his surname is never revealed) who, when a young ship's officer and "one of us", commits a single, impulsive act of cowardice: he jumps into a lifeboat from the *Patna*, a ship carrying 800 Muslim pilgrims from Singapore to Jeddah, following the rest of the European officers who think that the ship is about to sink, after a collision and in an approaching squall. In fact the damaged *Patna* reaches port, and Jim has to face an enquiry at which he loses his mate's certificate.[28] He spends the rest of his life trying to atone (primarily to himself) for the loss of his honour. He eventually becomes "Tuan" (Lord) Jim to the natives of a trading station up-river in Borneo; but, feeling himself to be responsible for the treachery of a gang of murderous European pirates, he offers himself as a sacrifice to the native Chief, who shoots him. Neither story nor structure are particularly complex, except in the manner of their narration (see *Narrative method*, below), and the novel's exciting sea-yarn supports the reader's interest in the exploration of Jim's character.

Characters: The centre of the novel is the psychodrama of Jim himself, whose character is examined and re-examined, both by his own self-enquiry and by the reports of the narrators and their informants. After Jim himself, the most important character turns out to be the leading narrator, Marlow, an ironical, discursive, Conrad-like former ship's officer who is also the narrator of two important novellas of the same period, *Youth* (1898) and *Heart of Darkness* (1899).[29] In relating Jim's story, and the stories of those connected with Jim, Marlow's own opinions and reactions tell us more and more about him, as someone we come to know as well as the

[27] It does seem odd that not only Dickens (who had a reason for it), but also George Eliot, and now Conrad, were all prepared to allow part or serial publication of a book to start before they had written the end of it. This was something that Trollope never did, for fear of letting his readers down.

[28] This part of the story is based on a similar event that actually occurred in 1880, when the pilgrim-ship *Jeddah* was thought to be sinking and was deserted by her European officers; but she did not in fact sink and was towed into Aden. The Master had his certificate suspended for three years.

[29] An altered Marlow reappears later as the narrator of *Chance* (1914).

characters he is describing. His persona is essential to an understanding of Jim.

Narrative method: Conrad employs three main narrative voices in *Lord Jim*. (1) For the first four chapters, he employs an omniscient third-person narrator, someone who understands professional seamen, and who judges them according to a strict moral code. (2) In chapter 5, Marlow takes over in the first person, and tells Jim's story and how he came to know it as a long yarn told to sympathetic, like-minded listeners as they talk the night away: "Perhaps it would be after dinner, on a verandah draped in motionless foliage and crowned with flowers, in the deep dusk speckled by fiery cigar-ends. The elongated bulk of each cane-chair harboured a silent listener ..."[30] One of these listeners is a "narrator's narrator", when Marlow's tale needs to be summarised or commented upon. (3) This takes us up to the end of chapter 35 when, Marlow's yarn having been carried on as long as might seem feasible,[31] it is succeeded by Marlow's written narrative, which he sends to a "privileged man" who has listened to the spoken tale (presumably the "narrator's narrator"), and who is now to be given the conclusion of the story, covering Jim's adventures in Borneo and his death. The different modes of these three main methods of narration – the stern, anonymous third-person narrator, Marlow's sympathetic, meditative talk, and his flatter written account of Jim's end – each show different aspects of what seems to have happened, and each throws a different light on Jim himself.

Here is Marlow's account of Jim telling him about his jump from the *Patna*, at the point when the captain and the other officers are already in the lifeboat, and are calling to George the donkey-man, who (unknown to them) has just died of a heart attack:

> "He shivered a little, and I beheld him rise slowly as if a steady hand from above had been pulling him out of the chair by his hair. Up, slowly – to his full height, and when his knees had locked stiff the hand let him go, and he swayed a little on his feet. There was a suggestion of awful stillness in his face, in his movements, in his very voice when he said 'They shouted' – and involuntarily I pricked up my ears for the ghost of that shout that would be heard directly through the false effect of silence. 'There were eight hundred people in that ship,' he said, impaling me to the back of my seat with an awful blank stare. 'Eight hundred living people, and they were yelling after the one dead man to come down and be saved. "Jump, George! Jump! Oh, jump!" I stood by with my hand

---

[30] *Lord Jim*, ch. 4.
[31] Conrad claimed that "all that part of the book which is Marlow's narrative can be read through aloud in less than three hours" (Author's Note, 1917); but it contains some 98,000 words, and the normal speed of reading fiction aloud is only about 12,000 words an hour.

on the davit. I was very quiet. It had come over pitch dark. You could see neither sky nor sea. I heard the boat alongside go bump, bump, and not another sound down there for a while, but the ship under me was full of talking noises. Suddenly the skipper howled, "Mein Gott! The squall! The squall! Shove off!" With the first hiss of rain, and the first gust of wind, they screamed, "Jump, George! We'll catch you! Jump!" The ship began a slow plunge; the rain swept over her like a broken sea; my cap flew off my head; my breath was driven back into my throat. I heard as if I had been on the top of a tower another wild screech, "Geo-o-o-orge! Oh, jump!" She was going down, down, head first under me ...'

"He raised his hand deliberately to his face, and made picking motions with his fingers as though he had been bothered with cobwebs, and afterwards he looked into the open palm for quite half a second before he blurted out –

"'I had jumped ...' He checked himself, averted his gaze. ... 'It seems,' he added.

"His clear blue eyes turned to me with a piteous stare, and looking at him standing before me, dumb founded and hurt, I was oppressed by a sad sense of resigned wisdom, mingled with the amused and profound pity of an old man helpless before a childish disaster.

"'Looks like it,' I muttered.

"'I knew nothing about it till I looked up,' he explained, hastily. And that's possible, too. You had to listen to him as you would to a small boy in trouble. He didn't know. It had happened somehow. It would never happen again. He had landed partly on somebody and fallen across a thwart. He felt as though all his ribs on his left side must be broken; then he rolled over and saw vaguely the ship he had deserted uprising above him, with the red side-light glowing large in the rain like a fire on the brow of a hill seen through a mist. `She seemed higher than a wall; she loomed like a cliff over the boat. ... I wished I could die,' he cried. 'There was no going back. It was as if I had jumped into a well – into an ever-lasting deep hole. ...'" (*Lord Jim*, ch. 9)

7. **Joyce** (James Joyce, 1882–1941)
Ulysses, 1922

Author: *Dubliners*, Joyce's[32] volume of short stories, was published (after difficulties with squeamish publishers) in 1914, and was followed by his autobiographical novel *A Portrait of the Artist as a Young Man* in 1916.[33] Following serial publication of the earlier episodes, *Ulysses* appeared in book form on Joyce's birthday, 2 February 1922, and was an immediate sensation, being banned in Britain and America until the mid-1930s on grounds of obscenity. Joyce's last work, *Finnegans Wake*, was published in 1939; trial versions of parts of the *Wake* had appeared earlier.

Text: Like *Lord Jim*, *Ulysses* was originally planned as a short story, but

[32] See p. 29 above.
[33] *A Portrait* was a wholly rewritten version of *Stephen Hero*, the surviving part of which was eventually published in 1944.

was then turned into a novel, which Joyce worked on from 1914 until the very last moment before publication in 1922. The 1922 text (set by French compositors) was full of errors but, if these are corrected – which is possible, for we have virtually all Joyce's manuscripts and proofs for the book – it remains the most satisfactory text of all. All the subsequent resettings accumulated further errors, and the "corrected text" produced by H. W. Gabler in 1984 wrongly introduces readings from a manuscript out of the main line of descent of the text. At the time of writing, there is no edition of *Ulysses* in print that is wholly satisfactory, but non-specialists will get along well enough with those that are available.[34]

Length: 264,500 words.[35]

Story and structure: The whole of the action of the story takes place in Dublin in less than twenty-four hours, from 8:00 a.m. on Thursday 16 June 1904 to the small hours of the following morning. It is divided into eighteen episodes that parallel, but do not slavishly follow, Homer's story of Ulysses – or Odysseus – on his adventurous journey home from Troy to Ithaca, and to his wife Penelope and his son Telemachus. In Joyce's story, Bloom is Ulysses, Molly is Penelope, and Stephen is Telemachus. During the course of Bloomsday in Dublin, Bloom has various adventures, paralleling those of Odysseus with the man-eating Lestrygonians, the musical Sirens, the one-eyed Cyclops, the seductive Nausicaa, and so on, and eventually makes his way home with Stephen, whom he has met on the way. Finally, after Stephen has left to make his own way in the world, Bloom gets into bed beside his sleeping wife, who has received a lover during the day, but who, in a long concluding monologue, asserts her essential fidelity to their partnership. In the course of the story, all three main characters discover their own ways forward: Stephen as an artist, Bloom as an all-accepting, all-round man; and Molly as embodying the female essence, earthy and all-embracing; while all three of them recognise in their different ways that the unifying principle of human existence is love.

The book is divided into three parts. Part I, the "Telemachia", consists of episodes 1–3, which describe Stephen's day from 8:00 a.m. to about noon on Thursday. Part II, which has no general title, follows Bloom's, and to a lesser extent Stephen's, activities and thoughts from 8:00 a.m. on Thursday to 1:00 a.m. on Friday in episodes 4–15. Part III contains the remaining episodes 16–18, the "Nostos" or "Homecoming", and covers

---

[34] See *Ulysses: A Review of Three Texts*, 1989, in which Philip Gaskell and Clive Hart offer a "repair kit" of emendations for three of the most easily available texts of *Ulysses*, including the World's Classics reprint of the uncorrected 1922 text.

[35] From the Concordance to Gabler's edition.

Bloom's return home with Stephen starting at 1:00 a.m. on Friday, Stephen's departure into the night, and Molly's final soliloquy which brings the book to a close at about 4:00 a.m.

The structure of the book, utterly unlike that of the other novels described here, is analysed in greater detail under *Narrative method*, below.

Characters: The three chief characters are Leopold Bloom, a Dublin Jew, aged 38, who works on commission as an advertisement canvasser for a Dublin newspaper; his wife Molly Bloom, 34, formerly a singer; and Stephen Dedalus (the hero of *A Portrait of the Artist as a Young Man*), 22, a writer and intellectual, employed as a temporary master at a small private day school. Bloom and Stephen are made known by their own thoughts, by their actions, and by the reports of others; but there are only scattered references to Molly until she speaks for herself in the last episode. In addition to these three, there is a huge cast of subsidiary characters who weave their way in and out of the course of the book, the whole of which is laced together with numerous cross-references.

Narrative method: Part of the point of *Ulysses* is the variety of narrative methods, used by Joyce not only to tell the story but also to investigate the uses and limits of language. To give a clearer picture of what Joyce is doing, here is an analysis of both structure and narrative method, episode by episode.[36]

Part I: Telemachia

1. *Telemachus* Stephen leaves the Martello tower in which he has been staying, after an altercation with his Dublin acquaintance Buck Mulligan, and Haines, an Englishman. Straight third-person narrative, with occasional interpolations of Stephen's thoughts.

2. *Nestor* Stephen teaches a class of small boys at the private school, and collects his wages for the month from the headmaster. Third-person narrative, with an increasing proportion of interpolations of Stephen's thoughts.

3. *Proteus* Stephen walks alone on the beach, wrestling with his thoughts, which are given wholly as interior monologue.[37]

Part II

4. *Calypso* Bloom, at home in Eccles Street, gets his own breakfast, and takes a tray up to Molly, who is in bed. Third-person narrative, blending into Bloom's interior monologue. (The thoughts of Bloom, who is

[36] The episodes are not named in the book, but the names by which we now know them were used by Joyce when he was writing it.

[37] See p. 41, n. 7 above.

everyman, are much easier to follow than those of Stephen, the intellectual.)

5. *Lotus eaters*   Bloom walks through Dublin to the public baths, attending to private business on the way. Third-person narrative, blending into Bloom's interior monologue.

6. *Hades*   Bloom and others travel across Dublin in a carriage to the city cemetery for the funeral of their acquaintance Paddy Dignam. He catches sight, first of Stephen, and then of Blazes Boylan who, he knows, has a romantic assignation with Molly later in the day. Third-person narrative, blending into Bloom's interior monologue.

7. *Aeolus*   Scene in a newspaper office. Stephen arrives and later goes off to a pub with a group of journalists and others, telling them a parable on the way. Bloom dodges in and out of the office, just failing to meet Stephen. Third-person narrative, broken up by descriptive "cross heads" (as if it were a newspaper article).

8. *Lestrygonians*   Bloom, in need of lunch, walks first to a restaurant (which disgusts him) and then to a pub where he has a sandwich and a glass of wine. Third-person narrative, blending into Bloom's interior monologue.

9. *Scylla and Charybdis*   Stephen, in the director's office of the National Library, discourses brilliantly on Shakespeare, with special reference to the relationship between fathers and sons in the dramatist's life and work. Third-person narrative, dipping into Stephen's interior monologue.

10. *Wandering rocks*   A number of Dubliners – all characters in the story – go about their business in the city in nineteen short sections, which form an entr'acte dividing the book into two unequal parts (the eight episodes that follow it being both longer and more daring technically than the nine that came before). Mostly third-person narrative, with a few excursions into interior monologue.

11. *Sirens*   Bloom visits the bar of a hotel, where he has a light meal, and again encounters Boylan, who is just off to his assignation with Molly. Third-person narrative blended with Bloom's interior monologue, but in a style that imitates musical forms in words.

12. *Cyclops*   An anonymous pub storyteller describes events in another Dublin pub. Bloom arrives and is attacked for being a liberal-minded Jew by a bigoted (one-eyed) Irish nationalist. Colloquial first-person narrative with interpolations of third-person commentaries in a variety of exaggerated literary and other styles.

13. *Nausicaa*   Daunted by the attack of the Cyclops, Bloom takes an evening walk on the beach (the same beach where Stephen was walking and thinking in the morning). Here he looks up the skirts of a young girl and

has an auto-erotic experience. The first part of the episode is a third-person narrative in the cloying style of a women's magazine, representing the girl's mental climate; the second part is mostly Bloom's interior monologue.

14. *Oxen of the sun*   After a number of near-misses during the day, Bloom and Stephen eventually meet at the maternity hospital, where Bloom has gone to enquire after an acquaintance who is in labour there, and where he finds Stephen carousing with a group of medical students. Third-person narrative in a series of styles which – on the analogy of the development of the foetus – follow the development of English as a literary language.

15. *Circe*   Bloom follows Stephen (who is drunk) to a brothel, where each of them has a series of more or less hallucinatory experiences which come up from their subconscious minds. Stephen eventually dashes raving into the street, where he is attacked and knocked out by a British soldier. Bloom saves Stephen from being arrested by the police, and says he will look after him. This, the longest and most complex episode, is in dramatic form with speech headings and stage directions.

Part III: Nostos

16. *Eumaeus*   Bloom takes Stephen, now sobering up, to a cabman's shelter, where he treats him to coffee and a bun, and they engage in tired, desultory conversation. They leave together for Bloom's home. Third-person narrative in an exhausted, hung-over style, ridden with clichés.

17. *Ithaca*   Bloom and Stephen discuss life, the universe, and everything in the basement kitchen of Bloom's house. Bloom offers to put Stephen up for the night, but Stephen declines, and leaves on his own. Bloom goes up to bed, where he finds Molly asleep. The whole episode is in the form of a series of "scientific" questions and answers, the answers being variously long and short, relevant and irrelevant to the story.

18. *Penelope*   Molly wakes up when Bloom has gone to sleep and thinks over the events both of the day just past and of her whole life. She finds that she prefers Bloom, despite all his shortcomings, to her virile lover Blazes Boylan; and ends with a rousing affirmation of life and love, her last word being "Yes". Molly's interior monologue is in eight enormous, unpunctuated sentences.

The styles used by Joyce are too various to be adequately illustrated, but here are specimens of the different styles of interior monologue used by the three main characters, taken from the 1922 text:[38]

---

[38] This text, as it happens, does not need correction in any of these extracts.

[Stephen] Wombed in sin darkness I was too, made not begotten. By them, the man with my voice and my eyes and a ghostwoman with ashes on her breath. They clasped and sundered, did the coupler's will. From before the ages He willed me and now may not will me away or ever. A *lex eterna* stays about Him. Is that then the divine substance wherein Father and Son are consubstantial? Where is poor dear Arius to try conclusions? Warring his life long on the contransmagnificandjewbangtantiality. Illstarred heresiarch. In a Greek watercloset he breathed his last: euthanasia. With beaded mitre and with crozier, stalled upon his throne, widower of a widowed see, with upstiffed omophorion, with clotted hinderparts. (*Proteus*, p. 38)

[Bloom] Other hand a sixfooter with a wifey up to his watchpocket. Long and the short of it. Big he and little she. Very strange about my watch. Wristwatches are always going wrong. Wonder is there any magnetic influence between the person because that was about the time he. Yes, I suppose at once. Cat's away the mice will play. I remember looking in Pill lane. Also that now is magnetism. Back of everything magnetism. Earth for instance pulling this and being pulled. That causes movement. And time? Well that's the time the movement takes. Then if one thing stopped the whole ghesabo would stop bit by bit. Because it's all arranged. Magnetic needle tells you what's going on in the sun, the stars. Little piece of steel iron. When you hold out the fork. Come. Come. Tip. Woman and man that is. Fork and steel. Molly, he. Dress up and look and suggest and let you see and see more and defy you if you're a man to see that and, like a sneeze coming, legs, look, look and if you have any guts in you. Tip. Have to let fly. (*Nausicaa*, pp. 356–7)

[Molly] theyre all so different Boylan talking about the shape of my foot he noticed at once even before he was introduced when I was in the D B C with Poldy laughing and trying to listen I was waggling my foot we both ordered 2 teas and plain bread and butter I saw him looking with his two old maids of sisters when I stood up and asked the girl where it was what do I care with it dropping out of me and that black closed breeches he made me buy takes you half an hour to let them down wetting all myself always with some brandnew fad every other week such a long one I did I forgot my suede gloves on the seat behind that I never got after some robber of a woman and he wanted me to put it in the Irish Times lost in the ladies lavatory D B C Dame street finder return to Mrs Marion Bloom and I saw his eyes on my feet going out through the turning door he was looking when I looked back and I went there for a tea 2 days after in the hope but he wasnt now how did that excite him because I was crossing them when we were in the other room first he meant the shoes that are too tight to walk in (*Penelope*, pp. 696–7)

The novel continued to be the dominant form of British literature during the rest of the twentieth century, both in a literary mode – by, for instance, Evelyn Waugh, Anthony Powell, Iris Murdoch, David Lodge, Pat Barker, Salman Rushdie, Martin Amis, and A. N. Wilson – and in the popular genres of romances, detective stories, thrillers, science fiction, and fantasy, all of which had their forerunners in the nineteenth century. Some of the formal and stylistic innovations of the modernists – especially Joyce – have found their way into most of these genres, though there have so far been no further major revolutions in the forms or styles of fiction. With few exceptions twentieth-century novels have been shorter, at 75,000–120,000 words, than their predecessors – our seven examples had a median length of 212,000 words – maybe because it is more profitable to both authors and publishers to produce and market them in smaller units, especially since the advent of paperbacks in the 1930s; it may also be that readers prefer shorter books. Surprisingly, perhaps, more fiction, both old and new, is bought and read now than ever before, not yet displaced by the TV screen or the computer terminal.

Chapter 3

Poetry

The Nature of Poetry

Poetry is the form of literature in which the words and meaning of language are manipulated to enhance what is to be communicated by ear or eye; and it is characterised by the special use of *rhythm*, *sound*, and *language*. The distinction between literature in prose and literature in verse is not always clear-cut, because prose writers, like poets, can manipulate the sound of their words, and they quite commonly use special language; they may even write in a way that has a rhythmical lilt. What they do not do is to arrange their words according to particular rhythmical patterns.

The prime technical characteristic of poetry, then, is that it is *metrical*; that is, that the words of a poem are arranged according to some sort of rhythmical scheme.[1] The second is that the effect of the rhythm is augmented by   *d* of the words, by the use of rhyme, and by such devices as alliteration and onomatopoeia. The third characteristic of poetry is that the meaning of the words is heightened by the *intensification of its language*, by compression and by the use of striking words, images, similes, puns, paradoxes, and other linguistic figures. We will consider each of these three major characteristics of poetry in turn.

Metre

The rhythmical scheme is the basic essential of poetry, the one characteristic that is not sometimes shared by prose; and the rhythm of poetry is indicated in different ways in different languages. In Greek, Latin, Arabic, and Persian, for instance, the rhythm is marked by "quantity", that is by a pattern of "long" and "short" syllables; the difference between long and short being something like the difference between the English received pronunciations of the words "beat" and "bet". French and Japanese, on the other hand, use syllabic patterns, the number of syllables in the line being

---

[1] Except in "free verse", a dubious form of poetry which is discussed on pp. 74–5 below.

the chief metrical unit. The point to grasp about verse in English and in the other Germanic languages, and also in Slavic languages such as Russian, is that its metre is based, not on quantity or on syllable counts, but on *stress*, which is the technical term for putting emphasis on a word.

In English, stress occurs in two forms. One is the stress pattern that belongs to words of more than one syllable; here, for example, we say "páttern", "belóngs", "sýllable", and "exámple". Words of four or more syllables usually have two stresses, one being the main stress and the other a lesser stress: thus "múltitúdinous" has the main stress on "túd" and the lesser stress on "múlt", while "incárnadíne" has the main stress on "cárn" and the lesser stress on "díne". The other form of stress in English is rhetorical stress, where we stress a particular word (of one or more syllables) to indicate our meaning, so that a simple sentence can have as many different meanings as there are words in it. For instance, the six-word sentence "Where can I sleep well tonight?" can be spoken without extra stress on any particular word as a plain, unweighted question about where I am going to sleep well; or it can be given any of six additional, special meanings by putting extra stress onto each of its six words in turn: "Whére can I sleep well tonight?", "Where cán I sleep well tonight?", and so on.

The study of metre is called "prosody", whereby poetry is "scanned" or analysed; and it is lumbered with a set of technical terms of ancient Greek origin for which there are no plain English equivalents. But be of good cheer: though alarming at first, these terms turn out to have simple meanings.

In English poetry, then, the metrical pattern is made up of stressed and unstressed syllables. Following classical practice, each word or group of words containing one stressed and one or more unstressed syllables is usually called a "foot", and names – also from classical sources – have been given to the several varieties of foot. The simplest, and also the commonest, pattern of stressed and unstressed syllables in English verse is the one that goes di-DA di-DA di-DA; and each di-DA is called an *iamb* or *iambic foot* (which occurs naturally in such words as "enóugh, befóre", and so on). Other patterns, which are used less often, are DA-di, DA-di, DA-di (*trochee, trochaic foot*; "wícked, márriage", and so on); DA-di-di, DA-di-di, DA-di-di (*dactyl, dactylic foot*; "ángrily, pósthumous", and so on); di-DA-di, di-DA-di, di-DA-di (*amphibrach, amphibrachic foot*; "outrágeous, uplífting", and so on); and di-di-DA, di-di-DA, di-di-DA (*anapaest, anapaestic foot*; "intercéde, unreformed", and so on).[2]

---

[2] These names can be remembered by using the mnemonic sentence "treason – implies – dangerous – ambition – at-the-least", where "tréason" is a *trochee*, "implíes" is an *iamb*, "dángerous" is a *dactyl*, "ambítion" is an *amphibrach*, and "at-the-léast" is an *anapaest*.

The classical foot called a *spondee* – which has two syllables of equal quantity – is occasionally found in stressed verse, DA-DA, DA-DA, as in "wéll-vérsed, héart-síck"; but in English such words or pairs of words tend to become either *iambs* ("well-vérsed") or *trochees* ("héart-sick").

Lines of English verse will have a certain number of stresses – we can now drop the term "foot" – in them, usually four (*tetrameter*) or five (*pentameter*) or six (*hexameter* or, if iambic, *Alexandrine*). Lines containing two or three or seven stresses are less common (seven-stress lines – *heptameters* or *fourteeners* – tend to break up into groups of four and three stresses); and lines with one stress or more than seven stresses in them are very rare.

If a line of verse is perfectly regular in stress (which is actually uncommon), the stressed syllables will be interspersed with a repeating pattern of unstressed syllables. For example,

a.   The cúrfew tólls the knéll of párting dáy   (Gray)

is a perfectly regular iambic pentameter or five-stress line; and

b.   The Assýrian[3] came dówn like a wólf on the fóld   (Byron)

is an equally regular anapaestic tetrameter or four-stress line. It will also be seen that in regular verse, iambic (or trochaic) lines will have twice as many syllables as there are stresses, and that anapaestic (or dactylic or amphibrachic) lines will have three times as many syllables as there are stresses – in these two examples, five stresses and ten syllables in *a*, and four stresses and twelve syllables in *b* (see also examples *c* and *i* below).

Regularity of this sort, if persisted in, quickly becomes tedious; perfectly regular verse, indeed, is said to be easy to write and boring to read. The secret of more advanced English versification is simply that the chosen metrical pattern is seldom completely regular but is more often subtly varied, which makes it much more interesting and pleasing. (There is an analogy here with music, in which a silent underlying beat has rhythmically varied melodies played over it.) Not only can the stresses in a line of verse be varied in position and strength, but the unstressed words and syllables can also be varied in strength and even number, provided only that the main beat of the line is not lost, and that words and phrases are not wrenched out of their usual form. (Despite this, it turns out that there are *usually* – but not always – twice as many syllables as there are stresses in an iambic or trochaic line; and three times as many syllables as there are stresses in a dactylic, amphibrachic, or anapaestic line.) Here are some examples of shifting stress in five-stress iambic lines, with the main stresses marked:

---

[3] "Assyrian" is scanned as a three-syllable word here.

c. Néar me hung Trínitý's loquácious clóck,
Who néver lét the quárters, níght or dáy,
Slíp by him únprocláimed, and tóld the hóurs
Twíce óver, with a mále and fémale vóice. (Wordsworth)

Each of these four lines has ten syllables, and the second of them is regular. In the first and third lines, the first iamb is exchanged for a trochee; and in the last line both the first two syllables are stressed, with their two unstressed syllables following them, and then three regular iambs.

d. A líttle léarning ís a dángerous thíng;
Drínk déep, or taste nót the Piérïan spríng. (Pope)

In the first line, Pope has slipped in the third syllable of "dángerous", making "-erous thíng" an anapaest, so that the line has eleven syllables; as does the second line, "Piérïan" having four syllables. The third stress in the second line could be scanned "táste not", but this seems weaker than "taste nót".

e. Dón Jósë and the Dónna Ínez léd
For sóme tíme an unháppy sórt of lífe,
Wíshing each óther, nót divórc'd, but déad. (Byron)

Although Byron keeps to the regularity of ten syllables a line, he shifts the stresses freely to give the rhetorical flavour of a raconteur at ease with his story (see also example *o*).

f. Ó that this too tóo sólid flésh would mélt,
Tháw, and resólve itsélf ínto a déw ... (Shakespeare)

The driving rhythms of Shakespeare's dramatic rhetoric encourage Hamlet to speak out here. In the first line it would obviously be wrong to say "O thát this tóo, too sólid flésh would mélt", but it would be possible to split the second stress between "too" and "too", to give the effect of a weak spondee. It is almost surprising to find that each line has exactly ten syllables.

g. To be, or not to be, that is the question:
Whether 'tis nobler in the mind to suffer
The slings and arrows of outrageous fortune ... (Shakespeare)

This beginning of another of Hamlet's soliloquies is more meditative than the last one, but is still strikingly dramatic. It has eleven syllables to the line, each of which ends with an unstressed syllable. How should the stresses be marked for an actor?

Although the iambic rhythm is the commonest form for English verse, other rhythms have also been used. Here are some eight-stress trochaics,

the line-ends being marked by the omission of the final unstressed syllables
as well as by rhyme:

h.   Óh Galúppi, Báldassáro, thís is véry hárd to fínd!
     Í can hárdly mísconcéive you; ít would próve me déaf and blínd;
     Bút althóugh I táke your méaning, 'tís with súch a héavy mínd!   (Browning)

The following four-stress quatrain has been described as having a dactylic
first line, an amphibrachic second line, an anapaestic third line, and an
amphibrachic fourth line; but in fact these supposedly different rhythms,
which all have one stressed and two unstressed syllables, blend together
here (the line endings being alternately unstressed and stressed):

i.   Knów ye the lánd where the cýpress and mýrtle
     Are émblems of déeds that are dóne in their clíme,
     Where the ráge of the vúlture – the lóve of the túrtle –
     Now mélt into sórrow – now mádden to críme?   (Byron)

The *line* being the next larger unit of the rhythmical scheme, it follows
that the end of each line is also the end of a rhythmical unit, and indicates
some sort of break or pause in the flow of the verse; an effect which can be
emphasised by the use of rhyme at the line ending (see **Sound** below). The
break can be a definite one, ending a sentence or clause, in which case the
line is said to be "end-stopped" (as in both lines of example *d* above); or the
sentence or clause can be continued from one line to another, in which case
it is said to "run on" (lines 3–4 of *c*, and lines 1–2 of *e*); but note that even
a run-on line has a slight pause at the end.

The effect of the line ending can also be altered by finishing it not (as
is more usual) with a stressed syllable (examples *a–f, h* above), but with
one or more unstressed syllables (example *g*, and lines 1 and 3 of *i*). These
are called "masculine" and "feminine" endings respectively; the feminine
endings of *g* seem to add to the pensive effect as Hamlet begins this
soliloquy.

Yet another variation of the rhythm of the line is the introduction of a
pause – or sometimes two pauses – in the body of it, called a *caesura*. The
commas in lines 2, 3, and 4 of example *c* have the effect of weak caesuras;
and there are strong caesuras after "Drínk déep" in line 2 of *d*, and at both
the commas in the first line of *g*.

After the line, the next unit up in the metrical scheme consists of groups
of lines called "stanzas". The forms that stanzas take will be discussed
under *Rhyme*, below.

"Free verse" is poetry without a particular scheme of rhythm or rhyme;
in expert hands (such as those of Blake, Whitman, D. H. Lawrence, or Ted
Hughes) it is given its own sort of rhythm by the juxtaposition of the

cadences of rhetorical or colloquial speech; but too often it is no more than heightened prose divided by clauses into lines of more or less arbitrary length. It has commonly been the resort – especially in the mid-twentieth century – of would-be poets who lacked the skill or energy to master the disciplines of versification; real poets seldom bother with it.

Sound

Rhyme

The purpose of using rhyme in poetry is not only to articulate the verse, adding vigour and momentum at the line endings, but also to give it a pleasant sound, and to make it easier to remember. Standard English is relatively poor in rhymes compared with Scots English and most other western languages, so that care has to be taken to see that the rhymes that are available do not become overused and stale (the *moon/June, love/dove* problem); it is hard to find suitable rhymes for such important words as *honour* and *spirit*.

An ordinary rhyme in English duplicates the sound, but not necessarily the spelling, of the last stressed syllable and all that follows it (*thing/spring; myrtle/turtle; foam/home; latter day/Saturday*). "Masculine" rhymes, like masculine endings, have no unstressed syllables after them (*found/ unbound*); while "feminine" rhymes, like feminine endings, do have unstressed syllables at the end (*loving/shoving; reporter/her daughter*); note the alternation of feminine and masculine endings and rhymes in example *i*. Rhymes of three or more syllables often sound comical, and are used for this effect by Byron (*ladies intellectual/have they not henpecked you all?*; and see example *o*).

Then there is para-rhyme,[4] a medieval device, later used by Emily Dickinson, Wilfrid Owen, and many twentieth-century poets; these are rhymes in which the consonants, but not the vowels, of the last stressed syllable and all that follows it are duplicated (*laughed/left; untold/distilled; spoiled/spilled; tigress/progress; skeleton/school at ten*). Occasionally eyerhymes are used, in which the spelling but not the sound is duplicated (for example, *trough/rough; one/alone; love/prove*).

Rhymes may be set within the lines ("internal rhymes") as well as at the ends of them, as in the third lines of some of the four-line stanzas of Coleridge's *Ancient Mariner*, which also have rhymes at the ends of lines 2 and 4:

---

[4] Also known as "off", "partial, "imperfect", or "slant" rhyme.

j.   The Sun came up upon the left,
      Out of the sea came he!
      And he shone bright, and on the right
      Went down into the sea.   (Coleridge)

Not all verse is rhymed. The poet may be discouraged by the paucity of rhymes in English, or he may want to avoid the jingle of rhyme, or he may be writing dramatic verse in which rhyme seems inappropriate. Most dramatic verse in English has in fact been written in unrhymed or "blank" five-stress lines; as have several long poems of dramatic or autobiographical character, such as Milton's *Paradise Lost* (1667), Wordsworth's *The Prelude* (1805, 1850), Tennyson's *Idylls of the King* (1859), Browning's *The Ring and the Book* (1868), and Betjeman's *Summoned by Bells* (1960).

Rhyme is intimately connected with the grouping of lines in a poem to form "stanzas".[5] Here the lines are laid out in sets of anything from two to fourteen lines each, nearly always with a rhyme-scheme that may be simple or complex, the rhymes being marked by means of a matching system of insets on the written or printed page.

The minimal form of stanza is the "couplet", two lines – usually of five or four stresses each – rhyming together (and in fact usually set out to follow each other on the page without a division between them). The five-stress couplet, although in regular use from Chaucer to the present day, was especially characteristic of neoclassical verse:

k.   Lo! thy dread Empire, CHAOS! is restor'd;
      Light dies before thy uncreating word:
      Thy hand, great Anarch! lets the curtain fall;
      And Universal Darkness buries all.   (Pope)

The four-stress couplet has commonly been used in English for lighter verse, where the lack of varied rhymes can be used to effect. Lighter does not necessarily mean less serious – as for instance in Marvell's "To His Coy Mistress" – but the form is particularly apt for comic verse:

l.   Matilda told such Dreadful Lies,
      It made one Gasp and Stretch one's eyes;
      Her Aunt, who, from her earliest youth,
      Had kept a Strict Regard for Truth,
      Attempted to believe Matilda:
      The effort very nearly killed her ...   (Belloc)

The association of four-stress rhymed lines with English light verse is a problem for the translators of German, Russian, and Scandinavian poets

---

[5] Stanzas (of hymns, for example) are sometimes confusingly called "verses"; technically "a verse" is a single line of poetry.

who wrote serious poems in this metre (Goethe's *Faust*, Pushkin's *Eugene Onegin*, Ibsen's *Brand*, and so on).

Three-line stanzas are relatively rare, but "quatrains", stanzas of four lines usually rhymed *abab* or *abcb*,[6] are common; quatrains are frequently made of four-stress lines, less often of five-stress lines, or lines alternating between four and three stresses ("ballad metre"; see example *j*). Here is a five-stress quatrain rhyming *aaba*:

m. A book of Verses underneath the Bough,
    A Jug of Wine, a Loaf of Bread – and Thou
      Beside me singing in the Wilderness –
    O Wilderness were Paradise enow!   (Fitzgerald)

The variety of possible stanza forms is potentially enormous, though in practice only a limited number have been in regular use in English poetry. A few of them are illustrated below: "rime royal" (seven five-stress lines rhyming *ababbcc*); "ottava rima" (eight five-stress lines rhyming *abababcc*); the "Spenserian stanza" (eight five-stress lines, and one six-stress line, rhyming *ababbcbcc*); and the various forms of "sonnet", the commonest being the "Italian sonnet" and the "English sonnet". Sonnets have fourteen lines, usually with five stresses in each, but exceptionally with six. In the Italian form of sonnet (used by Milton, Wordsworth, and others), the direction of the poem usually changes between the first eight lines (the "octave") and the last six lines (the "sestet"); and it has various rhyme-schemes on the lines of *abbaabba-cdecde*. In the English form (used chiefly by Shakespeare and his contemporaries), the division between the octave and the sestet is sometimes (but not always) absent, and a final couplet resolves the poem; the rhyme scheme is on the lines of *ababcdcdefef-gg*.

n.   *Rime royal*
    Through which I see that clean out of your mind
    Ye have me cast; and I ne can nor may
    For all this world, within my heartë find
    To unloven you a quarter of a day!
    In cursëd time I born was, wellaway,
    That you, that do me all this woe endure,
    Yet love I best of any creätúre.   (Chaucer)

o.   *Ottava Rima*
    But now at thirty years my hair is grey –
      (I wonder what it will be like at forty?

---

[6] In this system, the rhyme first encountered is labelled *a*, the second *b*, the third *c*, and so on; so that a quatrain rhyming *abab* has the first line rhymed with the third, and the second line rhymed with the fourth.

I thought of a peruke the other day –)
  My heart is not much greener; and, in short, I
Have squandered my whole summer while 'twas May,
  And feel no more the spirit to retort; I
Have spent my life, both interest and principal,
And deem not, what I deemed, my soul invincible.   (Byron)

p. *Spenserian stanza*
    Ere long they come, where that same wicked wight
      His dwelling has, low in an hollow cave,
    Farre underneath a craggie clift ypight,
      Darke, dolefull, drearie, like a greedie grave,
      That still for carrion carcases doth crave:
    On top whereof aye dwelt the ghastly Owle,
      Shrieking his balefull note, which ever drave
    Farre from that haunt all other chearefull fowle;
    And all about it wandering ghostes did waile and howle.   (Spenser)

q. *English sonnet*
    Since there's no help, come let us kiss and part.
      Nay, I have done; you get no more of me,
    And I am glad, yea, glad with all my heart,
      That thus so cleanly I myself can free;
    Shake hands for ever, cancel all our vows,
      And when we meet at any time again,
    Be it not seen in either of our brows
      That we one jot of former love retain.
    Now at the last gasp of Love's latest breath,
      When, his pulse failing, Passion speechless lies,
    When Faith is kneeling by his bed of death,
      And Innocence is closing up his eyes,
        Now if thou wouldst, when all have given him over,
        From death to life thou mightst him yet recover.   (Drayton)

r. *Italian sonnet*
    "Upon Westminster Bridge, Sept. 3, 1802"
    Earth has not anything to show more fair:
      Dull would he be of soul who could pass by
      A sight so touching in its majesty:
    This City now doth, like a garment, wear
    The beauty of the morning; silent, bare,
      Ships, towers, domes, theatres, and temples lie
      Open unto the fields, and to the sky;
    All bright and glittering in the smokeless air.
    Never did sun more beautifully steep
      In his first splendour, valley, rock, or hill;
    Ne'er saw I, never felt, a calm so deep!
      The river glideth at his own sweet will:

> Dear God! the very houses seem asleep;
> And all that mighty heart is lying still!   (Wordsworth)

Finally on this subject, it is a useful exercise to describe and scan a stanza of Masefield's "Cargoes":

s.   Dirty British coaster with a salt-caked smoke stack
      Butting through the Channel in the mad March days,
      With a cargo of Tyne coal,
      Road-rail, pig-lead,
      Firewood, iron-ware, and cheap tin trays.   (Masefield)

Other Sound Effects

"Alliteration" – using the same letter or sound at the beginning of (or occasionally within) several words in a line – was used, with a caesura pause, as a main principle in Old English verse; and, although verse depending primarily on alliteration died out in the Middle English period, it has continued to be used occasionally for the reinforcement of an important passage:

t.   In a somer seson whan soft was the sonne   (Langland)

u.   tongues in trees, books in the running brooks, sermons in stones
                                                          (Shakespeare)

v.   O Wild West Wind, thou breath of Autumn's being   (Shelley)

"Assonance" and "consonance" refer to resemblances or correspondences, of the sounds of vowels and consonants respectively, between syllables or words which enrich the movement of the verse:

w.   "O where are you going?" said reader to rider,
      "That valley is fatal when furnaces burn,
      Yonder's the midden whose odours will madden,
      That gap is the grave where the tall return."   (Auden)

"Onomatopoeia" – the matching of sound to sense – can be especially effective in verse when it involves phrases rather than single words such as "smack" or "cuckoo":

x.   The moan of doves in immemorial elms,
      And murmuring of innumerable bees.   (Tennyson)

"Movement" is the effect of making the verse drag or hurry along to emphasise its meaning:

y.   When Ajax strives some rock's vast weight to throw,
      The line too labours, and the words move slow;
      Not so, when swift Camilla scours the plain,
      Flies o'er th' unbending corn, and skims along the main.   (Pope)

Language

The language of poetry must always be to some extent artificial – we do not, after all, speak to each other in verse – both to accommodate poetic rhythm and sound, and to intensify what is said by the use of carefully selected words and rhetorical devices; and this "poetic licence" allows the poet to take liberties with the language. It will involve alterations of the normal word order, and a tendency to move away from the everyday and familiar. As we have seen, this appears to lead eventually to a degree of poetic artificiality that becomes intolerable – as in the eighteenth-century saying "the finny tribe" instead of "fish", a word thought not to be sufficiently "poetic" – and then to a revolution is taste and technique that returns to some approximation of "the real language of men".[7] But wherever we look in this cycle of change we will find that the use of striking images (similes and metaphors), and figures of speech such as metonymy and synecdoche, puns and double meanings, help to convey what the poet wants to say intensely and economically.

In poetry, *images* include *similes* introduced by "like" or "as" (example *b*, "The Assyrian came down like a wolf on the fold"); and *metaphors* which compare two things by saying one is the other (example *g*, "The slings and arrows of outrageous fortune"). Both similes and metaphors can be extended and elaborated to fill whole stanzas or short poems (the sestet of example *q*, in which Love is attended at his death-bed by Passion, Faith, and Innocence, is an extended metaphor; as is the whole of example *k*). *Antithesis* places opposing ideas against each other (example *g*, "To be, or not to be …").

Metonymy designates something by the name of something else associated with it ("The White House" for the President of the USA; and in example *d*, where Pope uses "the Pierian spring" – referring to the site on Mount Olympus that was the home of the Muses – to mean the source of art and wisdom); *allegory* is a special form of metonymy. *Conceits* are especially far-fetched comparisons. In *synecdoche*, either the part is made to stand for the whole (saying "all hands" when we mean all people), or the whole for the part (saying "England" when we mean the members of the English football team).

Irony is a fundamental device of satire; and *hyperbole*, intentional exaggeration, is an ironical device (example *k*). *Puns* and *double meanings* were much prized in Elizabethan and Jacobean verse, and seem to have fas-

---

[7] As Wordsworth put it in 1800; or, as T. S. Eliot said in 1942, poetry "has to be in such a relation to the speech of his time that the listener or reader can say 'that is how I should talk if I could talk poetry'" (see p. 102, n. 19 below).

cinated Shakespeare, the author of this final example: a sonnet which illustrates several of the devices that have been mentioned:

z. When my love swears that she is made of truth
   I do believe her though I know she lies,
   That she might think me some untutor'd youth
   Unlearnèd in the world's false subtleties.
   Thus vainly thinking that she thinks me young,
   Although she knows my days are past the best,
   Simply I credit her false-speaking tongue;
   On both sides thus is simple truth suppress'd.
   But wherefore says she not she is unjust,
   And wherefore say not I that I am old?
   O, love's best habit is in seeming trust,
   And age in love loves not to have years told.
      Therefore I lie with her, and she with me,
      And in our faults by lies we flatter'd be.   (Sonnet 138)

Poetry – and, to some extent, all literature – can be difficult to understand, not only because of the reorganisation and intensification of the language used by the poet, but also because of the cultural distance between poet and reader which will involve different uses of language, references to personal and historical events, and so on. Nevertheless the appeal of good poetry lies in its meaning as well as in its rhythm and sound: the poet has something to convey in extraordinary language, and it is worth the effort needed to understand it.

Good poems are on the whole easier to read than bad ones. They please the ear, like good music; they say something worthwhile in a small space, excluding everything that is not essential; and they use poetic language for the sake of what it can do, not just for the sake of using it.

Seven Poems

Seven annotated examples follow of good poems that were ahead of their time.

1. **Chaucer** (Geoffrey Chaucer, c.1343–1400)
   from the general *Prologue to the Canterbury Tales*

   Ther was also a Nonne, a Prioresse,
   That of hir smylyng was ful symple and coy;
   Hire gretteste ooth was but by Seinte Loy;
   And she was cleped madame Eglentyne.
   Ful weel she soong the service dyvyne   5
   Entunèd in hir nose ful semely;
   And Frenssh she spak ful faire and fetisly,
   After the scole of Stratford atte Bowe,

For Frenssh of Parys was to hire unknowe.
At metë wel y-taught was she with alle;   10
She leet no morsel from hir lippes falle,
Ne wette hir fyngres in her sauce depe;
Wel koude she carie a morsel and wel kepe
That no drope ne fille upon hir brest.
In curteisie was set ful muchel hir lest   15
Hir over-lippe wyped she so clene
That in her coppe ther was no ferthyng sene
Of grece, whan she dronken hadde hir draughte.
Ful semely after hir mete she raughte.
And sikerly she was of greet disport,   20
And ful plesaunt, and amyable of port,
And peyned hir to countrefete cheere
Of court, and to been estatlich of manere,
And to ben holden digne of reverence.
But for to speken of hire conscience,   25
She was so charitable and so pitous,
She wolde wepe, if that she saugh a mous
Kaught in a trappe, if it were deed or bledde.
Of smale houndes hadde she that she fedde
With rosted flessh, or milk and wastel-breed.   30
But soore wepte she if oon of hem were deed,
Or if men smoot it with a yerde smerte;
And all was conscience and tendre herte.
Ful semyly hir wympel pynched was,
Hir nose tretys, hir eyen greye as glas;   35
Hir mouth ful smal, and therto softe and reed.
But sikerly she hadde a fair forheed;
It was almoost a spanne brood, I trowe;
For, hardily, she was nat undergrowe.
Ful fetys was hir cloke, as I was war.   40
Of smal coral aboute hire arm she bar
A peire of bedes, gauded al with grene,
And theron heng a brooch of gold ful sheene,
On which ther was first write a crowned A,
And after *Amor vincit omnia.*   45

(*Prologue to the Canterbury Tales*, lines 118–62)

Text: *The Canterbury Tales* was so well liked that more than eighty
early manuscripts survive – though none from Chaucer's lifetime – plus
Caxton's first printed edition of 1478. These texts were rendered down by
nineteenth-century textual scholarship into W. W. Skeat's canonical version
of 1894–7 which is given here. Later texts make only small changes to
Skeat, and none of any importance in this extract.

Without practice, Chaucer can be hard to read in old spelling, quite apart from the obstacles presented by his vocabulary; and a version of this extract with the spellings, but not the words, modernised, and with some of the obsolete words glossed, is to be found in *NOBEV*, pp. 7-8. There is also Nevill Coghill's verse translation, which is an accurate representation of Chaucer's meaning in modern English, however much one may regret the loss of Chaucer's own words, and which may be used to elucidate the original:

> There also was a *Nun*, a Prioress;
> Simple her way of smiling was and coy.
> Her greatest oath was only "By St Loy!"
> And she was known as Madam Eglantyne.
> And well she sang a service, with a fine   5
> Intoning through her nose, as was most seemly,
> And she spoke daintily in French, extremely,
> After the school of Stratford-attë-Bow;
> French in the Paris style she did not know.
> At meat her manners were well taught withal;   10
> No morsel from her lips did she let fall,
> Nor dipped her fingers in the sauce too deep;
> But she could carry a morsel up and keep
> The smallest drop from falling on her breast.
> For courtliness she had a special zest.   15
> And she would wipe her upper lip so clean
> That not a trace of grease was to be seen
> Upon the cup when she had drunk; to eat,
> She reached a hand sedately for the meat.
> She certainly was very entertaining,   20
> Pleasant and friendly in her ways, and straining
> To counterfeit a courtly kind of grace,
> A stately bearing fitted to her place,
> And to seem dignified in all her dealings.
> As for her sympathies and tender feelings,   25
> She was so charitably solicitous
> She used to weep if she but saw a mouse
> Caught in a trap, if it were dead or bleeding.
> And she had little dogs she would be feeding
> With roasted flesh, or milk, or fine white bread.   30
> Sorely she wept if one of them were dead
> Or someone took a stick and made it smart;
> She was all sentiment and tender heart.
> Her veil was gathered in a seemly way,
> Her nose was elegant, her eyes glass-grey;   35
> Her mouth was very small, but soft and red,
> And certainly she had a well-shaped head,
> Almost a span across the brows, I own;

She was by no means undergrown.
Her cloak, I noticed, had a graceful charm.   40
She wore a coral trinket on her arm,
A set of beads, the gaudies tricked in green,
Whence hung a golden brooch of brightest sheen
On which there first was graven a crowned A,
And lower, *Amor vincit omnia*.   45

(*The Canterbury Tales*, tr. Nevill Coghill, Penguin Books 1951, pp. 28–9)

Context: Chaucer intended his twenty-nine pilgrims, journeying to Becket's tomb, to tell four stories each, two on the way from London to Canterbury and two on the way back; but the work was unfinished at the time of his death – even though it was already 17,000 lines long – and contained only twenty-four stories in all (one-fifth of what he had proposed) together with the general Prologue from which this extract is taken. Chaucer's narrator describes each pilgrim in turn in the general Prologue, and then the pilgrims themselves become the narrators of their own stories, sometimes adding individual prologues to introduce their tales.

The narrator's description of the Prioress – the Mother Superior of a Convent – is one of Chaucer's funniest and most ironical portraits, marked by his characteristic combination of detachment and sympathy. It quickly becomes apparent that the lady has no real vocation for the religious life, but follows – surely as a substitute for her lack of commitment to God – the ways of the fashionable world: taking a secular name, singing services in a seemly way, speaking French, exhibiting proper table manners, behaving with courtliness and dignity, weeping sentimentally over a mouse in a trap, pampering her pet dogs, being aware of her good looks and seemly habit, and displaying a jewelled rosary and a brooch with the courtly inscription "Love conquers all". It is a searching portrait of one who fails to be what she ought, or what she professes, to be: a nun bound by monastic vows.

Versification: Here Chaucer used what was to become one of the fundamental metres of English poetry, the five-stress iambic rhymed couplet; and it is the metre in which much, but not all, of *The Canterbury Tales* was written. Like virtually all the greatest English poets, Chaucer had a very good ear for rhythm and sound, though this is not always apparent now as we struggle with unfamiliar pronunciations and "e"s that might or might not have to be sounded. The modern reader may well wonder how to scan

And ful plesaunt, and amiable of port,
And peyned hir to countrefete chere
Of court, and been estatlich of manere,

if it is not understood that "plesáunt" and "manére" ("pleasant" and "manner") are stressed on the second syllable, not the first; and that Chaucer meant us to say "péynëd" and "cóuntreféte" ("pained" and "counterfeit"), and probably "chérë" and "manérë". But once such difficulties are overcome, it will be seen that in this passage Chaucer is writing regular iambic lines with little shifting of stress, the regularity being relieved not by rhythmical variety but by the apt choice of words and an intriguing story. The exceptions to this regularity here are that line 3 has only nine syllables, so that both "ooth" and "was" are stressed; and that lines 8, 13, 24, and 28 exchange the first iamb for a trochee. Word order was of course altered to suit the metre, but the tale is told without rhetorical frills; there are scarcely any figures of speech here, unless the possibly metaphorical "tendre herte" (tender heart, line 33) sounded fresher in the fourteenth century than it does today.

2. **Donne** (John Donne, c.1572–1631)
   "A nocturnall upon *S. Lucie's* day, Being the shortest day"

'Tis the yeare's midnight, and it is the daye's,
Lucie's, who scarce seaven houres herself unmaskes;
   The Sunne is spent, and now his flasks
   Send forth light squibs, no constant rays;
      The worlds whole sap is sunke;   5
The generall balme th' hydroptique earth hath drunk,
Whither, as to the bed's-feet, life is shrunk,
Dead and enterr'd; yet all these seem to laugh,
Compar'd with me, who am their Epitaph.

Study me then, you who shall lovers bee   10
At the next world, that is, at the next Spring:
   For I am every dead thing,
   In whom love wrought new Alchimie.
      For his art did expresse
A quintessence even from nothingnesse;   15
From dull privations, and lean emptinesse,
He ruin'd mee, and I am re-begot
Of absence, darknesse, death: things which are not.

All others, from all things, draw all that's good,
Life, soule, forme, spirit, whence they beeing have;   20
   I, by love's limbecke, am the grave
   Of all that's nothing. Oft a flood
      Have wee two wept, and so
Drownd the whole world, us two; oft did we grow
To be two Chaoses, when we did show   25
Care to ought else; and often absences
Withdrew our soules, and made us carcases.

> But I am by her death (which word wrongs her)
> Of the first nothing the Elixer grown;
>> Were I a man, that I were one,   30
>>> I needs must know; I should preferre,
>>>> If I were any beast,
> Some ends, some means; yea plants, yea stones detest
> And love; all, all some properties invest;
>> If I an ordinary nothing were,   35
> As shadow, a light, and body must be here.
>
> But I am None; nor will my Sunne renew.
> You lovers, for whose sake the lesser Sunne
>> At this time to the Goat is runne
>>> To fetch new lust, and give it you,   40
>>>> Enjoy your summer all;
> Since shee enjoyes her long nights festivall,
> Let mee prepare towards her, and let mee call
> This houre her Vigill, and her eve, since this
> Both the yeare's, and the daye's deep midnight is.   45
>>   (*Poems*, 1633, 1635, with grammatical punctuation)

Text: Nearly all of Donne's poems, including this one, remained un-printed until after his death, in the *Poems* of 1633 and (in a different order) of 1635; many manuscript copies also survive, but (with the exception of a manuscript of a single poem) they are not in Donne's own hand. Modern editors have concluded that the text is best represented by the first two printed editions, with such plausible emendations as the manuscripts suggest. The old-fashioned spelling of these texts will not bother the modern reader, but their apparently rhetorical punctuation, which *may* give some indication of how the poems were spoken, can be troublesome, and it has been changed here to a grammatical punctuation which makes the poem easier to understand. The only crux is the punctuation mark at the end of line 16: the early printed texts do not have one, so that the sentence reads "From dull privations, and leane emptinesse he ruin'd me, and I am re-begot ..."; some modern editors give the line a semi-colon, making it read "From dull privations, and leane emptinesse; he ruin'd me, and I am re-begot ...". I prefer the earlier version in which the art of love's alchemy governs the rest of the stanza, but I have put a comma after "and leane emptinesse," to balance "From dull privations,".

Context: Donne's poems cannot be precisely dated. The erotic love poems appear to belong to the 1590s, when Donne was in his twenties, but he seems to have gone on writing secular as well as religious poetry until considerably later in his life. This despairing nocturnal may have been written following the death (as a result of the stillbirth of their twelfth child) of his wife Anne in August 1617; at any rate no-one has proposed a more likely object for so extreme an expression of Donne's grief.

The argument of the poem is that the poet, having lost the one great love of his life to death, is now – on the longest night of the year – contemplating his utter and particular emptiness, especially compared with the fulfilment that other lovers will find in the coming year, and is preparing himself to join her. Presented as it is, however, in Donne's condensed syntax, and in the "metaphysical" imagery of the popular science of his time, the poem can be confusing at first. The following paraphrase should make all plain.

(*Stanza 1*)   On this shortest day of the year,[8] the festival of St Lucy (saint of light), who shows herself for a mere seven hours, the sun has expended his light, leaving only a fraction of it in the stars; the world's vital juices have sunk away and the thirsty earth has reabsorbed the essence of life, which is now dead and buried, in the same way as life retreats to the foot of the bed at the time of death; yet all this deadness is a joke compared with my funereal condition.

(*Stanza 2*)   Consider me, then, you who shall be lovers when the world is renewed next spring, for I represent every dead thing from which a new chemistry of love has distilled, even from nothingness, an essence of nothing, and has reconstituted me out of things that are lacking and empty, out of things that don't exist, such as non-presence, non-light, and non-life.

(*Stanza 3*)   All other beings derive the characteristics which give them existence – life, immortal soul, body, animating essence – from positive things, while I, by the transformation of love, am a receptacle of nothingness. You and I have often wept together and drowned the world with our tears; when we took our attention away from each other we became as formless as the universe before the creation; often when we were apart our souls left our bodies, which were then no more than dead meat.

(*Stanza 4*)   But as a result of the death of her (who cannot be considered truly dead), I have become the very essence of the formlessness that preceded the creation. If I were a man, I would be conscious of the fact; if I were an animal I would be able to choose one thing rather than another; even plants and rocks experience attraction and repulsion; everything has some distinguishing qualities; even if I were an ordinary non-thing like a shadow, there would have to be a light, and an object in front of it, for the shadow to be thrown.

---

[8] The nocturnal office of the Roman Catholic church leading to St Lucy's day took place on the night of 12–13 December. In Donne's time, this coincided with the winter solstice, beacause the Julian Calendar still in use was some nine days out of step with the solar year.

(*Stanza 5*)   But I am not any of these things, and the sun of my life will not rise again. All you lovers to come, for whom the sun in the sky is now moving into the sign of Capricorn to fetch goatish lust for you, enjoy your summer. Since the light of my life (like St Lucy) is now in her long darkness, let me get ready to join her, and let me call this time the eve of her holy day, for it is midnight both of the day and of the year.

It may be added that Donne, who was obsessed by death, was led to thoughts of suicide throughout his life; and that his parallel need to consider himself to be an exceptional person is expressed here in his paradoxical claim to be something that displays more nothingness than nothing itself.

Versification: The five nine-line stanzas of the "Nocturnall" are made up of two five-stress lines, two four-stress lines, one three-stress line, and four five-stress lines, which rhyme *abbacccdd*. At first the verse seems to be rough and angular; yet its rhythmical pulse is insistent even though the smooth lilt of regular iambics is so conspicuously absent. An analysis of the stress pattern in the fourth stanza – which is bound to be guesswork, for we do not know where Donne himself wanted the stresses to be placed – will demonstrate this.

> But Í ám by her déath (which wórd wróngs her)
> Of the fírst nóthíng the Elíxer grówn;
> Wére I a mán, that Í wére one,
> I néeds must knów; Í should preférre,
> If Í were ány béast,   5
> Some énds, some méans; yea plánts, yea stónes detést
> And lóve; all, áll sóme próperties invést;
> If Í an órdináry nóthing wére,
> As shádow, a líght, and bódy múst be hére.

Lines 5, 6, and 8 of this stanza are in regular iambics; but the poem gains its rugged strength from the obtrusive breaking of the iambic mould in the other lines, which may suggest the horrors underlying Donne's determinedly rational argument. In line 2, "nothing" is stressed here on both syllables, so that it becomes "no-thing", which not only makes sense but also avoids the need to stress "Of" or the second "the". Note, too, that despite the irregular rhythms the numbers of syllables in the lines are perfectly regular – that the five-stress lines all have ten syllables, that the four-stress lines have eight, and that the three-stress line has six.

3. **Milton** (John Milton, 1608–74)
   from *Paradise Lost*, 1667

> Forthwith upright he rears from off the pool
> His mighty stature; on each hand the flames
> Driven backward slope their pointing spires, and roll'd
> In billows, leave i' th' midst a horrid vale.
> Then with expanded wings he steers his flight   5
> Aloft, incumbent on the dusky air,
> That felt unusual weight; till on dry land
> He lights, if it were land that ever burn'd
> With solid, as the lake with liquid fire,
> And such appear'd in hue; as when the force   10
> Of subterranean wind transports a hill
> Torn from Pelorus or the shatter'd side
> Of thundering Etna, whose combustible
> And fuelëd entrails thence conceiving fire,
> Sublimed with mineral fury, aid the winds,   15
> And leave a singëd bottom all involv'd
> With stench and smoke: such resting found the sole
> Of unblest feet. Him follow'd his next mate,
> Both glorying to have 'scap'd the Stygian flood
> As gods, and by their own recover'd strength,   20
> Not by the sufferance of supernal power.
>   "Is this the region, this the soil, the clime,"
> Said then the lost archangel, "this the seat
> That we must change for Heaven? this mournful gloom
> For that celestial light? Be it so, since he   25
> Who now is sovereign can dispose and bid
> What shall be right: farthest from him is best,
> Whom reason hath equall'd, force hath made supreme
> Above his equals. Farewell, happy fields,
> Where joy forever dwells! Hail, horrors! hail,   30
> Infernal world! and thou, profoundest Hell,
> Receive thy new possessor, one who brings
> A mind not to be chang'd by place or time.
> The mind is its own place, and in itself
> Can make a Heaven of Hell, a Hell of Heaven.   35
> What matter where, if I be still the same,
> And what I should be, all but less than he
> Whom thunder hath made greater? Here at least
> We shall be free; th' Almighty hath not built
> Here for his envy, will not drive us hence.   40
> Here we may reign secure; and in my choice
> To reign is worth ambition, though in Hell:
> Better to reign in Hell than serve in Heaven.

But wherefore let we then our faithful friends,
Th' associates and copartners of our loss,   45
Lie thus astonish'd on th' oblivious pool,
And call them not to share with us their part
In this unhappy mansion, or once more
With rallied arms to try what may be yet
Regain'd in Heaven, or what more lost in Hell?"   50

(Paradise Lost, Book I, lines 221–70)

Text: *Paradise Lost* was written in 1658–63 when Milton was completely blind, composing substantial batches of the verses without the security of writing them down – sometimes as he lay awake at night – and dictating them later as opportunity offered. Although, in other hands, this method of transmitting a long poem might have resulted in a good many mistakes, Milton's extraordinary memory – which encompassed the whole complex plan of the poem as well as the memorised verses – and the control which this gave him over every detail of the work, suggest that he was able to ensure that the text was eventually as he wanted it down to the last comma. The resulting manuscript of *Paradise Lost* does not survive, and the authoritative text is that of the first edition of 1667, including the later issues of that edition for which Milton added the "Arguments" to each book; and of the second edition of 1674, which involved some rearrangement and small improvements.

Context: *Paradise Lost* is an epic of huge scope and complexity, dramatic not only in tone, but also in form with its long passages of direct speech. The cosmic struggle in the earlier books of the "heroic" Satan pitted against the forces of Heaven, descends to the earthly struggle of Adam and Eve against temptation, when Satan's character is debased, and Adam and Eve's humanity is confirmed even though Paradise is lost to them. The underlying theme is condemnation of the sin of pride, pride that causes Satan to rebel against God and to seduce Eve, pride that motivates Eve to test her own strength against temptation. Written in a language of extraordinary learning, strength, and beauty, it has remained unique in literature, a religious epic in which the climactic moment comes not in some great conflict or adventure, but when Eve eats the forbidden fruit.

The extract comes near the beginning of the poem, when Satan, cast down into Hell, is picking himself up and, with his "own recovered strength", is defying the "supernal power" that has sent him there: "Better to reign in Hell than serve in Heaven," he says, even though his Hell is both terrifyingly physical, with its landscape of perpetual fire, and even more terrifyingly mental: "The mind is its own place, and in itself / Can make a

Heaven of Hell, a Hell of Heaven".[9] Here the Fiend is at his most formidable, not yet degraded into the despicable tempter who later looks on Adam and Eve's happiness with "jealous leer malign".

Versification: The reader has no doubt that Milton's five-stress lines of blank verse have extraordinary power and resonance; but it is not easy at first to see quite how this has been achieved. On the face of it, the iambic rhythm is uncomplicated, often regular or nearly so, the stresses seldom extravagantly shifted; yet the lines roll on, one after another, like a series of great waves breaking on the shore, tireless and awesome. This rhythmical strength is supported by the opulence and sonority of the words themselves, and by the grand style of Milton's syntax; for he uses relatively few rhetorical figures – even similes – beyond the classical and other learned references that adorn a generally straightforward narrative. There have been critics from the eighteenth to the twentieth century who have found that *Paradise Lost* lacks human interest, and even that its verse is monotonous; yet few have denied the sombre beauty of Milton's diction, and the immense authority of his achievement.

Milton states his purpose in writing *Paradise Lost* at the very beginning of the poem with the famous invocation to his Heavenly Muse, transcribed below: a great sixteen-line sentence in two parts that outlines the general theme of the epic to come, and in its versification gives a foretaste of how it is to be realised.

> Of mán's first disobédience, ánd the frúit
> Of thát forbídden trée whose mórtal táste
> Broúght déath into the wórld, and áll our wóe,
> With lóss of Éden, till óne gréater Mán
> Restóre ús, and regáin the blíssful séat,   5
> Síng, Héavenly Múse, that on the sécret tóp
> Of Oreb, ór of Sínai, dídst inspíre
> Thát shépherd who first táught the chósen séed
> Ín the begínning hów the héavens and éarth
> Róse out of Cháos: ór, if Síon híll   10
> Delíght thee móre, and Síloa's bróok that flów'd
> Fást by the óracle of Gód, Í thénce
> Invóke thy áid to mý advénturous sóng,
> Thát with no míddle flíght inténds to sóar
> Abóve th' Aónian móunt, whíle it pursúes   15
> Thíngs unattémpted yét in próse or rhýme.
>
> (*Paradise Lost*, Book I, lines 1–16)

[9] As Mephistophilis says in Marlowe's *Dr Faustus*, when Faustus questions him about Hell: "Why, this is hell, nor am I out of it" (I.3.76); and again, "Hell hath no limits, nor is circumscribed / In one self place. But where we are is hell, / And where hell is there must we ever be" (I.5.124–6).

In this second extract the stresses are marked, showing a series of apparently minor shifts from line to line. Line 7 alone is in completely regular iambics; lines 11 and 13 are regular provided that the last two syllables of "Siloa's (line 11) and "adventurous" (line 13) are elided into one; and all the other lines have ten syllables, except lines 6 and 9, which have eleven each. The figures of speech are few. The word "fruit" in line 1 means both the apple itself and the result of eating it; metaphorical references to Moses and the Jews ("that shepherd", "the chosen seed", line 8) enable us to infer that Milton's "Heavenly Muse" is the Holy Spirit that inspired the writing of Genesis and the rest of the Pentateuch; and in the metaphor of his "song" soaring over "th' Aonian mount" (line 15), which is Mount Helicon, the home of the classical Muses, Milton invites comparison with Homer and Virgil.

4. **Pope** (Alexander Pope, 1688–1744)
   from *An Epistle from Mr. Pope, to Dr. Arbuthnot*, 1735

> (i)   Peace to all such! but were there One whose fires
> True Genius kindles, and fair Fame inspires,
> Blest with each Talent and each Art to please,
> And born to write, converse, and live with ease;
> Shou'd such a man, too fond to rule alone,   5
> Bear, like the *Turk*, no brother near the throne,
> View him with scornful, yet with jealous eyes,
> And hate for Arts that caus'd himself to rise;
> Damn with faint praise, assent with civil leer,
> And without sneering, teach the rest to sneer;   10
> Willing to wound, and yet afraid to strike,
> Just hint a fault, and hesitate dislike;
> Alike reserv'd to blame, or to commend,
> A tim'rous foe, and a suspicious friend,
> Dreading ev'n fools, by Flatterers besieg'd,   15
> And so obliging that he ne'er obliged;
> Like *Cato*, give his little Senate laws,
> And sit attentive to his own applause;
> While Wits and Templer ev'ry sentence raise,
> And wonder with a foolish face of praise.   20
> Who but must laugh, if such a man there be?
> Who would not weep, if *Atticus* were he!
> *(Epistle to Arbuthnot*, lines 193–214)

> (ii)   Let *Sporus* tremble – "What? that Thing of silk,
> *Sporus*, that mere white Curd of Ass's milk?
> Satire or Sense alas! can *Sporus* Feel?
> Who breaks a Butterfly upon a Wheel?"
> Yet let me flap this Bug with gilded wings,   5

This painted Child of dirt that stinks and stings;
Whose Buzz the Witty and the Fair annoys,
Yet Wit ne'er tastes, and Beauty ne'er enjoys,
So well-bred Spaniels civilly delight
In mumbling of the Game they dare not bite.   10
Eternal Smiles his Emptiness betray,
As shallow streams run dimpling all the way.
Whether in florid Impotence he speaks,
And, as the Prompter breathes, the Puppet squeaks;
Or at the ear of *Eve*, familiar Toad,   15
Half Froth, half Venom, spits himself abroad,
In Puns, or Politicks, or Tales, or Lyes,
Or Spite, or Smut, or Rhymes, or Blasphemies.
His Wit all see-saw between *that* and *this*,
Now high, now low, now Master up, now Miss,   20
And he himself one vile Antithesis.
Amphibious Thing! that acting either Part,
The trifling Head, or the corrupted Heart!
Fop at the Toilet, Flatt'rer at the Board,
Now trips a Lady, and now struts a Lord.   25
Eve's Tempter thus the Rabbins[10] have exprest,
A Cherub's face, a Reptile all the rest;
Beauty that shocks you, Parts that none will trust,
Wit that can creep, and Pride that licks the dust.
                    (*Epistle to Arbuthnot*, lines 305–33)

Text: Although *The Epistle to Arbuthnot* (also known as *The Prologue to the Satires*) was not published until 1735, it was made up partly of sections written at various earlier dates. The first satire extracted here, on Addison ("Atticus"), was originally drafted before Addison's death in 1719, and was revised several times before being incorporated in the *Epistle*. The subject of the second satire, Lord Hervey ("Sporus"), was attacked by Pope from 1732 onwards, the culmination of the offensive being this extract from the *Epistle*. Pope, a perfectionist, revised and re-revised his texts, to make sure that they reached his public – and posterity – just as he wanted them.

Context: Pope's general purpose in writing the *Epistle to Arbuthnot* was to put up a defence of himself and his work, chiefly by attacking those whom he saw as his enemies and detractors. His early relationship with Addison, as a coming young poet helped along by an established literary authority, was satisfactory to both of them; but then Addison began to be jealous of Pope's growing fame, and Pope reacted by resenting Addison's coldness and, as he saw it, hostility. The result is the satire perfected in the

[10] Rabbis.

Epistle, which is essentially Pope's description of how he saw Addison's later behaviour towards himself, especially in lines 5–12.

The assault on Lord Hervey shows how much more vicious Pope could be when he was not attacking an old friend. Some eight years younger than Pope, Hervey was an effeminate courtier and adviser to Queen Caroline, wife of George II, who had written an invective against Pope (including the cutting line "Hard as thy heart, and as thy birth obscure"), to which this ferocious satire was Pope's reply. Its scurrilous intent is plain enough, though perhaps it is paradoxical that Pope should compare Hervey's advice to Queen Caroline with the advice of Satan to Eve in that very different work *Paradise Lost.*[11]

Versification: In fact it would be hard to find two major works of English poetry in five-stress lines as different from each other in versification as the *Epistle to Arbuthnot* and *Paradise Lost.* Where Milton's blank verse rolls majestically on, the descriptive constructions occupying as many lines as they need, Pope's bitter wit is confined to sharply crafted, largely self-contained couplets or pairs of couplets; rarely does one of his sense-units run over more than four lines. The perfection of the verse, rhythmically as well as verbally, is astonishing, especially when it is seen that the rhythmical patterns are largely regular, Pope's favourite device for shifting the stress being merely to begin alternate (or third) lines with a trochee instead of an iamb. Not that Pope was incapable of great rhythmic originality when he needed it; the *Epistle* begins with the startling couplet:

> Shút, shut the dóor, good *Jóhn!* fatígued, I sáid,
> Tíe up the knócker, sáy I'm síck, I'm déad.

The first extract consists chiefly of a hostile description of Addison's character and behaviour (lines 5–20), adorned with a few similes (lines 6, 17) and metaphors (lines 2, 15, 20); but the description is elaborately set in the frame of an implied question (lines 1–4) which is answered (ambiguously) only in the final couplet.

In the second extract, the narrator's character of Hervey is introduced by a direct question from an interlocutor who doubts, insultingly, the need to attack so contemptible a foe (lines 1–4), whereupon a flood of savage invective is spilled over the rest of the paragraph, rich in cruel metaphor; metaphor so overwhelming in its spite that it almost defeats its own ends (bug, lines 5–8; spaniels, 9–10; shallow streams, 11–12; puppet master, 13–14; Eve's tempter, 15–18, 26–7; epicene ambiguity, 19–25); concluding

---

[11] The "familiar Toad" (line 15) refers to *Paradise Lost*, IV.799–803: "Him there they found / Squat like a toad, close at the ear of Eve, / Assaying by his devilish art to reach / The organs of her fancy, and with them forge / Illusions as he list, phantasms and dreams".

with the final assault on Hervey's "beauty, parts, wit," and "pride". One is led to wonder, did the butterfly really deserve so much abuse?

5. **Wordsworth** (William Wordsworth, 1770–1850)
   from "*The Ruined Cottage*", 1799

> ["]And so she lived
> Through the long winter, reckless and alone,
> Till this reft[12] house by frost, and thaw, and rain
> Was sapped; and when she slept the nightly damps
> Did chill her breast, and in the stormy day   5
> Her tattered clothes were ruffled by the wind
> Even at the side of her own fire. Yet still
> She loved this wretched spot, nor would for worlds
> Have parted hence; and still that length of road
> And this rude bench one torturing hope endeared,   10
> Fast rooted at her heart, and here, my friend,
> In sickness she remained, and here she died,
> Last human tenant of these ruined walls."
>   The old Man ceased: he saw that I was mov'd;
> From that low Bench, rising instinctively   15
> I turned aside in weakness, nor had power
> To thank him for the tale which he had told.
> I stood, and leaning o'er the garden-gate
> Reviewed that Woman's suff'rings, and it seemed
> To comfort me while with a brother's love   20
> I blessed her in the impotence of grief.
> At length towards the Cottage I returned
> Fondly, and traced with milder interest
> That secret spirit of humanity
> Which, 'mid the calm oblivious tendencies   25
> Of nature, 'mid her plants, her weeds, and flowers,
> And silent overgrowings, still survived.
> The old man, seeing this, resumed and said,
> "My Friend, enough to sorrow have you given,
> The purposes of wisdom ask no more;   30
> Be wise and chearful, and no longer read
> The forms of things with an unworthy eye.
> She sleeps in the calm earth, and peace is here.
> I well remember that those very plumes,
> Those weeds, and the high spear-grass on that wall,   35
> By mist and silent rain-drops silver'd o'er,
> As once I passed did to my heart convey
> So still an image of tranquillity,
> So calm and still, and looked so beautiful

---

[12] Bereft.

Amid the uneasy thoughts which filled my mind,   40
That what we feel of sorrow and despair,
From ruin and from change, and all the grief
The passing shews of being leave behind,
Appeared an idle dream that could not live
Where meditation was. I turned away   45
And walked along my road in happiness."
  He ceased. By this the sun declining shot
A slant and mellow radiance which began
To fall upon us where beneath the trees
We sate on that low bench, and now we felt,   50
Admonished thus, the sweet hour coming on.
A linnet warbled from those lofty elms,
A thrush sang loud, and other melodies,
At distance heard, peopled the milder air.
The old man rose and hoisted up his load.   55
Together casting then a farewell look
Upon those silent walls, we left the shade
And ere the stars were visible attained
A rustic inn, our evening resting place.
                       ("The Ruined Cottage", lines 480–538)

Text: "The Ruined Cottage" was first written in 1797–8, and was revised several times until it was incorporated in the first Book of *The Excursion* in 1814; it was not published as a separate work until 1949. The extract given here derives from Wordsworth's MS dated 1799.[13]

Context: "The Ruined Cottage" is the story of the silent suffering of poor Margaret, whose husband Robert has a breakdown at a time of near-famine, and deserts his family to enlist as a soldier. For five years she waits, looking up the road and hoping that he will return; but he never does, and both Margaret and her home decline until at last the cottage is a ruin, and Margaret dies. The story is told to the narrator by an old pedlar, who on his several returns to the district has witnessed or heard about it all: the original happy family, the absent husband, the ruin of Margaret and her home; and who ends his tale with his own resolution of the unspoken but central question: "Why should this have happened to the innocent Margaret?" (lines 29–46). Much of the strength of the poem derives from the involvement of the narrator (and thereby the reader) in a story which is not only poignant in itself, but which affects anyone – which is every-one – who asks why the innocent have to suffer.

Versification: After the inspiring orotundities of Milton and the brilliant

[13] From MS D, dated 1799, transcribed by James Butler in the Cornell Wordsworth "*The Ruined Cottage*" and "*The Pedlar*", 1979.

artificialities of Pope, Wordsworth's "real language of men" comes as a surprise, and perhaps as a relief. Here is a real revolution in English poetry, in which something simple but important is said in simple but moving words. The generally regular five-stress blank verse lines are saved from blandness by the subtle but undemanding shifts of stress:

> And só she líved
> Thróugh the lóng wínter, réckless and alóne,
> Till this réft hóuse by fróst, and tháw, and ráin
> Was sápped; and whén she slépt the níghtly dámps
> Did chíll her bréast, ánd in the stórmy dáy
> Her táttered clóthes were rúffled bý the wínd
> Éven at the síde of her ówn fire. Yet stíll …

The metre was a favourite one with Wordsworth, and he used it for many of his finest early poems of contemplation: "Tintern Abbey", "The Old Cumberland Beggar", "Michael", and the first version of "The Prelude", as well as "The Ruined Cottage". The calm rhythms, the absence of rhyme, and the avoidance of obtrusive figures of speech, all evoke the measured tones of the simple storyteller.

6. **Tennyson** (Alfred Lord Tennyson, 1809–92)
   from "*The Lotos-Eaters*", 1832, 1842

> "Courage!" he said, and pointed towards the land,
> "This mounting wave will roll us shoreward soon."
> In the afternoon they came unto a land
> In which it seemëd always afternoon.
> All round the coast the languid air did swoon, 5
> Breathing like one that hath a weary dream.
> Full-faced above the valley stood the moon;
> And like a downward smoke, the slender stream
> Along the cliff to fall and pause and fall did seem.
>
> A land of streams! some, like a downward smoke 10
> Slow-dropping veils of thinnest lawn, did go;
> And some thro' wavering lights and shadows broke,
> Rolling a slumbrous sheet of foam below.
> They saw the gleaming river seaward flow
> From the inner land: far off, three mountain-tops, 15
> Three silent pinnacles of agëd snow,
> Stood sunset-flush'd: and, dew'd with showery drops,
> Up-clomb the shadowy pine above the woven copse.
>
> The charmëd sunset linger'd low adown
> In the red West: thro' mountain clefts the dale 20
> Was seen far inland, and the yellow down

Border'd with palm, and many a winding vale
And meadow, set with slender galingale;
A land where all things always seem'd the same!
And round the keel with faces pale,   25
Dark faces pale against the rosy flame,
The mild-eyed melancholy Lotos-eaters came.

Branches they bore of that enchanted stem,
Laden with flower and fruit, whereof they gave
To each, but whoso did receive of them,   30
And taste, to him the gushing of the wave
Far far away did seem to mourn and rave
On alien shores; and if his fellow spake,
His voice was thin, as voices from the grave;
And deep-asleep he seem'd, yet all awake,   35
And music in his ears his beating heart did make.

They sat them down upon the yellow sand,
Between the sun and moon upon the shore;
And sweet it was to dream of Fatherland,
Of child, and wife, and slave; but evermore   40
Most weary seem'd the sea, weary the oar,
Weary the wandering fields of barren foam.
Then some one said, "We will return no more";
And all at once they sang, "Our island home
Is far beyond the wave; we will no longer roam."   45
                              ("The Lotos-Eaters", lines 1–45)

Text: "The Lotos-Eaters" was written in time for publication in Tennyson's *Poems* of 1832 (dated 1833). The collection was unfavourably reviewed, and Tennyson revised many of the poems in it (including "The Lotos-Eaters") for republication in the two-volume *Poems* of 1842; it is the later text that is given here.[14] The first five stanzas of the poem are followed by an irregular "Choric Song" of 128 lines divided into eight unequal parts.

Context: Odysseus (the "he" of line 1) tells in the *Odyssey* (IX: 82–97) how he and his companions came to the land of the Lotos-Eaters, where some of them tasted the lotos and were immediately bereft of any wish to return home; and how Odysseus had to force them back on board ship to continue their journey. Tennyson's retelling of the story uses as background the spectacular mountain scenery of Cauterets in Hautes-Pyrénées, which he visited with Hallam in 1832; and his description of the effects of the lotos on those who taste it (lines 30–6) suggests some personal experience with opium, or possibly even with hashish. The lengthy

---

[14] Tennyson's methods of revision can be examined in his poetry notebooks which are kept at Trinity College, Cambridge, and elsewhere.

"Choric Song" that follows the five stanzas of the extract explores the state of mind of the drugged sailors, and their determination never to return to their old life of struggle and deprivation, at the mercy of indifferent gods. Yet in the end, we know, Odysseus got his men back to the ships, and himself back to Ithaca; and Tennyson saw the poem as affirming his own need to engage in the struggle of life, and to overcome adversity however dark the outlook.

Versification: The extract consists of five Spenserian stanzas, each of eight five-stress lines and one six-stress line, rhyming *ababbcbcc*. The stresses shift indolently, it seems, within the lines:

> "Cóurage!" he sáid, and póinted towárds the lánd,
> "This móunting wáve will róll us shóreward sóon."
> In the áfternóon they cáme únto a lánd
> In whích it séemëd álways áfternóon.
> Áll round the cóast the lánguid áir did swóon,   5
> Bréathing like óne that háth a wéary dréam.
> Fúll-faced abóve the válley stóod the móon;
> Ánd like a dównward smóke, the slénder stréam
> Alóng the clíff to fáll and páuse and fáll did séem.

What is even more remarkable is the sense of languor and laziness that Tennyson evokes with word and phrase: with a slow, rolling rhythm; with repetitions (of the rhyme-words "land" in lines 1 and 3, and "adown" and "down" in lines 19 and 21; of "afternoon" in both lines 3 and 4; of the "downward smoke" of the waterfalls that "along the cliff to fall and pause and fall did seem", lines 8–11); and with the somnolent language of "the languid air did swoon, breathing like one that hath a weary dream", "the charmëd sunset linger'd low adown", "a land where all things always seemed the same", "most weary seem'd the sea, weary the oar, weary the wandering fields of barren foam" (lines 5–6, 19, 24, 41–2). The words come slowly and sleepily, echoing the exhaustion and delusions of the mariners.

"The Choric Song" that follows these stanzas continues in the same sensual style, but in irregular sections of lines of differing lengths, until in the sixth line of the last, longest section, the rhythms of sea and struggle intervene in rolling seven- and eight-stress lines, here trochaic rather than iambic:

> Wé have hád enóugh of áction, ánd of mótion wé,
> Rólled to stárboard, rólled to lárboard, whén the súrge was séething frée,
> Whére the wállowing mónster spóuted his fóam-fóuntains ín the séa.
>   ("The Lotos-Eaters", lines 150–2)

leading at the end to a final, defeated lament:

Súrely, súrely, slúmber is móre swéet than tóil, the shóre
Than lábour in the déep míd-ócean, wínd and wáve and óar;
O, rést ye, bróther márinérs, we wíll not wánder móre.

("The Lotos-Eaters", lines 171–3)

7. **T. S. Eliot** (Thomas Stearns Eliot, 1888–1965)
from *"The Love Song of J. Alfred Prufrock"*, 1917

And the afternoon, the evening, sleeps so peacefully!
Smoothed by long fingers,
Asleep ... tired ... or it malingers,
Stretched on the floor, here beside you and me.
Should I, after tea and cakes and ices,   5
Have the strength to force the moment to its crisis?
But though I have wept and fasted, wept and prayed,
Though I have seen my head (grown slightly bald) brought in upon a platter,
I am no prophet – and here's no great matter;
I have seen the moment of my greatness flicker,   10
And I have seen the eternal Footman hold my coat, and snicker,
And in short I was afraid.

And would it have been worth it, after all,
After the cups, the marmalade, the tea,
Among the porcelain, among some talk of you and me,   15
Would it have been worth while,
To have bitten off the matter with a smile,
To have squeezed the universe into a ball
To roll it towards some overwhelming question,
To say: "I am Lazarus, come from the dead,   20
Come back to tell you all, I shall tell you all" –
If one, settling a pillow by her head,
      Should say: "That is not what I mean at all.
      That is not it, at all."

And would it have been worth it, after all,   25
Would it have been worth while,
After the sunsets and the dooryards and the sprinkled streets,
After the novels, after the teacups, after the skirts that trail along the floor –
And this, and so much more? –
It is impossible to say just what I mean!   30
But as if a magic lantern threw the nerves in patterns on a screen:
Would it have been worth while
If one, settling a pillow or throwing off a shawl,
And turning toward the window, should say:
"That is not it at all,   35
That is not what I meant, at all."

*   *   *   *   *

No! I am not Prince Hamlet, nor was meant to be;
Am an attendant lord, one that will do
To swell a progress, start a scene or two,
Advise the prince; no doubt, an easy tool,   40
Deferential, glad to be of use,
Politic, cautious, and meticulous;
Full of high sentence, but a bit obtuse;
At times, indeed, almost ridiculous –
Almost, at times, the Fool.   45

I grow old ... I grow old ...
I shall wear the bottoms of my trousers rolled.

Shall I part my hair behind? Do I dare to eat a peach?
I shall wear white flannel trousers, and walk upon the beach.
I have heard the mermaids singing, each to each.   50

I do not think that they will sing to me.

I have seen them riding seaward on the waves
Combing the white hair of the waves blown back
When the wind blows the water white and black.

We have lingered in the chambers of the sea   55
By sea-girls wreathed with seaweed red and brown
Till human voices wake us, and we drown.

("The Love Song of J. Alfred Prufrock", lines 75–131)

Text: Written in 1910–11, "The Love Song of J. Alfred Prufrock" first appeared in an American periodical in 1915, but it was its publication in England in book form as the first poem in *Prufrock and Other Observations*, 1917, that caught the literary establishment's attention. As with Tennyson, many of Eliot's working manuscripts survive, but it is the book text – of which Eliot himself later became the publisher – that is followed here.

Context: "Prufrock" is "a portrait of failure, or of a character which fails".[15] The narrator (who speaks to a listener, perhaps his own inner self) wants to be a success, especially with women, but is prevented by his social and sexual inhibitions from being one. In this second half of the poem, he admits his fear (line 12), which is a fear of failure itself, and thinks (not for the first time) of what he might have attempted, what he might have achieved, and – if it were worth the risk – what he might yet attempt; and concludes that there is nothing to be done, that he will hear the call but be unable to answer it.

[15] Ezra Pound to Harriet Monroe, 31 January 1915.

Partly influenced by the Symbolists,[16] Eliot alludes to external writings and other matters in the poem, though less obtrusively than he was to do in some of his later work. Obvious allusions here are to the Bible (lines 7–9, 20–1), to other works of literature, (lines 18, 37–45), and to current events (lines 5, 14–15, 46–9[17]).

The "Prince Hamlet" paragraph (lines 37–45), is slightly out of key with the rest of the poem, a bit too slick, as Ezra Pound quickly saw. He tried, unsuccessfully, to persuade Eliot to leave it out, but (as he explained in his letter to Harriet Monroe) "it is an early and cherished bit and T.E. won't give it up, and as it is the only portion of the poem that most readers will like at first reading, I don't see that it will do much harm".[18]

Versification: Eliot wrote later that he would like a reader to be able to say "that is how I should talk if I could talk poetry",[19] and the colloquial tone of this first great poem is as original and successful in this respect as was Wordsworth's "real language of men". The deliberate irregularity of its rhythms, rhymes, and stanzas suggests patterns of ordinary speech; yet it is nevertheless ordinary speech "talking poetry".

The metre of "Prufrock" is based on the iambic pentameter, but the regular lines are repeatedly interrupted by other stress-patterns. The first of the three twelve-line stanzas at the beginning of the extract (lines 1–12, 13–24, 25–36) has 5, 3, 3, 5, 5, 5, 5, 8, 5, 5, 7, and 3 stresses; the second has 5, 5, 6, 3, 5, 5, 5, 5, 5, 5, 5, and 3 stresses; while the last of the three is yet more irregular, with 5, 3, 5, 9, 3, 5, 8, 3, 6, 4, 3, and 4 stresses. Here is the third stanza with the suggested stresses marked:

> And wóuld it have béen wórth it, áfter áll,   25
> Wóuld it have béen worth whíle,
> Áfter the súnsets and the dóoryards and the sprínkled stréets,
> Áfter the nóvels, áfter the téacups, áfter the skírts that tráil alóng the flóor –
> And thís, and só much móre? –
> Ít is impóssible to sáy júst what I méan!   30
> But as íf a mágic lántern thréw the nérves in pátterns ón a scréen:
> Wóuld it have béen worth whíle
> If óne, séttling a píllow or thrówing óff a sháwl,
> And túrning towárd the wíndow, should sáy:

---

[16] See p. 42, n. 9 above.

[17] Line 47, "I shall wear the bottoms of my trousers rolled", has puzzled some readers. It refers to turn-ups (or cuffs) at the bottoms of trouser legs, which were just then coming in as a youthful fashion.

[18] Pound was more successful in persuading Eliot to remove parts of *The Waste Land* that he didn't like, to the great improvement of the poem; see *The Waste Land*, a facsimile and transcript of the manuscript, edited by Valerie Eliot, 1971.

[19] "The Music of Poetry", 1942 (T. S. Eliot, *Selected Prose*, 1953, p. 58).

"Thát is not ít at áll,   35
Thát is nót what I méant, at áll."

The later stanzas tend to greater regularity; in the "Prince Hamlet" stanza
(lines 37–45) all but the first and last of its nine lines (which have six and
three stresses respectively) have five stresses each; and all six lines of the
last two stanzas (lines 52–4 and 55–7) have five stresses. It might be thought
that this degree of irregularity would nullify the rhythmic strength of the
poem, but it does not do so; here, as in most of his later work, the underlying rhythm implied by Eliot is always present as an unsounded beat,
rather as a regular beat may underlie and control a piece of syncopated
music without having to be stated. Although he did not manifest it in the
way that Tennyson, say, or Auden did, Eliot's mastery of metre in his
poetry was always absolute.

The rhyme-scheme of "Prufrock" is likewise irregular, but is again
strong enough to make its binding force effective. The rhymes of the first
three stanzas go a*bbaccdeeffd*, *abbccadeaeaa*, and *abcddeebafaa*; those of the
"prince Hamlet" stanza are *abbcdedec*; and it is not until we get to the three
three-line stanzas at the end (lines 48–50, 52–4, and 55–7) that we have the
regularity of *aaa*, *abb*, and *abb* respectively. Some of the rhymes appear to
be deliberately absurd and "unpoetic": especially *ices/crisis* (lines 5–6), but
perhaps also *platter/matter* (lines 8–9) and *old/rolled* (lines 46–7).

The stanzas, finally, are just as obviously irregular, having 12, 12, 12, 9,
2, 3, 1, 3, and 3 lines respectively, suggesting perhaps the increasing
incoherence of the narrator's thoughts.

As with fiction, the form of poetry has not changed much during the rest
of the twentieth century; but, unlike fiction, it has become generally less
rather than more widely read. John Betjeman, it is true, had a considerable
following, but there has been nothing to equal the immense popularity
of Tennyson. That there is nevertheless a steady readership for poetry is
shown by the long series of collections and anthologies of contemporary
work published by Penguin Books; and by the success of several fine poets
who have been able to speak to us in our own "real language of men", such
as W. H. Auden, Philip Larkin, Ted Hughes, and Seamus Heaney. Auden
was also the century's outstanding master of formal technique in poetry,
though his actual innovations were few. As with fiction, we still await the
next revolution in poetic form.[20]

[20] The "Beat" poetry of the mid-century was an attempt at poetic innovation but, since it
took the form of dispensing with the disciplines of poetic technique, it was not a lasting
success.

Chapter 4

Drama

The Nature of Drama

Drama – the art form that is primarily intended for theatrical performance and is written down by a dramatist in prose or verse dialogue – differs essentially from fiction and poetry in that the artist's intention is fulfilled, not by people reading or reciting his work, but by its presentation to a live audience by his collaborators (the play's director, actors and theatre staff) using theatrical devices. Indeed, plays are so different from books that they might well be classed as belonging to another art form altogether, but they are generally considered to be part of literature because they can be communicated in a secondary way as written texts, and because such texts are all that remain to us of the plays of the past.

Even the written texts of drama differ in an important way from those of literature intended to be read as books, for they are subject to modification, not only by the dramatist, but also by his collaborators. Play texts go through three main stages. The words of a play exist first as the dramatist's *script*, the written version of what he or she originally intended to be said and done on stage. Secondly, they exist as a *performance text*, what is actually said and done in one or more performances of the play, commonly following changes introduced by the director and actors, with or without the dramatist's knowledge or consent. Thirdly, they appear as a *reading text*, the version published by author or editor as a saleable record of what might or should have been said and done on stage, based either on the script or on the performance text, or on a combination of the two; reading texts normally appear after a play has been produced, but sometimes on or before the first night.

Another major difference between drama and books is that, even when a dramatic text has stabilised – as it usually has with the classic drama of the past – its effect on its audience can vary greatly in different productions as a result of changed outlook and fashion, of new theatres and changed settings, of differing approaches and interpretations by director and actors, and of myriad other things; its effect can also change from night to night if the performances are uneven, or if the audiences differ in composition.

Before going on to look at drama in more detail, four allied forms should be mentioned: closet plays; cinema films; plays written for television; and plays written for radio. *Closet plays*, which are plays (usually in verse) written to be read, not performed, are really a form of written literature. They seldom achieve popular success, but there have been exceptions, notably Ibsen's great verse-dramas *Brand* and *Peer Gynt*, which were intended to be read, not performed, and which were immediately appreciated as major works of Scandinavian literature (and which, incidentally, were later successfully produced on stage in abbreviated versions).

It is worth emphasising that, unlike much closet drama, real stage plays are very well worth reading; a good stage play, indeed, can be as gripping and rewarding as a good novel, the experienced reader "producing" it in his or her head while reading.

There are obvious similarities between live drama and *cinema films* in that both are presentations for an audience, using actors and theatrical or technical devices. But, whereas a play performed in a theatre is a presentation of a dramatist's work in live interaction between performers and audience, which must be repeated *ab initio* each time it is to be experienced, a cinema film is built up in advance of its showing by the collaborative work of producers, scriptwriters, director, cinematographer, actors, and film-editors; and the resulting film, like a book, can be experienced again and again without further effort by its makers. The scriptwriter, unlike the playwright, is usually a relatively unimportant figure, his work being liable to being revised or replaced by others, and to being amended during shooting by the director. You cannot have a great stage play without a great dramatist, but you can have a great film without a great scriptwriter; and the scripts even of good films make poor reading compared with the texts of good plays. Although successful stage plays are sometimes adapted for the cinema, they not only lose the immediacy of the live theatre, but they can seldom take advantage of the wide range of cinematic effects that give films their life.

Television plays are similar to cinema films in that they are built up in advance of transmission by teams of collaborators.[1] Television playwrights, however, tend to be more important and influential figures than film script-writers; and television has the advantage over cinema of being able to

---

[1] In the early days of television, plays were broadcast live; but, now that they can be recorded on videotape, this is no longer done.

produce much longer works, transmitting them in parts over several days or weeks. Television is especially good at adapting fiction, especially long, classic novels, for its small screen; and its relatively limited range of effects, combined with its intimacy, make it a more suitable medium than cinema for the adaptation of stage plays.

Compared with cinema and television plays, *radio plays* are relatively simple and inexpensive productions, which can if necessary be broadcast live (though they are normally prerecorded), and which can be an effective form given the limitation that they can only be heard, not seen. To hear a radio play is in fact very like attending a play-reading; and, provided that any necessary dialogue and effects are added to make up for being unable to see the action, stage plays can work well on radio – or, as is more usual nowadays, on tapes or CDs of audio productions of stage plays. Radio plays can also be good to read.

Techniques and Constraints

The medium of drama is *dialogue*, which purports to represent people communicating through speech. This dialogue, which can be in verse or prose, can be obviously artificial or (apparently) realistic; or – the most usual form, as in the dialogue of a novel[2] – it can compromise between artificiality and realism. Truly realistic dialogue, given at length with its repetitions, hesitations, omissions, and redundancies, would be as intolerable on the stage as it would be in fiction.

Obviously artificial dialogue
Dumaine   But what to me, my love? But what to me?
  A wife?
Catherine   A beard, fair health, and honesty.
  With three-fold love I wish you all these three.
Dumaine   O, shall I say "I thank you, gentle wife"?
Catherine   Not so, my lord. A twelvemonth and a day
  I'll mark no words that smooth-faced wooers say.
  Come when the king doth to my lady come;
  Then if I have much love, I'll give you some.
Dumaine   I'll serve thee true and faithfully till then.
Catherine   Yet swear not, lest ye be forsworn again.
  (Shakespeare, *Love's Labour's Lost*, V.2.808–18)

Apparently realistic dialogue
Rosencrantz (*cutting his fingernails*)   Another curious scientific phenomenon is
  the fact that the fingernails grow after death, as does the beard.

---

[2] See pp. 39–40 above.

Guildenstern   What?
Rosencrantz (*loud*)   Beard!
Guildenstern   But you're not dead.
Rosencrantz   I didn't say they *started* to grow after death! (*pause, calmer*)
   The fingernails also grow before birth, though *not* the beard.
Guildenstern   *What?*
Rosencrantz (*shouts*)   Beard! What's the matter with you? (*reflectively*)
   The toenails, on the other hand, never grow at all.
Guildenstern (*bemused*)   The toenails on the other hand never grow at all?
Rosencrantz   Do they?
(Stoppard, Rosencrantz and Guildenstern Are Dead, Act I)

Compromise between artificial and realistic dialogue
Androcles   Easy, Ferrovius, easy: you broke that last man's jaw.
   (*Lentulus, with a moan of terror, attempts to fly; but Ferrovius holds him ruthlessly*)
Ferrovius   Yes, but I saved his soul. What matters a broken jaw?
Lentulus   Don't touch me, do you hear? The law –
Ferrovius   The law will throw me to the lions tomorrow; what worse could it
   do if I were to slay you? Pray for strength; and it shall be given to you.
Lentulus   Let me go. Your religion forbids you to strike me.
Ferrovius   On the contrary, it commands me to strike you. How can you turn
   the other cheek, if you are not first struck on the one cheek?
Lentulus (*almost in tears*)   But I'm convinced already that what you said is quite
   right. I apologise for striking you.
Ferrovius (*greatly pleased*)   My son: have I softened your heart? Has the good
   seed fallen in a fruitful place? Are your feet turning towards a better path?
Lentulus (*abjectly*)   Yes, yes. There's a great deal in what you say.
Ferrovius   Join us. Come to the lions. Come to suffering and death.
Lentulus (*falling on his knees and bursting into tears*)   Oh, help me. Mother!
   Mother!
(Shaw, Androcles and the Lion, Act I)

Structure

Most drama, like most fiction, is constructed on the three-part plan of situation/action/resolution; this applies to comedy as well as to tragedy. But, unlike a novel which can be of almost any length, a play has to be witnessed in a short and continuous time, so that the dramatist must be economical, telescoping events that in reality would develop over a longer period, and introducing encounters and coincidences that might seem unrealistic in fiction, let alone in ordinary life. In some of the dramatic traditions of the past, moreover (though seldom in British drama of any period), it was considered desirable that dramatists should attempt to observe *the three unities*, of action, time, and place. In theory this meant that a play should deal with one main subject; that it be shown in real time; and that the scene should not be moved from place to place. In practice it was generally taken to meant that a play should follow one main subject, without sub-plots; that a period of not more than twenty-four hours should be represented; and that the action should take place in one area, such as a single palace. This was supposed to keep the audience from becoming confused. No-one flouted the unities more thoroughly than Shakespeare, whose *Winter's Tale*, for instance, has a double plot, covers a period of sixteen years, and shifts its scene back and forth between Sicily and Bohemia, apparently without confusing the audience.

Traditionally, plays have been thought of as being either tragedies or comedies, or as being some mixture of the two. A *tragedy* is a drama dealing with serious themes ending in the suffering or death of one or more of the principal characters. Aristotle's *Poetics* proposed that the tragic hero should be of high worth or standing, but not perfect (though from Ibsen onwards an imperfect ordinary person could be the *protagonist*, the leading figure, in tragedy). A tragic flaw, weakness, or transgression (*hamartia*), or an excess of arrogant ambition (*hubris*), should lead to the reversal (*peripeteia*) of the protagonist's position, bringing him down. The effect of the inevitable disaster (*catastrophe*) on the spectators would be the purgation or cleansing (*catharsis*) of the emotions of pity and terror through what they have seen. With the possible exception of the theory of catharsis, this archaic formula is still generally applicable to dramatic tragedy.

Comedy, on the other hand, is the element in drama that makes people laugh. If tragedy purges the emotions, comedy protects them by neutralising what might otherwise be frightening or embarrassing. Comedy rests on human error, social blunders, mistaken identity, awkward meetings, and verbal humour; comedy can be romantic, satirical, or social; and characters in comedy are in general less subtle and dignified than the characters in tragedy.

Characters

Just as the dramatist has to tell his story economically, he must be just as economical in presenting his characters. Characters may be depicted as great people, leaders of the community and powerful in its destiny, or, as is more usually the case in modern drama, as ordinary people. They must be quickly introduced to the audience and become familiar in a short time. They are created through the words they speak, their actions in the play, and what other characters report of them; leading characters are supported by minor roles. The quality of a great dramatist such as Shakespeare is shown by his skill in making his characters individual and credible, even in the dramatic conventions of four centuries ago. Stage directions may aid the actor or the reader, but on the stage itself there is not much room for detached narrative or authorial comment; the ancient Greek theatre, which made do with only two or three actors, used the device of a "Chorus" to comment on the action, but it has rarely been used in later drama.

Production

Until very recent times, production techniques had moved gradually but steadily towards greater realism. Early drama was generally written in verse, and acted in declamatory styles, with stylised costumes and minimal scenery. Actors in ancient Greece and Rome wore masks, and performed on a platform in a large semicircular open-air theatre. Medieval plays were acted in the open on temporary scaffolds or moveable wagons, without scenery, but with costumes and properties. Elizabethan and Jacobean actors still declaimed verse in the open air on a projecting ("open") stage – or occasionally in a private hall – with a stylised back to the stage and a few properties, and wore grand clothes that usually had little connection with what the characters would actually have worn; but there was a move towards a more naturalistic style of acting (Hamlet's speech to the players is chiefly a call to actors for greater realism in *speaking* actors' parts). The indoor theatre with its stage behind a proscenium arch and artificial lighting followed in the later seventeenth century, but scenery and properties were still limited and unrealistic until well into the nineteenth century – there was usually no more than a canvas backdrop with, say, walls and furniture painted on it, and sets of moveable wings, each set of which could be used in the same sort of scene in a number of plays; the auditorium remained lit during performance; costumes became something of an indication of the character that was being played, but were still liable to be anachronistic. Prose began to be used for comedy in the eighteenth century, but tragedy was still usually in verse until the mid-nineteenth century.

There were precursors, but the greatest change came in the second half of the mid-nineteenth century when Ibsen, the originator of modern prose drama, began to write plays about ordinary people in ordinary situations. Everyday words were spoken in an everyday way; there were accurate costumes and carefully realistic sets, with all the necessary properties; the auditorium was darkened; and the actors spoke to each other, rather than to the audience.

It is only from the mid-twentieth century that there has been a return to simplified sets and costumes, and even to open stages, though the style of acting generally remains realistic.

Origins and Early Development

Ritual

It has long been recognised that some aspects of drama appear to derive from ritual practices. Ritual and drama have it in common that both deal with social, ethical, and spiritual relationships by having them acted out by living people. It is demonstrable, moreover, that the Athenian drama of the fifth century BC – the earliest western drama of which we have texts – had links with the religion of ancient Greece. It is also true that dramatic features are identifiable in surviving rituals; in the Christian Eucharist, the priest acts the part of Christ at the last supper, and the communicants act the part of the disciples. However, the purpose of ritual is to bind its participants to one particular end, whereas that of drama is to instruct and entertain a non-participating audience by means of repeatable performances; so that it could be said that, at a wedding, the priest, the bride, and the bridegroom (and their acolytes) are taking part in a ritual, and that the wedding guests are attending a drama.

Ancient Greek Drama

Although they dealt with religious themes, the sombre plays of Aeschylus, Sophocles, and Euripides, written for the public theatre in Athens in the fifth century BC, were dramas in this sense, not rituals; as were the exuberant satires of their younger contemporary Aristophanes. The theatrical conventions of the time are unfamiliar to us, yet these ancient dramatists approached story, character, and dialogue in ways that we can recognise, and their plays can still be successfully performed. This can be illustrated by an examination of what is generally considered to be the dramatic masterpiece of the Greek theatre, Sophocles's *Oedipus the King*; this play was also picked out by Aristotle as the perfect example of dramatic tragedy.

Sophocles took as the story for his play the culmination of a well-known myth. The tale was that, when Laius, king of Thebes, and Jocasta, had a baby boy, the oracle of Apollo warned them that he would kill his father and marry his mother. In order that this fate should be avoided, the baby, who was Oedipus, was exposed on Mount Cithaeron with his ankles pinned together, so that he would die there or be eaten by wild beasts. Although lamed, Oedipus was rescued by a shepherd, and was then taken away to be brought up as the son of the king and queen of Corinth. As a young man, Oedipus himself was told by the oracle that he would kill his father and marry his mother and, in another effort to avoid this fate, he left Corinth for Thebes where he unwittingly fulfilled both predictions; he killed Laius in an affray at a place where three roads met; and then, having destroyed the murderous sphinx that was terrorising the city, he married the widowed Jocasta and became king of Thebes himself. He proved to be a good king, with the Athenian virtues of being swift and strong to act, and if he had been content with that, all might have been well.

It is at this point that the play of *Oedipus the King* begins. Oedipus learns from Delphi that Thebes can only be saved from a plague that has fallen on the city by the discovery and exile of Laius's murderer. Tiresias, the blind seer, is summoned to reveal the truth, which is known to him; at first he refuses, but is then forced to give a true but riddling answer. Still suspecting only that Creon, Jocasta's brother, is plotting against him, Oedipus learns from a messenger that he is not in fact the son of the king and queen of Corinth, for it was the same messenger who had brought him as a baby from Mount Cithaeron to Corinth. Against advice, Oedipus sends for the shepherd from whom the messenger had received the baby, and who also happened to have been present at the death of Laius; and he forces the old man to reveal the truth about him. Appalled to discover that he is himself his father's murderer and his mother's husband, he is now told that Jocasta has hanged herself. He rushes frantically offstage and blinds himself with her brooch. He returns to be confronted by Creon, who succeeds him as king of Thebes, and accedes to his wish that he should be sent into perpetual exile.

It is a gripping and intricately constructed plot, in which the protagonist brings about his own downfall as a result of his excessive self-confidence, precipitates the catastrophe and suffers a complete reversal of fortune. The dialogue, which is in verse, is realistic, the character of Oedipus is convincingly presented, and the minor persons in the play are well distinguished from each other. If we cannot see it in quite the same way as could its ancient Athenian audience, it is because they not only knew the whole story in advance, but they also firmly believed that oracular predictions were bound to be fulfilled. They knew, too, that the oracle had said nothing more about what would happen to Oedipus than that he would kill his father and marry his mother, as did indeed happen; and that it was therefore chiefly owing to his own hubristic detective work that he and Jocasta ultimately came to grief.

Here is part of the climactic scene in which Oedipus forces the shepherd to tell him who he is:

Messenger (*to the shepherd*)   Come, tell me,
    you gave me a child back then, a boy, remember?
    A little fellow to rear, my very own.
Shepherd   What? Why rake that up again?
Messenger   Look, here he is, my fine old friend –

the same man who was just a baby then.

Shepherd   Damn you, shut your mouth – quiet!

Oedipus   Don't lash out at him, old man –
you need lashing more than he does.

Shepherd   Why,
master, majesty – what have I done wrong?

Oedipus   You won't answer his question about the boy.

Shepherd   He's talking nonsense, wasting his breath.

Oedipus   So, you won't talk willingly –
then you'll talk with pain.   (*the guards seize the shepherd*)

Shepherd   No, dear god, don't torture an old man!

Oedipus   Twist his arms back quickly!

Shepherd   God help us, why? –
what more do you need to know?

Oedipus   Did you give him the child? He's asking.

Shepherd   I did … I wish to god I'd died that day.

Oedipus   You've got your wish if you don't tell the truth.

Shepherd   The more I tell, the worse the death I'll die.

Oedipus   Our friend here wants to stretch things out, does he?
                                    (*motioning to his men for torture*)

Shepherd   No, no, I gave it to him – I just said so.

Oedipus   Where did you get it? Your house? Someone else's?

Shepherd   It wasn't mine, no, I got it from … someone.

Oedipus   Which one of them?
(*looking at the citizens*)   Whose house?

Shepherd   No –
god's sake, master, no more questions!

Oedipus   You're a dead man if I have to ask again.

Shepherd   Then – the child came from the house …
of Laius.

Oedipus   A slave? or born of his own blood?

Shepherd   Oh no.
I'm right at the edge, the horrible truth – I've got to say it!

Oedipus   And I'm at the edge of hearing horrors, yes, but I must hear!

Shepherd   All right! His son, they said it was – his son!
But the one inside, your wife, she'd tell it best.

Oedipus   My wife – *she* gave it to you?

Shepherd   Yes, yes, my king.

Oedipus   Why, what for?

Shepherd   To kill it.

Oedipus   Her own child, how could she?

Shepherd   She was afraid – frightening prophecies.

Oedipus   What?

Shepherd   They said – he'd kill his parents.

Oedipus   But you gave him to this old man – why?

Shepherd   I pitied the little baby, master,
hoped he'd take him off to his own country,

far away, but he saved him for this, this fate.
If you are the man he says you are, believe me,
you were born for pain.
Oedipus   Oh god –
all come true, all burst to light!
O light – now let me look my last on you!
I stand revealed at last –
cursed in my birth, cursed in marriage,
cursed in the lives I cut down with these hands! (*rushing through
                                            the doors with a great cry*)
                        (*Oedipus the King*, tr. Robert Fagles, Penguin 1982, pp. 227–32)

These astonishing Greek plays were imitated but not improved on
by Roman dramatists such as the comedians Plautus (254–184 BC) and
Terence (185–159 BC), and the tragedian Seneca (4 BC–AD 65); and it
was the Roman dramatists, not the Greek, who were the chief classical
influence on the sixteenth- and seventeenth-century dramatists of the
renaissance. Roman drama subsequently gave way for the most part to
games and spectacles, and ended with the barbarian invasions of the sixth
century AD.

Ancient Theatres

The earliest structures for theatrical performances in the ancient world
were probably scaffolds – or even moveable wagons – of wood, and virtually
no details or remains of them survive. Many Greek and Roman stone
theatres, on the other hand, do survive, and follow a generally similar
arrangement of an arc, of slightly more than a semicircle, of rows of
seats rising up from and partly surrounding a circular or semicircular
"orchestra" (dancing place), behind which was a shallow stage and a
"scene" building. The Greek actors performed in masks, and there appears
to have been some stylised scenery, and crude machinery for "flying", and
so on. The Roman theatres seem to have been used more for spectacles and
public meetings than for seeing plays performed. The acoustics of these
stone theatres were excellent, but they were generally oriented so that the
central seats faced south, backlighting the stage and the action.

Medieval Drama

Although the medieval period was a long one – from the eleventh to the
fifteenth century is as great a span of time as from the sixteenth to the
twentieth – the surviving evidence of medieval drama is exiguous and
defective. Such texts as we have indicate that, besides *liturgical drama*,
which dates back at least to the tenth century, there were English *mystery*

plays[3] (civic cycles illustrating biblical events from the creation to the ascension, presented by trade guilds, and dating from about the twelfth to the sixteenth century); *saints' plays* (lives of saints) and *miracle plays* (miracles of saints and the Virgin); and, later, *morality plays* (allegorical presentations of the struggle between good and evil, dating from the fifteenth and sixteenth centuries).

The most approachable of the surviving medieval plays are some of the fifteenth-century texts of plays in the mystery cycles, and the early sixteenth-century morality play *Everyman*. The best of the mystery plays (such as the *Second Shepherds' Play* from the Wakefield cycle, and the *York Play of the Crucifixion*), which show great skill as well as humour in building dialogue and developing character, are however difficult for ordinary readers because they are written in a northern dialect of English which is actually more obscure than Chaucer's south-eastern dialect of 100 years earlier. Here, in modernised spelling, are three of the easier stanzas from the *Second Shepherds' Play*, in which Mak's trick in trying to pass off a stolen lamb as his wife's newborn baby is discovered by his fellow-shepherds Coll, Gib, and Daw. The relevance of this story to that of the Nativity is as a sardonic parallel to the newborn Lamb of God, who was also recognised in the cradle by three wise men.

Daw	Give me leave him to kiss, and lift up the clout.
	What the devil is this? He has a long snout.
Coll	He is markèd amiss. We wot ill about.
Gib	Ill-spun weft, ywiss, ay comes foul out.
	Aye so!
	He is like to our sheep.
Daw	How, Gib, may I peep?
Coll	I trow kind will creep
	Where it may not go.

Gib	This was quaint gaud and a fair cast.
	It was a high fraud.
Daw	Yea, sirs, was't.
	Let burn this bawd and bind her fast
	A false scaud hang at the last:
	So shall thou.
	Will you see how they swaddle
	His four feet in the middle?
	Saw I never in cradle
	A horn'd lad ere now.

---

[3] The term "mystery" is taken here, not from the mysteries of religion, but from the medieval Latin word *misterium*, meaning an occupation or craft; cf. medieval French *mestier*, modern *métier*.

Mak	Peace bid I! What, let be your fare!
	I am he that him gat, and yond woman him bare.
Coll	What devil shall he hat? Mak? Lo, Gib, Mak's heir!
Gib	Let be all that: now God give him care –
	I sawgh.
Gill	A pretty child is he
	As sits on a woman's knee,
	A dillydown, pardie,
	To gar a man laugh.

(Second Shepherd's Play, lines 584–610)

The allegorical morality play *Everyman*, which dates originally from around 1500, is in much easier English, and seems familiar because of its similarity to the first part of Bunyan's *The Pilgrim's Progress* of 1678. Everyman is summoned by Death, but his companions Fellowship, Kindred, Cousin, and Goods all find excuses at the last moment not to go with him; and he finds out at last what is necessary for his salvation. This is part of his discourse with Fellowship, again in modernised spelling:

Fellowship   Sir, I say as I will do, indeed.
Everyman   Then be you a good friend at need.
   I have found you true herebefore.
Fellowship   And so ye shall evermore.
   For, in faith, and thou go to hell,
   I will not forsake thee by the way.
Everyman   Ye speak like a good friend. I believe you well.
   I shall deserve it, and I may.
Fellowship   I speak of no deserving, by this day!
   For he that will say and nothing do
   Is not worthy with good company to go.
   Therefore show me the grief of your mind,
   As to your friend most loving and kind.
Everyman   I shall show you how it is:
   Commanded I am to go on a journay,
   A long way, hard and dangerous,
   And give strait count, without delay,
   Before the high judge Adonai.
   Wherefore I pray you bear me company,
   As ye have promised, in this journay.
Fellowship   This is matter indeed! Promise is duty –
   But, and I should take a voyage on me,
   I know it well, it should be to my pain.
   Also it maketh me afeard, certain.
   But let us take counsel here, as well as we can –
   For your words would fear a strong man.
Everyman   Why, ye said if I had need,

Ye would me never forsake, quick ne dead,
   Though it were hell, truly.
Fellowship   So I said, certainly,
   But such pleasures be set aside, the sooth to say.
   And also, if we took such a journay,
   When should we again come?
Everyman   Nay, never again, till the day of doom.
Fellowship   In faith, then, will not I come there!
   Who hath you these tidings brought?
Everyman   Indeed, Death was with me here.
Fellowship   Now by God that all hath bought,
   If Death were the messenger,
   For no man that is living today
   I will not go that loath journay –
   Not for the father that begat me!

(*Everyman*, lines 227–69)

Medieval Staging

Almost anywhere could serve as a place to put on a play in medieval times – a church or churchyard, a private or public hall, the market place, a street, a field – and there were likewise several methods of staging. The most usual were *multiple staging*, where scenes were acted, either alternately or one after another, at a number of linked locations which might be fixed or moveable structures around a central stage; and *single-focus staging*, which might take place on an open space, a moveable pageant-wagon, a fixed scaffold or booth stage, or anywhere indoors. Audiences were accommodated as convenience and the possibility of obtaining money from spectators allowed, a specially good viewing place being in the upstairs window of a house overlooking the performance. Although these locations were unelaborate, costumes, properties, and special effects could be provided on lavish scales. Until the late fifteenth century, actors were not professionals in the sense that they earned their living by acting, but great care seems to have been taken with every detail of a production; broad gestures and clear enunciation to the audience would often have been necessary; and women's parts were played by men and boys.

Later Development

There is no room here for a history of drama – even an abbreviated history of English drama – from the sixteenth century to the twentieth, and we shall therefore focus on two outstanding periods of our early dramatic history, the late Elizabethan and Jacobean period, the golden age of English drama; and the neoclassical period, from Dryden to Sheridan. This is followed by an account of the theatrical revolution initiated by the Norwegian dramatist Henrik Ibsen in the late nineteenth century, and its effect, through the work of Bernard Shaw, on British theatre of the early twentieth century.

London Theatres, 1576–1642

The first building in London dedicated to the performance of plays and other spectacles was James Burbage's "Theatre" of 1576, in Shoreditch just outside the City. When its lease ran out in 1598, its timbers were carried across the river and used in the construction of the "Globe", in which Shakespeare was one of six financial partners from 1599 to 1608, the period when some of his finest plays were staged there. The Globe was a polygonal structure, with three tiers of spectators' galleries running round the inside, and a pit open to the sky with a rectangular stage under a canopy projecting into it; it could accommodate an audience of something like 3,000. There were two doors at the back of the stage, and possibly a "discovery" space curtained off between them, with a balcony above. (The recently built replica of the Globe near its original Bankside site shows better than any words what it was like.) Other early theatres of similar form were the "Rose" (1587), the "Swan" (1595), and the "Fortune" (1600). As well as these open-air theatres, the Blackfriars, an intimate indoor theatre with a capacity of little more than 100, was operated in the old Blackfriars monastery from 1576 to 1584, and again with increased capacity from 1600 to 1642. The open stage may have accommodated a form of multiple staging for plays in which many short scenes followed quickly one after another (in *Antony and Cleopatra*, for instance); the style of acting appears to have been semi-realistic (Hamlet's exhortation to the players gives an idea of what went on[4]); costumes were gorgeous but scenery was minimal; and women's parts were still played by men and boys.[5] In 1642, the Globe and all the other theatres were closed by Parliament, with Puritan encouragement, for fear of political and moral unrest among the mixed crowds who frequented the public theatres, so bringing the great age of English drama to an end.

[4] *Hamlet*, III.2.1–45.
[5] The resulting sexual ambiguities, now lost to the stage, were exploited with relish. In *As You Like It*, the character Rosalind (played by a young man or a boy) disguises herself as a young man, Ganymede, and, as Ganymede, requires Orlando, the man she loves, to make love to her as "Rosalind"; and, still as Ganymede, she is made love to by the shepherdess Phoebe (also played by a young man or a boy).

Late Elizabethan and Jacobean Drama

Although English poetry and, to a lesser extent drama, developed steadily under renaissance influences[6] during the middle years of the sixteenth century, nothing prefigured the astonishing outburst of dramatic genius that transformed the stage from the late 1580s to the 1630s. It began with two dramatists – one great, one superlative – who were born in the same year, 1564. The simultaneous emergence of Marlowe and Shakespeare was a wonder, for it was their brilliance that initiated the upsurge of great drama in the years following 1600, and which was then a profound influence on all their successors.

Christopher Marlowe (1564–93), poet, playwright, and spy, wrote half a dozen plays before he was murdered at the age of 29. The first of them, *Tamburlaine* in two parts (1587), was a popular success; but it is his two last plays – *Edward II* (c.1592) and *Doctor Faustus* (c.1592–3)[7] – that suggest the heights that he might have reached had he outlived his twenties.[8]

Edward II is a well-constructed and gripping history play, written in a plainer blank verse than Marlowe had used hitherto. In it, the homosexual King is defeated by a combination of disloyal barons with his estranged Queen and her lover Mortimer; his favourites Gaveston and Hugh le Despenser are successively killed; and the King himself is degraded and eventually murdered, slowly and sadistically, at Berkeley Castle.

Doctor Faustus, which survives only in two different, corrupted texts of 1604 and 1616, is a dramatisation of the medieval legend of the magus who bargains his soul away to the Devil. Faustus (identified here with Dr Georg Faust, a German sorcerer of c.1500), wearying of academic science, turns to magic and calls up Mephistophilis, through whom he makes a fatal contract with the Devil: Faustus is to have twenty-four years on earth with Mephistophilis as his servant to do all he asks, at the end of which the Devil is to have Faustus's immortal soul. Faustus proceeds to get what he can from the bargain, with an ever-increasing lust for power, though predictably the Devil cheats him of any real benefit from it. He is encouraged by his good angel to repent and be saved, but is persuaded by his bad angel to accept that he is already damned, and to carry on with his futile self-

---

[6] See p. 12 above.

[7] Apart from *Tamburlaine*, none of Marlowe's plays can be dated with much confidence, and some authorities assign an earlier date to *Doctor Faustus*.

[8] The dating of Shakespeare's earliest plays is also notoriously difficult, but it seems likely that those he wrote before Marlowe's death in 1593 include only one major work, *Richard III*; which may have been preceded by the relatively minor *Two Gentlemen of Verona*, *The Taming of the Shrew*, *Henry VI* parts I–III, and *Titus Andronicus*.

indulgence. The middle section of the play includes some crude knock-about comedy, which may or may not have been written by Marlowe, and which sorts badly with the high style and psychological sophistication of the main story. The play ends with Faustus's magnificent, despairing monologue as he waits at the eleventh hour for the Devil to come and fetch his soul, when he realises the worthlessness of what he has had from the Devil's bargain, and cries out to his Saviour to let him repent even now. But it is too late, and the Devil's servants carry him away to hell.

> (*the clock strikes eleven*)
>
> Faustus   Ah Faustus,
>   Now has thou but one bare hour to live,
>   And then thou must be damn'd perpetually.
>   Stand still, you ever-moving spheres of heaven,
>   That time may cease, and midnight never come.
>   Fair nature's eye, rise, rise again, and make
>   Perpetual day. Or let this hour be but
>   A year, a month, a week, a natural day,
>   That Faustus may repent and save his soul.
>   *O lente, lente, currite noctis equi.*[9]
>   The stars move still, time runs, the clock will strike.
>   The devil will come, and Faustus must be damn'd.
>   Oh, I'll leap up to my God: who pulls me down?
>   See, see, where Christ's blood streams in the firmament.
>   One drop would save my soul, half a drop. Ah, my Christ!
>   Ah, rend not my heart for naming of my Christ!
>   Yet will I call on him. Oh, spare me, Lucifer! …
>
>   (*the clock strikes twelve*)
>   Oh it strikes, it strikes! Now body turn to air,
>   Or Lucifer will bear thee quick to hell.
>   (*thunder and lightning*)
>   Oh soul, be changëd into little water drops
>   And fall into the ocean, ne'er be found.
>   (*thunder; enter the devils*)
>   My God, my God, look not so fierce on me,
>   Adders and serpents, let me breathe awhile.
>   Ugly hell, gape not, come not Lucifer!
>   I'll burn my books. Ah, Mephistophilis! (*exeunt with him*)
>   (*Doctor Faustus*, V.2.143–59, 193–200)

It is worth remembering that sorcery, damnation, hell, and the devil all seemed very real threats to almost everyone in Marlowe's original audiences.

---

[9] "O run slowly, slowly, you horses of the night" (from Ovid's *Amores*).

William Shakespeare (1564–1616)[10] needs no introduction or commentary here, except to repeat that in his greatest plays he outclassed all his contemporaries in his psychological insight, in the harmony of his blank verse, and in his management of dramatic effect; and that he has been a powerful and virtually inescapable influence on the subsequent development, not only of European drama, but of western literature as a whole.

To reaffirm his quality, here is a splendid yet mellifluous piece of rhetoric to be enjoyed and, if possible, located:

> Time hath, my lord,
> A wallet at his back, wherein he puts
> Alms for oblivion, a great-sized monster
> Of ingratitudes. Those scraps are good deeds past,
> Which are devour'd as soon as they are made,
> Forgot as soon as done. Perséverance, dear my lord,
> Keeps honour bright. To have done is to hang
> Quite out of fashion, like a rusty mail
> In monumental mock'ry. Take the instant way,
> For honour travels in a strait so narrow,
> Where one but goes abreast. Keep then the path,
> For emulation hath a thousand sons
> That one by one pursue: if you give way,
> Or hedge aside from the direct forthright,
> Like to an enter'd tide they all rush by
> And leave you hindmost;
> Or, like a gallant horse fall'n in first rank,
> Lie there for pavement to the abject rear,
> O'errun and trampl'd on. Then what they do in present,
> Though less than yours in past, must o'ertop yours.
> For Time is like a fashionable host,
> That slightly shakes his parting guest by th'hand,
> And, with his arms outstretch'd as he would fly,
> Grasps in the comer. Welcome ever smiles,
> And Farewell goes out sighing. O let not virtue seek
> Remuneration for the thing it was;
> For beauty, wit,
> High birth, vigour of bone, desert in service,
> Love, friendship, charity, are subjects all
> To envious and calumniating time.
> One touch of nature makes the whole world kin –
> That all with one consent praise new-born gauds,
> Though they are made and moulded of things past,
> And give to dust that is a little gilt
> More laud than gilt o'er dusted.

[10] See pp. 13–14 above.

Ben Jonson (1573–1637), a Londoner of extravagant personality and multiple talents, was in his plays pre-eminently a satirist. Unlike Shakespeare, who wrote quickly and unfastidiously, and who at the time of his death neither knew, nor can have seriously cared, whether some of his best plays would ever be published,[11] Jonson was meticulous both in writing and in editing his texts, and went so far as to produce a collected edition of his own *Works* in 1616. *Volpone* (1606) and *The Alchemist* (1610) are his greatest satiric comedies, and the first of these is perhaps his masterwork. Written in little more than a month (an indication – as is the workmanlike competence of the blank verse – of Jonson's outstanding professionalism), *Volpone* is a fable of greed deluded and thwarted by guile, its animal names and animal imagery a respectful nod to Aesop. The scene is supposedly Venice,[12] but the application of this funniest and most mischievous of satires to the middle classes of Jonson's London must always have been plain enough. Volpone (fox), assisted by his servant Mosca (fly), puts it about that he is dying, confident that he will be sought out by greedy legacy-hunters; and, sure enough, various leading citizens walk into his trap. In order to secure Volpone's fortune, the lawyer Voltore (vulture) will break the law; Corbaccio (crow) will disinherit his own son; and Corvino (raven) will prostitute his own wife to Volpone. Volpone then goes too far and, having made Mosca his heir, pretends to be dead. Mosca blackmails Volpone, who has to return to life, and to reveal the whole plot to the authorities. In the end, both trappers and trapped are suitably punished, only Corbaccio's son and Corvino's wife being rewarded. Besides all this, there is a sub-plot involving a foolish Englishman, Sir Politic Would-be, and his hectoring, deceitful wife Lady Politic. In the following extract, Corvino is trying persuade Celia, his innocent wife, to go to Volpone's bed, while Volpone pretends to be too ill to make use of her:

> Corvino (*to Celia*)   I've told you reasons:
>   What the physicians have set down; how much
>   It may concern me; what my engagements are;
>   My means; and the necessity of those means,

---

[11] Among the plays which remained unpublished until the appearance of the first folio of 1623, seven years after Shakespeare's death, were *Antony and Cleopatra, As You Like It, Julius Caesar, Macbeth, Measure for Measure, Othello* (following a quarto of 1622), *The Tempest, Twelfth Night,* and *The Winter's Tale.* It is most improbable that Shakespeare could not have arranged for their publication in his lifetime if he had wanted to.

[12] This play, and the two plays by Webster and Ford that follow it here, are all set in an imaginary renaissance Italy – a land of vice, betrayal, torture, murder, scheming, and corruption – which both fascinated and appalled the English society that dreamed it up, and in which dramatists and storytellers found a suitable location for their wilder fantasies.

For my recovery: wherefore, if you be
Loyal and mine, be won, respect my venture.
Celia   Before your honour?
Corvino   Honour! tut, a breath;
   There's no such thing in nature. A mere term
   Invented to awe fools. What is my gold
   The worse for touching, clothes for being looked on?
   Why, this's no more. An old decrepit wretch,
   That has no sense, no sinew; takes his meat
   With others' fingers; only knows to gape
   When you do scald his gums; a voice, a shadow;
   And what can this man hurt you?
Celia (*aside*)   Lord! what spirit
   Is this hath enter'd him?
Corvino   And for your fame,
   That's such a jig; as if I would go tell it,
   Cry it on the Piazza! Who shall know it,
   But he that cannot speak it, and this fellow,
   Whose lips are in my pocket? Save yourself
   (If you'll proclaim't, you may), I know no other
   Should come to know it.
Celia   Are Heaven and saints then nothing?
   Will they be blind or stupid?
Corvino   How!
Celia   Good sir,
   Be jealous still, emulate them; and think
   What hate they burn with toward every sin.
Corvino   I grant you; if I thought it were a sin,
   I would not urge you. Should I offer this
   To some young Frenchman, or hot Tuscan blood
   That had read Aretine, conn'd all his prints,
   Knew every quirk within lust's labyrinth,
   And were professëd critic in lechery,
   And I would look upon him, and applaud him,
   This were a sin: but here, 'tis contrary,
   A pious work, mere charity, for physic,
   And honest polity to assure mine own.
Celia   O heaven! canst thou suffer such a change?
Volpone (*aside to Mosca*)   Thou art mine honour, Mosca, and my pride,
   My joy, my tickling, my delight! Go bring them.
Mosca (*to Corvino*)   Please you draw near, sir.
Corvino (*to Celia*)   Come on, what –
   You will not be rebellious? By that light –
Mosca   Sir,
   Signor Corvino here is come to see you –
Volpone   O!

Mosca   And hearing of the consultation had,
  So lately, for your health, is come to offer,
  Or rather, sir, to prostitute –
Corvino   Thanks, sweet Mosca.
Mosca   Freely, unasked, or unentreated –
Corvino   Well.
Mosca   As the true fervent instance of his love,
  His own most fair and proper wife, the beauty
  Only of price in Venice –
Corvino   'Tis well urg'd.
Mosca   To be your comfortress, and to preserve you.
Volpone   Alas, I'm past, already! Pray you, thank him
  For his good care and promptness; but for that,
  'Tis a vain labour e'en to fight 'gainst heaven,
  Applying fire to stone – uh, uh, uh, uh! (*coughing*) –
  Making a dead leaf grow again. I take
  His wishes gently, though; and you may tell him
  What I've done for him: marry, my state is hopeless.
  Will him to pray for me; and to use his fortune
  With reverence, when he comes to't.
Mosca   Do you hear, sir?
  Go to him with your wife.
Corvino (*to Celia*)   Heart of my father!
  Wilt thou persist thus? Come, I pray thee, come.
  Thou seest 'tis nothing. Celia! By this hand,
  I shall grow violent. Come, do't, I say.
Celia   Sir, kill me, rather: I will take down poison,
  Eat burning coals, do anything.

(*Volpone*, III.7.32–94)

Later, Volpone, throwing off his pretence of sickness, does make an attempt on Celia's virtue, but is frustrated by Bonario, Corbaccio's disinherited son.

John Webster (c.1580–c.1625): little is known about Webster but that he was a middle-class Londoner and unsuccessful law student, who was probably supported financially by his father. He began as a dramatist by working from about 1602 as a collaborator with Dekker and others; and he wrote his two great tragedies, *The White Devil* and *The Duchess of Malfi*, in 1612–13. He worked slowly and carefully, building up his plays by the commonly used method of reworking material gathered from his own reading; and, like Jonson but unlike Shakespeare, he took the trouble to see that his plays were correctly printed. An admirer of Donne, his blank verse could be harsh and fractured; but this was intentional, for he could change to a smoother style when it was appropriate, and he was able to turn out well-crafted, melodious lyrics. Both *The White Devil* and *The Duchess of Malfi* are "revenge tragedies", a genre which centred on murder, and especially on murder in revenge for murder, with the involvement of a malcontent;[13] and Webster makes the most of it, piling horror on morbid horror. But *The Duchess of Malfi* has a further dimension in the Duchess herself, whose moral stature increases with her troubles. Webster is concerned here, moreover, both as artist and citizen, not merely with violence, but with the social problems of lawlessness and tyranny, and the ethical problems of vengeance, human and divine. The story, set in the cruel, conspiratorial Italy of English imagination, tells of a Duchess, a high-spirited widow, who is in love with her steward Antonio, and who secretly marries him even though she knows that her brothers, a Duke and a Cardinal, are opposed to her remarrying. The brothers place a spy, the malcontent Bosola, in her household, who betrays her to them. She is captured, mentally tortured, and finally murdered. The Duke goes mad; the Cardinal is murdered by the now remorseful Bosola; Bosola, having murdered Antonio by mistake for the Cardinal, is himself is murdered by the mad Duke, but survives long enough to see the Duke killed by Antonio's friends. This is a bloody tale indeed; but Webster's poetic imagination has contrived to make of it an intimate and poignant study of human nature *in extremis*. Here is an extract which shows both the dignity of the Duchess as she faces her executioners, and Bosola's indifferent cruelty as he orders the murder of her waiting woman Cariola:

> Bosola   Doth not death fright you?
> Duchess   Who would be afraid on't?
>   Knowing to meet such excellent company
>   In th'other world.
> Bosola   Yet, methinks,
>   The manner of your death should much afflict you,
>   This cord should terrify you?
> Duchess   Not a whit:
>   What would it pleasure me, to have my throat cut
>   With diamonds? or to be smother'd
>   With cassia? or to be shot to death, with pearls?
>   I know death hath ten thousand several doors
>   For men to take their exits: and 'tis found
>   They go on such strange geometrical hinges,
>   You may open them both ways: any way, for heaven sake,
>   So I were out of your whispering. Tell my brothers
>   That I perceive death, now I am well awake,
>   Best gift is, they can make, or I can take.
>   I would fain put off my last woman's fault,
>   I'ld not be tedious to you.

---

[13] *Hamlet*, with its multiple revenges, is the best-known example.

Executioners   We are ready.

Duchess   Dispose my breath how please you, but my body
    Bestow upon my women, will you?

Executioners   Yes.

Duchess   Pull, and pull strongly, for your able strength
    Must pull down heaven upon me:
    Yet stay, heaven gates are not so highly arch'd
    As princes' palaces: they that enter there
    Must go upon their knees. Come, violent death,
    Serve for mandragora to make me sleep;
    Go tell my brothers, when I am laid out,
    They then may feed in quiet.
        they strangle her

Bosola   Where's the waiting woman?
    Fetch her. Some other strangle the children.
        exeunt executioners; enter one with Cariola
    Look you, there sleeps your mistress.

Cariola   O you are damn'd
    Perpetually for this. My turn is next,
    Is't not so order'd?

Bosola   Yes, and I am glad
    You are so well prepar'd for it.

Cariola   You are deceiv'd sir,
    I am no prepar'd for't. I will not die,
    I will first come to my answer; and know
    How I have offended.

Bosola   Come, dispatch her.
    You kept her counsel, now you shall keep ours.

Cariola   I will not die, I must not, I am contracted
    To a young gentleman.

Executioner   Here's your wedding-ring.

Cariola   Let me but speak with the Duke. I'll discover
    Treason to his person.

Bosola   Delays: throttle her.

Executioner   She bites: and scratches.

Cariola   If you kill me now
    I am damn'd. I have not been at confession
    This two years.

Bosola   When!

Cariola   I am quick with child.

Bosola   Why then,
    Your credit's saved.   *Cariola is strangled*

        (*The Duchess of Malfi*, IV.2.199–244)

John Ford (c.1586–c.1640): Ford was a Devonshire man who spent most
of his life in the Middle Temple, though he was not called to the bar.
Having published some poetry and prose, he collaborated with Dekker and

others on various plays from 1621 to 1625, and then wrote some eighteen plays on his own, seven of which are lost. Ford was particularly concerned to investigate moral paradox in his studies of human dignity, suffering, and endurance; and, although his tragedies are shot through with the violence so characteristic of the period, all his plays are suffused with a sympathetic melancholy. This mood of acquiescent sadness is expressed in dramatic blank verse of great beauty; more successfully than any other dramatist of the period, Ford has adapted the style of Shakespeare's dramatic poetry, tuning it perfectly to his own voice; so that the contrast between the poignant music of Ford's blank verse, and Jonson's colloquial rhythms or Webster's toughness, could hardly be greater.

Ford's most enduring play is *'Tis Pity She's a Whore* (c.1625–33), a tragedy of great psychological intensity set yet again in Italy, and centring on the incestuous love between a brother and his sister, a taboo subject which Ford treats seriously and honestly. The siblings, Giovanni and Annabella, confess that they are in love with each other, knowing that it is forbidden; but they are then obliged to carry on their affair clandestinely, while Annabella has to deal with the wish of their father that she should marry, and with the approaches of three suitors for her hand. They remain faithful to each other but, while Annabella goes on to endure the misery of marriage to one of the suitors with some fortitude, Giovanni's mind becomes unhinged and, recognising that they cannot continue to be all in all to each other, he kills his sister-lover. He bears her heart on his dagger to her husband, kills him, and is killed in his turn. In this extract Giovanni and Annabella reveal their love to each other:

Giovanni   Here.   (*offers his dagger to her*)
Annabella   What to do?
Giovanni   And here's my breast, strike home.
  Rip up my bosom, there thou shalt behold
  A heart in which is writ the truth I speak.
  Why stand 'ee?
Annabella   Are you earnest?
Giovanni   Yes, most earnest.
  You cannot love?
Annabella   Whom?
Giovanni   Me. My tortured soul
  Hath felt affliction in the heat of death.
  O Annabella, I am quite undone.
  The love of thee, my sister, and the view
  Of thy immortal beauty hath untun'd
  All harmony both of my rest and life.
  Why d'ee not strike?

Annabella   Forbid it, my just fears.
  If this be true, 'twere fitter I were dead.
Giovanni   True, Annabella; 'tis no time to jest.
  I have too long suppress'd the hidden flames
  That almost have consum'd me; I have spent
  Many a silent night in sighs and groans,
  Ran over all my thoughts, despis'd my fate,
  Reason'd against the reasons of my love,
  Done all that smooth'd-cheek virtue could advise,
  But found all bootless; 'tis my destiny
  That you must either love, or I must die.
Annabella   Comes this in sadness from you?
Giovanni   Let some mischief
  Befall me soon if I dissemble aught.
Annabella   You are my brother Giovanni.
Giovanni   You
  My sister Annabella; I know this:
  And could afford you instance why to love
  So much the more for this; to which intent
  Wise nature first in your creation meant
  To make you mine; else't had been sin and foul
  To share one beauty to a double soul.
  Nearness in birth or blood doth but persuade
  A nearer nearness in affection.
  I have ask'd counsel of the holy church,
  Who tells me I may love you, and 'tis just
  That since I may, I should; and will, yes, will.
  Must I now live, or die?
Annabella   Live. Thou has won
  The field, and never fought; what thou has urg'd
  My captive heart had long ago resolv'd.
  I blush to tell thee – but I'll tell thee now –
  For every sigh that thou hast spent for me
  I have sighed ten; for every tear shed twenty:
  And not so much for that I lov'd, as that
  I durst not say I lov'd, nor scarcely think it.
                        (*'Tis Pity She's a Whore*, I.2.203–47)

The Neoclassical Period

When theatrical production was permitted again after eighteen years of
prohibition, following the restoration of the monarchy in 1660, it was
theoretically limited in London to two patent holders, though the patents
were frequently infringed; the first two patent holders controlled the
King's Men in a new theatre at Drury Lane, and the Duke's Men in a
converted tennis court at Lincoln's Inn Fields. The old open-air "wooden

Os" were quickly replaced by new indoor theatres with proscenium arches; these were at first fairly small buildings seating 200–300 people, but by the early eighteenth century theatres were being built for audiences of 2,000 and more. Another major change was that women's parts were no longer played by men and boys, but by professional actresses; though, unfortunately for them, actresses, however accomplished, were not considered to be wholly respectable members of society for another 200 years.

For the first few years, the companies had little option but to revive old plays – Jacobean tragedies were especially popular – but new plays then began to appear; the two favourite genres were old plays cast in new forms, and – most successful of all – comedies of manners, which flourished and continued to develop until late in the eighteenth century; these were funny, often outrageous, satires on the failings and absurdities of contemporary society, with witty dialogue and clever plotting, but without profound characterisation. We look at three of the best of them here, though there were many others almost as good – Farquhar's *The Beaux' Stratagem*, Steele's *The Conscious Lovers*, and Gay's *The Beggar's Opera*, for instance. Tragedy, on the other hand, whether or not influenced by Corneille and Racine, rarely reached as high a standard.

John Dryden (1631–1700)[14] dominated the development of the London theatre from the restoration of Charles II in 1660 until the removal of James II in 1688, when, as a Catholic convert, he was ejected from the Poet Laureateship, and had to scrape a living as a hack playwright and compiler of miscellanies. Besides his outpouring of satirical and other poetry, he composed both comedies and tragedies; and he also wrote *An Essay of Dramatick Poesie* (1668), the first major work of dramatic criticism in English, in which he was able to deploy his extensive knowledge of literature and criticism, ancient and modern. Here, and in his prefaces, Dryden established a set of neoclassical critical principles which were to serve the new literary age which he was instrumental in forming.

The play of his which has lasted best is *All for Love*, Dryden's neoclassical version of *Antony and Cleopatra*. Although it is a tragedy in blank verse that covers the same great theme – should Antony choose honour or love? – and some of the same events as Shakespeare's play, and although Dryden says frankly in his preface to the play that "in my style I have professed to imitate the divine Shakespeare", the play is Dryden's, not merely Shakespeare revised; a version for Dryden's own time. To continue with Dryden's preface:

[14] See pp. 16–17 above.

All reasonable men have long since concluded that the hero of the poem ought not to be a character of perfect virtue, for then he could not, without injustice, be made unhappy; nor yet altogether wicked, because he could not then be pitied: I have therefore steered the middle course ... That which is wanting to work up the pity to a greater height was not afforded me by the story: for the crimes of love which they [Antony and Cleopatra] both committed were not occasioned by any necessity or fatal ignorance, but were wholly voluntary, since our passions are, or ought to be, within our power. The fabric of the play is regular enough ... and the unities of time, place, and action more exactly observed than, perhaps, the English theatre requires. Particularly, the action is so much one that it is the only of the kind [of plays on this theme] without episode or underplot, every scene in the tragedy conducing to the main design, and every act concluding with a turn of it.

But, although our passions "ought to be within our power" according to the strictest neoclassical doctrine, Dryden knows that they are not always so, and in presenting his hero he compromises what ought to be with what is, accepting what is practicable rather than what would be ideal as a sufficient – if not a perfect – cause for Antony's giving up all for love.

He writes, too, with affection as well as admiration for Shakespeare, and Shakespearean echoes are heard throughout the play; consider Dryden's version of Enobarbus's famous description of Cleopatra on the water in *Antony and Cleopatra* ("The barge she sat in, like a burnished throne, / burn'd on the water ...", II.2.190–222):

> Antony   ... Her galley down the silver Cydnos rowed,
> The tackling silk, the streamers wav'd with gold;
> The gentle winds were lodg'd in purple sails;
> Her nymphs, like Nereids, round her couch were plac'd,
> Where she, another sea-born Venus, lay. ...
> She lay, and leant her cheek upon her hand,
> And cast a look so languishingly sweet
> As if, secure of all beholders' hearts,
> Neglecting she could take 'em. Boys like Cupids
> Stood fanning with their painted wings the winds
> That play'd about her face; but if she smil'd,
> A darting glory seem'd to blaze abroad,
> That men's desiring eyes were never wearied,
> But hung upon the object. To soft flutes
> The silver oars kept time; and while they play'd,
> The hearing gave new pleasure to the sight,
> And both to thought. 'Twas Heaven, or somewhat more;
> For she so charm'd all hearts, that gazing crowds
> Stood panting on the shore, and wanted breath
> To give their welcome voice.
>
>   (*All for Love*, III.162–82)

But, however Shakespearian in flavour, *All for Love* is still a neoclassical play, not a renaissance one; controlled rather than exuberant, and obeying formal rules of structure and language.

John Vanbrugh (1664–1726), born exactly 100 years after Shakespeare, was not only possessed of extraordinary artistic talent, but he was also a man of abounding energy, wit, and charm. After a brief career as a soldier and suspected spy (he was arrested in France in 1688, and imprisoned in Vincennes and the Bastille before being exchanged in 1692), he became a leading spirit in London social and intellectual circles. He wrote his first comedy, *The Relapse*, in 1696. It was a great and lasting success, and was followed by another fine comedy, *The Provok'd Wife* (1697); but his dramatic activity then tailed off, though it did not cease completely for several years more. In 1699 he designed a new house for the Earl of Carlisle, who supported his appointment as Comptroller of the Board of Works (1702). From now on, he found the major outlet for his creativity in architecture. Castle Howard (1702) was followed by Blenheim Palace (1704–16), and other well-designed, if less grandiose, buildings. An ardent Hanoverian, Vanbrugh was the first man to be knighted in the reign of George I (1714).

The Relapse (1696) was vivacious, funny, bawdy, and outrageous; it succeeded immediately, was produced at least once in each of the next fifty years, and has held its place on the stage ever since. It began as a sequel to *Love's Last Shift*, a lesser play by Colley Cibber in which the unworthy Loveless is reconciled to his virtuous wife Amanda, with comic relief in the self-preoccupation of the would-be beau Sir Novelty Fashion. Vanbrugh's play is an ironical development of Cibber's situation. Loveless again betrays the determinedly faithful Amanda, seducing her not-unwilling best friend; but Sir Novelty has bought a peerage and expanded to become Lord Foppington, one of the great comic characters of the English stage. Foppington, who speaks a ludicrously self-conscious "court" dialect (saying "a" for "o", as in "stap my vitals"), proposes to marry a boisterously self-seeking country girl, Miss Hoyden, but is outsmarted by his sneakily self-seeking brother, Young Fashion, who secretly marries her first; while other disreputable characters step in and out of the main town-and-country plot. All the characters, except the boringly virtuous Amanda, are moved primarily by self-interest, expressed as sexual appetite, social ambition, and the pursuit of financial gain; and the moral of the play lies in its scandalous immorality, which insists that we consider the possibility of higher values. Here, at the very end of the play, Foppington decides (in his private voice) to bear his discomfiture gracefully, and then (in his beau's voice) he gives his brother Tom his good wishes, and praises Miss Hoyden for the qualities she conspicuously lacks. Young Fashion spurns him; but then, taking his wife's hand, he is inspired to make a final, monstrous suggestion:

> Lord Foppington (*aside*) Now for my part, I think the wisest thing a man can do with an aching heart is to put on a serene countenance, for a philosophical air is the most becoming thing in the world to the face of a person of quality. I will therefore bear my disgrace like a great man, and let the people see I am above an affront. (*to Young Fashion*) Dear Tam, since things are thus fallen aut, prithee give me leave to wish thee jay; I do it *de bon cœur*, strike me dumb! You have married a woman beautiful in her person, charming in her airs, prudent in her canduct, canstant in her inclinations, and of a nice marality, split my windpipe!
>
> Young Fashion Your lordship may keep up your spirits with your grimace if you please; I shall support mine with this lady, and two thousand pound a year. – (*taking Miss Hoyden's hand*) –
> Come, madam: –
> We once again, you see, are man and wife,
> And now, perhaps, the bargain's struck for life.
> If I mistake, and we should part again,
> At least you see you may have choice of men:
> Nay, should the war at length such havoc make,
> That lovers should grow scarce, yet for your sake,
> Kind heaven always will preserve a beau:
> (*pointing to Lord Foppington*)
> You'll find his lordship ready to come to.
>
> Lord Foppington
> Her ladyship shall stap my vitals, if I do. (*exeunt*)
>
> (*The Relapse*, V.5.246–70)

There is of course an element of farce here, but farce does seem to be an essential constituent of the best comedy. It is absent from *The Way of the World*, the comedy of Vanbrugh's contemporary William Congreve (1670–1729) which is usually judged his best; it was a flop when it was first staged and, for all its wit and ingenious plotting – or perhaps partly because of them – it lacks some spark of theatrical life. Congreve, incidentally, who was brought up in Ireland, was the first of the string of major English dramatists who began life as Anglo-Irishmen: Goldsmith, Sheridan, Wilde, and Shaw.[15]

Oliver Goldsmith (c.1730–1774) was the son of a country clergyman of the Church of Ireland, but lived most of his life in London. Whether failing or succeeding, he was chronically short of money, and sought to relieve this condition by writing much hack work, a number of competent essays,

---

[15] Synge and Beckett were also Irishmen of Protestant stock, but Synge remained in Ireland, and Beckett emigrated not to England but to France.

histories and anthologies, and three masterpieces: two poems, *The Traveller* (1764, deriving from memories of his beggar's grand tour of Europe as a young man) and *The Deserted Village* (1770, looking back to his childhood in Ireland); and *She Stoops to Conquer* (1773), the better of his two comedies. This last has all the ingredients that have enlivened comedy from *A Midsummer Night's Dream* to *The Importance of Being Earnest*: wit, a clever plot, funny and almost credible characters, and a dash of farce; and it also succeeded in satirising the current "sentimental comedy" that had developed in reaction to the crudities of the Restoration stage. Two young men from London, going courting in the country, arrive at their host's country house having been led to believe that it is an inn; they treat this peppery old gentleman as a common innkeeper, and his virtuous daughter (who, unlike her father, has been let into the joke) as the barmaid. Goldsmith carries off this central jest, and several associated confusions, with a miraculous lightness of touch, and with exactly the right balance of sense and sensibility to carry his audience with him (though the theatre owners were at first dubious about putting on what they saw as an attack on contemporary taste). It was an immediate and continuing success, and has held the stage ever since. Here the two young men, Marlow and Hastings, mistake Mr Hardcastle for an innkeeper:

> Hardcastle   Gentlemen, once more you are heartily welcome. Which is Mr Marlow? Sir, you're heartily welcome. It's not my way, you see, to receive my friends with my back to the fire. I like to give them a hearty reception in the old style at my gate. I like to see their horses and trunks taken care of.
>
> Marlow (*aside*)   He has got our names from the servants already. (*to him*) We approve your caution and hospitality, sir. (*to Hastings*) I have been thinking, George, of changing our travelling dresses in the morning. I am grown confoundedly ashamed of mine.
>
> Hardcastle   I beg, Mr Marlow, you'll use no ceremony in this house.
>
> Hastings   I fancy, Charles, you're right: the first blow is half the battle. I intend opening the campaign with the white and the gold.
>
> Hardcastle   Mr Marlow – Mr Hastings – gentlemen – pray be under no constraint in this house. This is Liberty-Hall, gentlemen. You may do just as you please here.
>
> Marlow   Yet, George, if we open the campaign too fiercely at first, we may want ammunition before it is over. I think to reserve the embroidery to secure a retreat.
>
> Hardcastle   Your talking of a retreat, Mr Marlow, puts me in mind of the Duke of Marlborough, when we went to besiege Denain.[16] He firstsummoned the garrison.

---

[16] Part of the joke is that Hardcastle cannot have been at the siege of Denain, which took place in 1712, and from which Marlborough was also absent.

Marlow   Don't you think the *ventre d'or* waistcoat will do with the plain brown?

Hardcastle   He first summoned the garrison, which might consist of about five thousand men –

Hastings   I think not: brown and yellow mix but very poorly.

Hardcastle   I say, gentlemen, as I was telling you, he summoned the garrison, which might consist of about five thousand men –

Marlow   The girls like finery.

Hardcastle   Which might consist of about five thousand men, well appointed with stores, ammunition, and other implements of war. Now, says the Duke of Marlborough, to George Brooks, that stood next to him – You must have heard of George Brooks; I'll pawn my Dukedom, says he, but I take that garrison without spilling a drop of blood. So –

Marlow   What, my good friend, if you gave us a glass of punch in the meantime, it would help us to carry on the siege with vigour.

Hardcastle   Punch, sir! (*aside*) This is the most unaccountable kind of modesty I ever met with.

Marlow   Yes, sir, punch. A glass of warm punch, after our journey, will be comfortable. This is Liberty-Hall, you know.

(*She Stoops to Conquer*, II.1.146–90)

Richard Brinsley Sheridan (1751–1816) was born into the theatre, his father being an Irish actor-manager, and his mother a novelist and playwright. He wrote his great comedies of manners while still in his twenties, and he later became sole proprietor of Drury Lane. Yet he did not really like the theatre, and never saw a play unless he had to; what he most wanted to be, and to be remembered as, was a politician. He did succeed in this ambition up to a point, being an MP from 1780 to 1811, including a brief period as a minister, and being celebrated as an orator in the Commons. At the same time he was improvident and unbusinesslike, letting the huge sums of money he earned and borrowed slip through his fingers; he was arrested for debt in 1813, and died admired but insolvent. Nowadays it is the politician who is largely forgotten, the playwright who is remembered.

The School for Scandal (1777) is Sheridan's most masterly comedy, and is still regularly staged.[17] It satirises with acid humour the worthless scandalmongers and backbiters of fashionable London. The story, which is complex but plain enough in the theatre, concerns the Surface brothers – Joseph, a sanctimonious hypocrite, and Charles, a good-hearted improvident charmer (not unlike Sheridan himself) – their rich uncle Oliver newly returned from India, and the quarrelsome Sir Peter and Lady Teazle. After much intrigue, plot, and counter-plot, all comes right in the end; as in Miss Prism's definition of Fiction, "the good ended happily,

---

[17] Sheridan's other plays include a polite version of *The Relapse* called *A Trip to Scarborough*.

and the bad unhappily".[18] But, splendid entertainment as this is, it is the exposure and indictment of the scandalmongers that is the play's greatest strength. This extract, in which a completely fictitious quarrel between Sir Peter Teazle and one or other of the Surface brothers is dreamed up, shows the rumour mill in action:

Lady Sneerwell   So, my dear Mrs Candour, here's a sad affair of our friend Lady Teazle!

Mrs Candour   Ay, my dear friend, who would have thought –

Lady Sneerwell   Well, there is no trusting to appearances; though indeed she was always too lively for me.

Mrs Candour   To be sure, her manners were a little too free; but then she was so young!

Lady Sneerwell   And had, indeed, some good qualities.

Mrs Candour   So she had, indeed. But have you heard the particulars?

Lady Sneerwell   No; but everybody says that Mr Surface –

Sir Benjamin   Ay, there; I told you Mr Surface was the man.

Mrs Candour   No, no; indeed the assignation was with Charles.

Lady Sneerwell   With Charles! You alarm me, Mrs Candour.

Mrs Candour   Yes, yes: he was the lover. Mr Surface, to do him justice, was only the informer.

Sir Benjamin   Well, I'll not dispute with you, Mrs Candour; but, be it which it may, I hope that Sir Peter's wound will not –

Mrs Candour   Sir Peter's wound! Oh, mercy! I didn't hear a word of their fighting.

Lady Sneerwell   Nor I, a syllable.

Sir Benjamin   No! what, no mention of a duel?

Mrs Candour   Not a word.

Sir Benjamin   Oh, yes: they fought before they left the room.

Lady Sneerwell   Pray let us hear.

Mrs Candour   Ay, do oblige us with the duel.

Sir Benjamin   "*Sir*," says Sir Peter, immediately after the discovery, "*you are a most ungrateful fellow.*"

Mrs Candour   Ay, to Charles –

Sir Benjamin   No, no – to Mr Surface – "*a most ungrateful fellow; and old as I am, sir,*" says he, "*I insist on immediate satisfaction.*"

Mrs Candour   Ay, that must have been to Charles; for 'tis very unlikely Mr Surface should fight in his own house.

Sir Benjamin   'Gad's life, ma'am, not at all – "*giving me immediate satisfaction.*" – On this, ma'am, Lady Teazle, seeing Sir Peter in such danger, ran out of the room in strong hysterics, and Charles after her, calling out for hartshorn and water; then, madam, they began to fight with swords –

(enter Crabtree)

Crabtree   With pistols, nephew – pistols! I have it from undoubted authority.

---

[18] *The Importance of Being Earnest*, Act II.

Mrs Candour   Oh, Mr Crabtree, then it is all true!

Crabtree   Too true, indeed, madam, and Sir Peter is dangerously wounded –

Sir Benjamin   By a thrust in second quite through his left side –

Crabtree   By a bullet lodged in the thorax.

Mrs Candour   Mercy on me! Poor Sir Peter!

Crabtree   Yes, madam; though Charles would have avoided the matter, if he could.

Mrs Candour   I knew Charles was the person.

Sir Benjamin   My uncle, I see, knows nothing of the matter.

Crabtree   But Sir Peter taxed him with the basest ingratitude –

Sir Benjamin   That I told you, you know –

Crabtree   Do, nephew, let me speak! – and insisted on immediate –

Sir Benjamin   Just as I said –

Crabtree   Odds life, nephew, allow others to know something too!

(*The School for Scandal*, V.2)

Ibsen's Revolution

From the late eighteenth century, English – and much other European – drama fell into a decline that was to last for the best part of a century. The quality of acting and production was usually adequate, and there were always the great plays of the past to fall back on, but there was a dearth of good new plays. The vacuum was filled by plays imported from abroad – notably the work of the German dramatist August von Kotzebue (1761– 1819), and his imitators – and, increasingly, by melodrama and farce, which took the place of tragedy and comedy. Not that theatre was unpopular as a form of entertainment in the nineteenth century; on the contrary, its popularity was enormous, and greater then, perhaps, than ever before or since. But there was to be no great improvement in serious drama until the influence of Ibsen – and especially of his twelve great social dramas of the period 1877 to 1899 – began to be felt outside Scandinavia in the 1880s and 1890s.

It would hard to exaggerate the importance of the revolution initiated by the Norwegian poet and dramatist Henrik Ibsen (1828–1906), whose plays from *Catiline* (1849–50) to *When We Dead Awaken* (1899) exactly spanned the second half of the nineteenth century; rather as Wordsworth invented modern poetry, so Ibsen invented modern drama. Coming from a provincial, middle-class background in southern Norway, Ibsen had a difficult childhood and youth. His father's business failed, and it was rumoured that Ibsen was the son of another man who had had an affair with his mother; so that he was not only extremely poor but also felt himself despised and rejected. Writing in such spare time as he had from being an apothecary's assistant, Ibsen developed as a poet with great facility and technical skill; and he also showed talent as a draughtsman and painter. In 1846 he had a brief love affair and fathered an illegitimate son. He wrote his first play in 1849–50, and had a second play performed in 1850. From 1851 to 1857 he was employed as stage-manager, playwright, and general dogsbody to a new, unskilled but enthusiastic company of players in Bergen, which often put on a new show every *week*. This was followed (1857–62) by a theatrical appointment in Christiania (Oslo), a better-paid but less satisfying position than before. During this period he continued to write plays, mostly in verse; he got married in 1858, and had a legitimate son in 1859; and he became progressively disenchanted with his country and its people, which he found narrow and inhibiting. From 1864, the Ibsens left Norway for voluntary exile in Rome, then Dresden, then Munich, remaining abroad until 1891, when they returned to live near Christiania, and where Ibsen died in 1906 after a series of strokes.

Ibsen's first two masterpieces, the great verse dramas *Brand* and *Peer Gynt*, appeared in 1866 and 1867, and were a sensation in Scandinavia. Intended to be read rather than performed, they argued that the individual conscience, however much impeded by personal weakness and self-indulgence, was the only battleground for a man's victory over the difficulties of life. Two prose works followed – *The League of Youth* (1869), a political farce, and *Emperor and Galilean* (1873), an immensely long closet drama concerning the Emperor Julian's apostasy and tyranny – but it took another four years for Ibsen to make up his mind to abandon verse completely and to write social dramas in prose. The first of them was *Pillars of the Community* (1877; a study of a hypocritical leader), which was followed at approximately two-year intervals by a further eleven plays, culminating in his last work, *When We Dead Awaken*, in 1899. It was these twelve plays that forced the revolution in European drama. They concerned ordinary people such as might be met with every day, not the great men and women of classical tragedy; their dialogue was written in ordinary, everyday language, not heightened by verse or artificial rhetoric; and they addressed problems that recognisably affected every thinking man and woman in late nineteenth-century European society. The real breakthrough came with *A Doll's House* (1879), in which a simple housewife comprehends with horror her abject place in marriage and society; and, in finding herself, rejects it. With tight, economical dialogue, a small cast of credible characters, gripping development, and an uncompromising outcome, the play swept through the theatres of Scandinavia and Germany, changing the intellectual climate as it went.

Ibsen's remaining ten social dramas continued to evolve and develop, breaking new ground, addressing old but hitherto ignored or suppressed social, moral, artistic, and spiritual problems: *Ghosts* (1881; extramarital sex, incest, syphilis); *An Enemy of the People* (1882; profit preferred to public safety, and the whistle-blower defeated); *The Wild Duck* (1884; the advantages and disadvantages of telling the truth). The last six plays deal with the trolls within rather than the trolls without: *Rosmersholm* (1886; the desire to live up to radical ideals frustrated by inner weakness); *The Lady from the Sea* (1888; infatuation for a demon lover defeated by a deeper love); *Hedda Gabler* (1890; arrogance compensating for self-contempt); *The Master Builder* (1892; talented youth comes knocking at the door of declining age); *Little Eyolf* (1894; sensual man cannot live up to his own ideals); *John Gabriel Borkman* (1896; the quest for material success may lead to emotional bankruptcy); and *When We Dead Awaken* (1899; Ibsen's epilogue: fame achieved at the expense of personal happiness, the only way out being upwards to the spiritual heights beyond life).

In his own life, Ibsen always put art first, and humanity second. His creed was to be true and faithful to oneself, and to will what one must. Ibsen saw himself as supporting "the revolution of the spirit"; and understood, as Shaw remarked in connection with *The Wild Duck*, that "people cannot be freed from their failings from without. They must free themselves."[19] Truth to oneself mattered more to Ibsen than social questions, even matters of importance to him such as women's rights. He was intuitively perceptive but not widely educated; he read newspapers in preference to books, and there were large gaps in his general knowledge (for instance in science). As a person he was a loner, an egocentric introvert, and determinedly private. He could be kind and charming, and he could be malicious and cruel; he ruthlessly cast off the girl who bore his illegitimate son, and refused as far as possible to acknowledge the child. Living parsimoniously, he loved, supported and worked hard for his wife and legitimate son. He was timid physically but not in print; he dressed smartly, loved medals and decorations, and was jealous of protocol. He could drink too much, but did not allow drink to affect his work, which he put before everything else, and which he performed with meticulous regularity.[20]

Ibsen's plays, with their ordinary people apparently carrying on their ordinary lives, required new standards of realism in dramatic production, which they duly received. Increasingly from the 1880s, scenery, mostly

[19] *The Quintessence of Ibsenism*, 1913, p. 98. There is a parallel here with the "self-realisation" of the great religions.
[20] This sketch may put the reader in mind of other artists of the first rank who were not the easiest of men to live with – among great writers, Milton, Tolstoy, and Joyce come to mind – and it may be wondered why it is that Shakespeare, about whose personality and behaviour we know virtually nothing, is commonly assumed not to have been difficult in this sort of way.

of interiors, reproduced as closely as possible the rooms and other environments in which ordinary people lived, while furniture and other properties were the real thing; costumes were simply the clothes that people wore every day; and the style of acting gave the impression of people conversing naturally, speaking to each other rather than out into the auditorium.

Ibsen's influence on western drama was widespread and profound. Some countries – England amongst them – resisted it for longer than others, but in the end western theatre was irreversably changed. In England, Ibsen's views were propagated – rather quirkily – by Bernard Shaw in *The Quintessence of Ibsenism* (1891, expanded edition 1913), and Ibsen's techniques were copied by Shaw in his own plays from 1892 to 1948.

George Bernard Shaw (1856–1950) was primarily a polemicist and prophet who, finding that fiction and journalism did not give him an adequate platform for his views, became a dramatist and made the theatre into an effective medium for what he wanted to say and the way in which he wanted to say it. In some fifty plays, from *Widowers' Houses* (1892) to *Buoyant Billions* (1948), he justified his belief that controversial ideas outside the theatre could best be argued within it; and he demonstrated a genius for dramatising debate on the great political and social issues of his time. In doing this he was, of course, partly following the lead of Ibsen, whom he greatly admired; Ibsen, however, had not only used his plays for political and social argument, but had also probed deeply into the souls of his characters, exploring the human being in the social situation. This was not Shaw's way: incisive, irreverent, paradoxical, suspicious of established wisdom, he performed brilliantly on the surface of life, always more interested in clever ideas than in people's inner being. Technically, too, Shaw followed Ibsen in his realistic approach to the staging and performance of his plays, though his irresistible urge to amuse and scandalise with wit and paradox produced dialogue that was unrealistically brilliant. For all this, Shaw's plays did very well in the theatre, once the initial shock to convention had been assimilated, and he was the outstanding playwright in English of the first half of the twentieth century. The following extract from *Saint Joan* (1923) shows Shaw's debt both to Ibsen, and to an earlier tradition of wit in English comedy; and, like all of Shaw's best plays, it makes excellent theatre and is a wonderfully good read. It also shows Shaw's propensity for combining the serious (here the politico-theological debate about how to arrange for a young girl to be burned alive) with the frivolous (the farcical jokes about the number of counts of the indictment, the language spoken by Joan's voices, and the theft of the Bishop's horse). This technique is immediately attractive – the audience or reader can enjoy the illusion of being involved in an intellectual process, while the humour diverts them from its underlying horror – but its shallowness trivialises feeling and emotion.

Cauchon [*Bishop of Beauvais*]   Good morning, Master de Stogumber. (*to the Inquisitor*) Chaplain to the Cardinal of England.

The Chaplain (*correcting him*)   Of Winchester, my lord. I have to make a protest, my Lord.

Cauchon   You make a great many.

The Chaplain   I am not without support, my lord. Here is Master de Courcelles, Canon of Paris, who associates himself with my protest.

Cauchon   Well, what is the matter?

The Chaplain (*sulkily*)   Speak you, Master de Courcelles, since I do not seem to enjoy his lordship's confidence. (*he sits down in dudgeon next to Courcelles, on his right*)

Courcelles   My lord: we have been at great pains to draw up an indict ment of The Maid on sixty-four counts. We are now told that they have been reduced, without consulting us.

The Inquisitor   Master de Courcelles: I am the culprit. I am overwhelmed with admiration for the zeal displayed in your sixty-four counts; but in accusing a heretic, as in other things, enough is enough. Also you must remember that all the members of the court are not so subtle and profound as you, and that some of your very great learning might appear to them to be very great nonsense. Therefore I have thought it well to have your sixty-four articles cut down to twelve –

Courcelles (*thunderstruck*)   Twelve!!!

The Inquisitor   Twelve will, believe me, be quite enough for your purpose.

The Chaplain   But some of the most important points have been reduced almost to nothing. For instance, The Maid has actually declared that the blessed saints Margaret and Catherine, and the holy Archangel Michael, spoke to her in French. That is a vital point.

The Inquisitor   You think, doubtless, that they should have spoken in Latin?

Cauchon   No: he thinks they should have spoken in English.

The Chaplain   Naturally, my lord.

The Inquisitor   Well, as we are all here agreed, I think, that these voices of The Maid are the voices of evil spirits tempting her to her damnation, it would not be very courteous to you, Master de Stogumber, or to the King of England, to assume that English is the devil's native language. So let it pass. The matter is not wholly omitted from the twelve articles. Pray take your places, gentle-men; and let us proceed to business.

(*all who have not taken their seats, do so*)

The Chaplain   Well, I protest. That is all.

Courcelles   I think it is hard that all our work should go for nothing. It is only another example of the diabolical influence which this woman exercises over the court. (*he takes his chair, which is on the Chaplain's right*)

Cauchon   Do you suggest that I am under diabolical influence?

Courcelles   I suggest nothing, my lord. But it seems to me that there is a conspiracy here to hush up the fact that The Maid stole the Bishop of Senlis's horse.

Cauchon (*keeping his temper with difficulty*)　This is not a police court. Are we to waste our time upon such rubbish?

Courcelles (*rising, shocked*)　My lord: do you call the Bishop's horse rubbish? ...

The Inquisitor　I submit to you, with great respect, that if we persist in trying The Maid on trumpery issues on which we may have to declare her innocent, she may escape us on the main issue of heresy, on which she seems so far to insist on her own guilt.

(Saint Joan, scene 6)

And yet ... despite Shaw's determination to be jester, gadfly, and conscience to the nation all at the same time, his great talent for comedy made his best plays – *Major Barbara* (1905), *Pygmalion* (1912), and *Androcles and the Lion* (1916), for instance – supremely entertaining.

Along with Shaw's plays, the 1920s and 1930s saw a number of witty stage comedies, such of these of Noël Coward, and a great improvement in the staging and speaking of classic drama, especially Shakespeare; but there was no British modernist theatre in the early 1920s in the way that there was modernist fiction and modernist poetry. European modernist plays such as Pirandello's *Six Characters in Search of an Author* (1921) and Brecht's *Threepenny Opera* (1928) had no great effect here; and it was not until 1955 that Beckett's *Waiting for Godot* was staged in London – five years after Shaw's death and the year before the appearance of John Osborne's *Look Back in Anger* – and set off the next great, unfinished revolution in English theatre.

Creative Writing – Creative Reading

Creative Writing and the Study of Literature

The reason for including an appendix on creative writing in this guide is that the best way for students and general readers of literature to find out about the problems that face a writer of fiction or poetry or drama, and to explore their possible solutions, is for them to try writing a novel or a poem or a play for themselves. Very likely some readers will have tried their hands at some form of creative writing already. Both for them, and for those who have not yet got an unpublished novel or collection of poems, or an unperformed play, tucked away in a bottom drawer, this appendix aims to give some practical advice.

In theory, the quality of what is written for the purpose of learning something about literature is not of great importance; but in practice those who make a serious attempt at creative writing will probably find that they are carried away by an ambition to do it well, and that the result is actually better than they expected. It might even be publishable. But trying to write well is never easy. Anyone seriously attempting it is going to need:

motivation: the need·to write and communicate.
self-discipline: the willingness to learn a difficult craft.
stamina: the power to keep going when enthusiasm flags.
dissatisfaction with what has been achieved so far.
confidence that something better can be achieved.·
faith in the result, even if it is not immediately appreciated.

Taken together, these qualities make for *professionalism* in a writer. Literature is not for dilettantes.

Despite all this, serious attempts to write will be made, and the rest of this appendix offers a miscellany of information and advice; not about structure, characterisation, and dialogue in fiction and drama, or about the technicalities of metre and sound in poetry, all of which have been covered in the previous chapters; but about practical, workaday matters of the writer's trade that students attending classes in creative writing have found useful. It is particularly relevant to the writing of fiction – which is what is most often attempted – but the main principles apply to poetry and drama as well.

The Writer's Materials

Reading

All writers should be great readers; and, if they want to write drama, they should be great playgoers as well, and if possible should have some actual experience, however humble, of working in a theatre. Unless they are thoroughly familiar with the work of others in their medium, past as well as present, would-be writers will never fully understand what is possible, and what will be required of them. Likewise, they should get from their reading or playgoing – as well as from a manual such as this – an understanding of the essential characteristics of the form they would attempt: in fiction the possibilities and requirements of structure, of characterisation, and of dialogue; in poetry the use and manipulation of metre, sound, and language; in drama, the art of compression in plotting, characterisation, and dialogue.

Language

Besides knowing their medium, writers need a technical equipment of their own; and, before anything else, they must know and love language. Language is the writer's basic raw material, rather as musical notes and musical instruments are the musician's raw material, or as coloured shapes on a two-dimensional surface are the painter's raw material. And, just as the musician has to learn to read and play music, and the painter has to learn how to draw, to mix colours, and to wield a brush, so the writer has to learn how to make language say just what he wants it to say. The English language can be a difficult mistress, but she is an infinitely fascinating one, and will reward all the devotion we can give her. There are, fortunately, many excellent dictionaries, grammars, manuals of usage, histories, and other guides to understanding and using English (some of which are listed in the Annotated Bibliography following this appendix), but it is worth summarising here the three technical aspects of written language which are of immediate importance to writers: vocabulary, grammar, and punctuation.

Vocabulary

The vocabulary of a language is its total word-stock, and a personal vocabulary is the total of words that a person can recognise and – not quite the same thing – use effectively. Personal vocabularies are usually much larger than people think, running to several – perhaps many – tens of thousands of words.[1] Writers must master the vocabulary appropriate to what they want to write; and besides this they should always look up the meanings of words they do not understand when they are at the essential business of reading what others have written. Here is a list of sixty-two words which are commonly misunderstood or confused, some more obscure than others; a well-educated person might be expected to define at least three-quarters of them correctly without using a dictionary.

abrogate/arrogate (verbs)	exiguous (adjective)
affect/effect (verbs *and* nouns)	explanation/explication (nouns)
aggravate (verb)	fictitious/factitious (adjectives)
alternate/alternative (adjectives)	hopefully (adverb)
ante-/anti- (prefixes)	hyper-/hypo- (prefixes)
aphasia/ataxia (nouns)	infer/imply (verbs)
appraise/apprise (verbs)	inter-/intra- (prefixes)
centenary/centennial (nouns)	ontology/teleology (nouns)
convince (verb)	paradigm/parameter (nouns)
cybernetic (adjective)	picaresque (adjective)
decimate (verb)	prevaricate/procrastinate (verbs)
disinterested/uninterested (adjectives)	satire/satyr (nouns)
eclectic (adjective)	semantic/semiotic (adejctives)
egregious (adjective)	sinecure/cynosure (nouns)
epicene/epicentral (adjectives)	super-/supra- (prefixes)
epistemology (noun)	supercargo/superego (nouns)
esoteric/exoteric (adjectives)	synecdoche/metonymy (nouns)
exegesis (noun)	venal/venial (adjectives)
exigent (adjective)	

It is also important in practice to know how to spell correctly, and for those whose spelling (or typing) is shaky, it is best to get help, either from a friend or from the spellcheck programme of a word-processor. Note:

[1] This depends, obviously, on how "word" is defined: whether for instance each part of a verb (love, loving, loves, loved) is counted as a separate word, or how the multiple idiomatic uses of some words are counted (turn about, turn away, turn back, turn off, turn on [and turn-off, turn-on], turn out [and turn-out], turn over, turn round, turn turtle, turn up, and many other idioms based on "turn").

spelling variations (English): such as *connection/connexion*; *gaol/jail*; *judgement/judgment*; *theorise/theorize*;

spelling variations (English/American): such as *centre/center*; *colour/ color*; *programme/program*; *tyre/tire*

its and *it's* are not interchangeable

all right is two words (*alright* is all wrong)

Grammar

Grammar is a way of analysing and describing how the words of a language are used in relation to each other to convey meaning. We understand the common terms that refer to parts of speech – nouns, verbs, adjectives, and so on – and we can recognise simple rules for their relationship, such as that a singular subject is followed by a singular, not a plural, verb. Some grammatical rules, and the jargon in which they are expressed, can seem complicated, but there is no need to be alarmed because we learned as small children how the grammar of our native language works in practice – indeed we may have been born with our brains specially arranged for learning language – and we do not need to know how to describe it technically.

What we mean when we speak of our own or someone else's "bad grammar" is usually no more than a small number of common mistakes of form and usage, which are relatively easy to put right; things such as case and number confusions, double possessives, false subjunctives, misplaced apostrophes, and so on. Here are some examples of such errors:

number (changing number during a sentence)

> *There is likely to be differences between us*
> *The last crop to be harvested were potatoes*
> *The* BBC *does their classic drama very well*

case (especially with pronouns: "I" and "me", "he" and "him", and so on; "who" and "whom")

> *They kindly invited my husband and I to dinner* (the way to test this one is to leave out "my husband and", whereupon it is obvious that *They kindly invited I to dinner* is wrong)
> *It might have been him and not the Prime Minister who made the speech*
> *I am afraid that the culprit is me* (though *It's me*, *That's him*, and so on, are good colloquial English)
> *Who shall he give it to?*
> *Let the final arbiter be whom he may*

possessives (double possessives; apostrophes)

> *He praised the eccentric novel of Sterne's* (but *He praised an* [or *this*]

eccentric novel of Sterne's is right)
Note that the following forms deriving from "Jones" are all correct:
*The Jones family/Keeping up with the Joneses/The Joneses' house/
Mrs Jones's dress*
<u>subjunctives</u> (false subjunctives with *if*)
If he were there, he was in the wrong place
If the vote is close, and if a recount be demanded, he will retire
<u>obsolete conjugations</u> (dost, doth, and so on)
Dost he attend the court?
Thou understandeth not
She givest of her best

Punctuation

Punctuation matters a great deal more than spelling, for it can affect the meaning and nuance of what is written. Anyone who is at all uneasy about punctuation should consult the excellent specialist articles and books on the subject (see the Annotated Bibliography, below). Meanwhile, here are some notes on common problems:

general: Though it is usually something of a compromise, punctuation can tend either towards a *grammatical* form, marking the construction of the sentences by clauses (suitable for explication), or towards a *rhetorical* form (suitable for dialogue), indicating how the sentences are spoken. This book tends towards grammatical punctuation.

comma: Commas are chiefly used to mark pauses, clauses, minor parentheses, and items enumerated within a sentence. It is easy to use too many or too few commas; if in doubt, the sentence should be read aloud to see where a definite pause is required to make the sense clear. In enumerations, it is best not to omit the comma before the final *and*.

semicolon: Best used to link two balanced sentences, or blocks of words, that are too closely related to be divided by full stops.

colon: Fowler (1926) remarks briskly that the colon has acquired the special function of delivering the goods that have been invoiced in the preceding words. *Hart's Rules* (1983) adds that it generally marks a step forward, from introduction to main theme, from cause to effect, from premiss to conclusion; though in some of these cases a semicolon would do just as well.

full stop: Full stops, which bring sentences to an end, can be tiresome if they are used to break prose up into ridiculously short sentences, or verb-less blocks of words (unless the punctuation is intended to be rhetorical). Abbreviations should be terminated with a full stop only where the abbreviated form does not end with the last letter of the full form of the word (thus *Dr*, *Mr*, *Mrs*, *Bart* do not have full stops; but *etc.*, *fig.*, *N.B.* do have them); note however that there is a modern tendency to omit full stops from all abbreviations.

exclamation mark: Used for exclamations (*oh!*, *damnation!*), and exclamatory sentences (*What an extraordinary thing!*), but to be avoided for marking the merely odd or funny.

question mark: Sometimes wrongly omitted because the writer has forgotten that what he or she has written is a question. To put either an exclamation mark or a question mark in round brackets, to indicate an authorial comment on what is said, can seem painfully arch.

quotation marks ("*inverted commas*"): British editors and printers prefer single inverted commas to mark quotations or direct speech, while American ones prefer double. It does not matter which sort is used (unless work is submitted as a computer disk for making camera-ready copy), provided that the other sort is used for interior quotations. A full stop (or exclamation mark or question mark) ending a sentence is often placed inside closing inverted commas; other punctuation marks are placed outside closing inverted commas. See Judith Butcher, *Copy-editing*, 3rd edn, Cambridge 1992.

apostrophe: Apostrophes are *not* used to make plurals (*banana's 49p*). In direct speech, *do not*, and so on, indicates a different pronunciation, and probably a different emphasis, from *don't*, and so on. See also the note on possessives, above.

hyphens: Used in compound nouns and adjectives. Note the different meanings of *a little used car/a little-used car, the two year-old babies/the two-year-old babies*.

italics (shown by underlining): Used to mark emphasis on a particular (usually unexpected) word; but italicising whole sentences can be a mistake. Italics, not inverted commas, are used for the titles of books, inverted commas for the titles of articles.

brackets: Round brackets ( ) are used for parenthetical clauses that need something stronger than paired commas; square brackets [ ] are used for parentheses inside round brackets, and also to mark material supplied editorially.

dashes: May be used in pairs instead of round brackets for parenthetical clauses. Single dashes may sometimes be used to indicate a pause in direct speech, but only rarely as a substitute for some other punctuation mark (see the next sentence).

ellipses (three dots – not four or five): Used to mark words omitted; and occasionally to indicate a pause, usually in direct speech.

Setting out Dialogue in Fiction

A new paragraph should be used for each new speaker. If this is done for dialogue between two people, it is theoretically possible for the reader to know who is speaking however many speeches there are, but after half a page of it readers are liable to lose track and to suffer the annoyance of having to go back to the beginning and note the alternation of the speeches to find out where the dialogue has got to. This can be avoided by putting in an occasional "he said", "she said", "said John", and so on, at appropriate points. Although the repetition of words would normally be avoided, "said" is a neutral word in this context, and it can be used frequently; "asked" and "replied" are also fairly neutral words here, but "he laughed", "she gasped", and so on, are less neutral and may sound mannered if they are used more than once in a particular dialogue.

Usage

The usage of language means the way in which the elements of language – the words and the grammar with which they are related – are customarily used to produce meaning. Besides grammatical constructions, this includes pronunciation, stress, spelling, punctuation, words (in the sense of which words are chosen), and, most difficult of all for non-native speakers, idiom. Idiom means both the specific character of the language, and the use of phrases such as expressions which carry meanings other than their face value (*carry the can, kick the bucket, put a sock in it*), and such as the vast range of different meanings that can be derived from a single word such as *hand*: *at first hand, change hands, a dab hand, a free hand, in hand, offhand, hands off, high hand, take in hand, underhand, the upper hand*, and dozens of others.[2] Native speakers of English are indeed fortunate that they do not have to learn idioms as strange and as numerous as these.

Clichés

Prose fiction (and poetry and drama) can be written in any number of forms and styles, and there is no saying which is right and which wrong. But, unless they are used to make a point, it is worth avoiding clichés – tired metaphors and similes – such as: *a bolt from the blue, dead as a doornail, quick as a flash, avoid like the plague, stick out like a sore thumb, the calm before the storm, as old as the hills, leave no stone unturned, at the end of the day, explore*

---

[2] David Crystal's *Cambridge Encyclopedia of the English Language*, 1995, p. 163, gives a list, "which makes no claim to completeness", of over *eighty* different idioms deriving from *hand* and *hands*. See also the idioms based on "turn", p. 143, n. 1 above.

every avenue, food for thought, keep a low profile, trouble is brewing. There are tired non-metaphorical clichés to avoid, too, such as: *far be it from me to, in this day and age, for love or money, last but not least, at this moment in time, from time immemorial.* However, there are a few clichés, mostly of a proverbial character, that are unobjectionable because they express concisely what it would take too many words to say otherwise: *better safe than sorry, better late than never, easier said than done, a miss is as good as a mile, a stitch in time, spilt milk, swan song.*

Forms of Address

Native English writers often make mistakes with titles and forms of address. If nobs, or references to nobs, are to be introduced, their titles, and the way they are addressed, should be got right. The rules are complex, as the following summary of some of them shows, and for serious study a manual of forms of address should be consulted. For instance:

Royalty: addressed in person as "Ma'am" and "Sir". It is technically wrong to refer to the late Diana, Princess of Wales, as "Princess Diana", but right to refer to the Princess Royal as "Princess Anne".

The peerage: the order of precedence is Dukes and Duchesses, Marquesses (or Marquises) and Marchionesses, Earls and Countesses, Viscounts and Viscountesses, Barons and Baronesses. Dukes and Duchesses are always referred to as "the Duke of So-and-so", "the Duchess of So-and-so", but other peers are usually referred to as "Lord So-and-so", "Lady So-and-so". In conversation, an acquaintance (not an intimate) would say "Good morning, Duke", "Good morning, Duchess", and "Good morning, Lord So-and-so", "Good morning, Lady So-and-so"; but a servant would say "Good morning, Your Grace", "Good morning, my Lord", "Good morning, my Lady". The elder sons of senior peers (Dukes, Marquesses, and Earls) have courtesy titles and are addressed as if they were peers; but the younger children of Dukes and Marquesses, and the daughters of Earls, are called "Lord John Surname", "Lady Mary Surname". The younger sons of Earls, and the children of junior peers (Viscounts and Barons), are called "the Honourable John Surname", "the Honourable Mary Surname". ("Right Honourables" are Privy Counsellors.)

Baronets and knights: baronetcies are hereditary knighthoods, and both baronets and knights are addressed as "Sir John", and so on. The wives of baronets and knights are addressed as "Lady Surname", not "Lady Mary" or "Lady Mary Surname".

Foreign Languages

It is perfectly all right to use words, phrases, and even sentences in foreign languages provided that they are readily understandable; but if they are not, a translation should be provided. Words and phrases in foreign languages are normally underlined for italicisation, but foreign words and phrases (such as legal and medical terms in Latin) which have become thoroughly acclimatised are not italicised. Quotations in foreign languages should be used sparingly, and should always be checked.

Planning and Research for Fiction

A certain amount of planning in advance is essential if the writer is to avoid wasting time and effort on false starts. There are various ways of planning a book, but the traditional, and probably most effective, method is to write a synopsis. For a novel, this could begin with a list of characters, plus a brief biography of each one; could proceed to a summary of the main lines of the story; and could be completed with notes of what is to happen in each chapter. There is no need to regard such a synopsis as immutable – stories have a way of developing as they are written, sometimes in unexpected directions – but it will still be necessary for the author to have a good idea before starting of what the book is going to be about, and how the story is going to be resolved; it will not matter if a few things have to be changed later.

If the story is set in a location, period, and milieu with which the writer is thoroughly familiar – and the more a writer sticks to what he or she knows about personally, the better – there is not much more preparation to be done; but often research on the background of the story will be required. To take as examples two novels by Pat Barker: her first novel *Union Street* (1982) consists of the interlinked stories of a number of fictional working-class women in an unnamed northern industrial city, for which she could draw directly on her own youthful experience of Middlesbrough, her home town, and of the sort of people and situations she knew there; this cannot have required much research. In *Regeneration* (1991), however, the first volume of Pat Barker's trilogy set in the First World War, the story includes a semi-fictionalised account of the relationship between certain real people in 1917, and much of the action takes place in a hospital for shell-shocked officers in Edinburgh that really existed. Here she was undoubtedly involved in a formidable amount of research: reading histories of the First World War, soldiers' memoirs, politicians' autobiographies, technical works on the army, old maps, the files of old newspapers, probably visits to the Public Record Office at Kew and other archives, and much more. It is well to remember that most public libraries stock encyclopaedias; dictionaries and lexicons for a range of languages; dictionaries of biography, proverbs, quotations, personal names, place names; atlases, gazetteers, local directories; and many specialist reference books. One final point, small but important: quotations and references should always be checked, preferably at source, never taken from memory alone.

Revision

Revision is absolutely essential to the production of good work. Hardly anyone – professionals included – can get everything right in a first draft, and nearly all good writers put time and effort into revising their work. The first thing to do, each time writing begins, is to read through and correct what was written last time; which has the additional advantage of getting oneself into the mood for the next stint. Then whole chapters can be revised, and parts of them rewritten if necessary, as they are completed; and finally the book should be put away for as long as possible after it is finished – preferably for two or three months – and read again with a fresh eye. A final polishing may be enough at this point; but it sometimes happens that substantial parts of the book will demand to be rewritten, and in an extreme case it may seem best to write the whole book out again, with concurrent revision. If it does, so be it: anything is worth sacrificing for the sake of quality.

Relatively minor things like spelling mistakes and bad grammar, repetitions, awkward phrasing, and ambiguities, will probably be dealt with in the earlier revisions. In later revisions, larger themes such as construction, consistency, clarity of expression (which usually means simplicity), rhythm and pacing, interest and suspense may be tackled. Perhaps most importantly, anything that does not contribute to the meaning and impact of the book should be cut. This means cutting not only unnecessary verbiage and words and phrases that are used too often, but also explanations of what should be self-evident, anything that is not strictly relevant to the work, such as the fascinating results of peripheral research, and anything that follows the ending of the main theme. Passages that the author thinks particularly fine, which are likely enough to be inessential, should also considered for removal. Writers often have to scrap whole chapters that have not worked, and sometimes have to discard as much as a year's work on a book. Less often than superfluities, under-writing may be identified, which is when a passage is actually too short to do the job it is meant for; an explanation, for instance, that needs to be expanded, or a character who needs further development.

When all this is done, the book may not be a masterpiece, but it will be much better than it was before.

Equipment for Writing

Every writer has his or her own way of writing. Some have to write with pencil or pen (either because it is the only way that works for them, or because they cannot type), while others can write straight onto a typewriter or word-processor. Two things should be borne in mind: one is that nobody will be eager nowadays to read anything written by hand, and that manuscripts are definitely not acceptable to publishers or their professional readers; and the other is that the process of typing out a manuscript gives an excellent opportunity for revising it. Better still is to use a word-processor, on which revision can be a virtually continuous process from first draft to last, and which, if the author is up to it, can produce a disk or disks to accompany the author's printout, disks which contain the whole book ready to be reproduced as "camera-ready copy" without having to be transcribed again. For a writer, the moral of this is: if you can't type, learn how.

Publication

The Typescript or Printout

When a typescript or printout is sent to a publisher, it is in effect being offered for sale, and it is both polite and sensible to present it in the way that is most likely to appeal to its potential customer. It should be in a form that is neat, without spelling mistakes, and that is easy both to read and to turn into a printed book. The main points are:

(1) The book should be typed (or printed out) on one side only of sheets of medium-weight, white, A4 paper. The typing should be at least competent, and its appearance should not be spoiled by too many manuscript corrections and alterations; it is better to retype a heavily corrected page. The typewriter or printer ribbon should be replaced as soon as the page begins to look grey, and (if a typewriter is used) the carbon paper should be changed frequently; it is never worth being mean about paper, ribbons, and carbons.

(2) Lines should be one-and-a-half or double spaced, with a margin of at least an inch all round the page. Paragraphs should be indented four or five spaces, but there should not be a blank line between paragraphs unless there is to be a "white line" (indicating a break in the text) on the printed page. There should be the same number of lines on each full page of the

typescript. There is no need to justify the right-hand margin, even if the typewriter or word-processor will do it.

(3) Each chapter should begin on a new page.

(4) The pages should be numbered consecutively in the top right-hand corner from the beginning of the typescript to the end. The pages of each chapter should not be numbered separately. It is a good idea to precede each page number with an acronym which identifies the book. The last page of the book should be unambiguously marked as such.

(5) In addition to the cover sheet – which gives the author's name and address, biographical notes, and the number of words in the book – it is wise to write the author's name and address again on the first and last pages of the text.

(6) The pages should not be bound or otherwise fastened together. They should be put in a folder or a cardboard box (the sort that the typing paper comes in), tied round with string.

(7) If the typescript has to be resubmitted to another publisher, it may be freshened up by retyping or reprinting any pages – for instance the first and last pages – that have become creased or thumbed during the earlier submission.

(8) The author should never let the typescript leave his or her hands without keeping a copy.

Approaching Publishers

Writers' manuals offer plenty of advice about how to get a book – usually a novel – published. It can be summarised in the following main points:

(1) The typescript – or a synopsis plus a sample chapter – should be submitted to a reputable publisher, not to a "vanity publisher" (a shark who advertises his willingness to publish any writer's book, and will charge him hundreds or thousands of pounds to do so). It is worth writing to a named individual (see *The Writers' and Artists' Yearbook* for useful names).

(2) The publisher should be one who publishes the sort of book that is being submitted; see *The Writers' and Artists' Yearbook*.

(3) If an agent is prepared to take a writer on – and agents can be even more choosy than publishers – he or she will be well worth the commission charged.

(4) Publishers can take some time – weeks or even months – to decide whether or not to accept a book.

(5) If the book is accepted, it may be on condition that changes are made; and even if changes are not required, the book will be "copy-edited" to bring it into line with the publisher's "house style".

(6) The first contract offered to an author should be checked by an independent solicitor familiar with publishing.

(7) Rejection should not cause despair. Many good books are turned down, and it is worth resubmitting a first effort to other publishers; if it has real quality, it will be accepted in the end.

(8) Very few novelists, and no poets, make a living from their writing.

Copyright

So long as a work remains unpublished, the author retains copyright in it; that is, he or she owns its text, and it may not be copied, printed, or otherwise reproduced without the author's permission. This still applies even if the physical manuscript or typescript is given away; for instance, if A writes and sends a letter to B, B owns the physical document because A has given it to him; but A still owns the text of what he has written, and neither B nor anyone else may copy, reproduce, or publish that letter without A's permission. When a work is submitted for publication, it is understood that the author is offering to lease the copyright in it to the publisher, and the author's rights in the matter will be established by contract between them. The author could agree to sell the copyright of his book to the publisher outright – as a journalist may sell the copyright in his work to his employer – but this would be improvident, and the usual practice is for the author to retain ownership of the copyright and for the publisher to pay the author a royalty on sales. Copyright in unpublished work is perpetual; but copyright in published work runs out seventy years after the author's death, after which it may be republished by anybody without further permission or payment.[3]

It should be remembered, incidentally, that copyright works both ways, and that no-one may use another author's work, or even quote substantially from it without permission, at the risk of litigation if permission is not granted.

[3] This paragraph outlines the basic law of copyright. In practice, with the use of photocopying machines, and especially today with the growth of the Internet, the letter of the law is unenforceable and is widely disregarded; see ch. 25 of Barry Turner, *The Writer's Companion*, London 1996.

Annotated Bibliography

As far as possible, the bibliography lists works of reference that can usually be found in public libraries; and biographies and texts, often including critical material, that have been published in paperback editions (marked * for paperback; but note that particular titles may have gone into or out of print as paperbacks since this bibliography was compiled). It is arranged as follows:

I. Language
1. general guides
2. dictionaries
3. grammars
4. usage

II. Literature
1. guides
    a. general guides *b*. subject guides
2. subject dictionaries
3. bibliographies
4. authors: fiction
    a. Cervantes *b*. Richardson *c*. Austen *d*. Dickens
    e. George Eliot *f*. Conrad *g*. Joyce
5. authors: poetry
    a. Chaucer *b*. Spenser *c*. Donne *d*. Milton
    e. Dryden *f*. Pope *g*. Johnson *h*. Blake
    i. Wordsworth *j*. Byron *k*. Tennyson *l*. T. S. Eliot
6. authors: drama
    a. Sophocles *b*. mystery and morality plays *c*. Marlowe
    d. Shakespeare *e*. Jonson *f*. Webster *g*. Ford
    h. Dryden *i*. Vanbrugh *j*. Goldsmith *k*. Sheridan
    l. Ibsen *m*. Shaw

154

III. Creative writing
  1. guides
  2. language and usage
  3. publication

I. Language

1. General Guides

The Oxford Companion to the English Language, ed. Tom McArthur, Oxford 1992, is a superb A–Z survey of the language in all its strange and wonderful manifestations: English as differently spoken by dozens of nations and communities; English as a lingua franca for the world; English dissected and analysed; and, for us, English as the language of an astonishing and invaluable literature, including articles on the technicalities of fiction, poetry, and drama.

Two well-illustrated encyclopaedias by David Crystal also offer a mass of useful information, covering much of the same ground by subjects: *The Cambridge Encyclopedia of Language*, Cambridge 1987*; and, even better, *The Cambridge Encyclopedia of the English Language*, Cambridge 1995.

Steven Pinker, *The Language Instinct: The New Science of Language and Mind*, London 1994*, argues that language is not a cultural artifact that we learn, but is a distinct piece of the biological make-up of our brains. Fascinating, whether one agrees with the argument or not, and an excellent introduction to linguistics.

2. Dictionaries

The Oxford English Dictionary, 2nd edn, Oxford 1989 (*OED*) – the great lexicon that is the one indispensable tool for the serious study of the English language and English literature – is available not only in libraries in its twenty massive volumes, but also for home use in a single "compact" volume (new edn, 1991), and on CD-ROM. Of the many good single-volume desk dictionaries of English, two are outstanding: *The Concise Oxford Dictionary of Current English*, 9th edn, Oxford 1995 (*COD*), has definitions of great authority in lapidary form; while the *Collins English Dictionary*, 3rd edn, Glasgow 1991 (*Collins*), adds concise encyclopaedic entries, biographical, geographical, and historical.

3. Grammars

Sylvia Chalker and Edmund Weiner, *The Oxford Dictionary of English Grammar*, Oxford 1994, is a modern A–Z approach; Sidney Greenbaum and Randolph Quirk, *A Student's Grammar of the English Language*,

Harlow 1990*, is a systematic grammar; both are authoritative, but are not for the faint-hearted.

4. Usage

The classic text is "Fowler": H. W. and F. G. Fowler, *A Dictionary of Modern English Usage*, Oxford 1926, splendidly revised in a third edition by R. W. Burchfield, Oxford 1996* (though the first edition is still worth consulting). Also valuable are Eric Partridge, *Usage and Abusage: A Guide to Good English*, rev. edn, London 1965, which, like Fowler, is arranged A–Z; and two guides arranged by subjects, Sir Ernest Gowers, *The Complete Plain Words*, 2nd edn, HMSO 1973 (republished by Penguin, 1973*); and E. S. C. Weiner and Andrew Delahunty, *The Oxford Guide to English Usage*, 2nd edn, Oxford 1993.

II. Literature[1]

1. Guides

a. *General guides*

Two pairs of guides stand out above the rest; all four are alphabetical in arrangement, and will between them answer most questions: they are *The Oxford Companion to English Literature*, ed. Margaret Drabble, 6th edn, Oxford 1995, and *The Oxford Companion to the Theatre*, ed. Phyllis Hartnoll, 4th edn, Oxford 1983; together with *The Cambridge Guide to Literature in English*, ed. Ian Ousby, 2nd edn, Cambridge 1993, and *The Cambridge Guide to Theatre*, ed. Martin Banham, 3rd edn, Cambridge 1995. *The Norton Anthology of English Literature*, ed. M. H. Abrams, 6th edn, New York 1993*, is (inevitably) short on fiction, but is otherwise an admirable and comprehensive collection, with excellent biographical and critical introductions to each author. Harold Bloom's *The Western Canon*, London 1994, is stimulating, idiosyncratic, and thoroughly readable. On printing, publishing, and editorial method, see Philip Gaskell, *A New Introduction to Bibliography*, Winchester 1995*, and the same author's *From Writer to Reader*, Winchester 1998*.

b. *Subject Guides*

The *Cambridge Companions* to literature (all *) include collections of essays

---

[1] It is worth mentioning that some excellent readings of unabridged classic novels have been published on audio tape by Chivers/Sterling Audio Books, and that much poetry and many plays are similarly available. But beware of the abridged novels which form the bulk of the audio catalogues: they are as undesirable as are "condensed books" in print.

on *Medieval English Theatre*; *English Poetry, Donne to Marvell*; *English Renaissance Drama*; and *British Romanticism*. A valuable guide to the technicalities of fiction by a practising novelist is David Lodge, *The Art of Fiction: Illustrated from Classic and Modern Texts*, London 1992*; for the history of literary criticism and modern critical theory, see Harry Blamires, *A History of Literary Criticism*, Macmillan 1991*, and Chris Baldick, *The Concise Oxford Dictionary of Literary Terms*, Oxford 1990*. A good general description of the techniques of poetry is the article "Poetic Forms and Literary Terminology" printed at the end of both volumes of *The Norton Anthology of English Literature*, 6th edn, 1993*.

2. Subject Dictionaries

Biographical dictionaries include the indispensable *Chambers Biographical Dictionary*, 5th edn, Edinburgh 1990*; and, for Britain, *The Dictionary of National Biography* (*DNB*), with its supplements up to 1990, and *The Concise Dictionary of National Biography*, new edn, Oxford 1992. See also the annual British *Who's Who*; when its subjects die, their final entries are collected in the five-yearly volumes of *Who Was Who* (from 1897). There are also dictionaries of quotations, first names, surnames, place names, proverbs, and many other special subjects, which are usually available in public libraries.

3. Bibliographies

The handiest concise bibliography of works of literature (but not of works about them) is *Annals of English Literature 1475–1950*, 2nd edn, Oxford 1961; this remarkable compilation brings together all the important – and many less important – literary publications year by year from the late fifteenth to the mid-twentieth century, and indexes them by authors. *The Shorter New Cambridge Bibliography of English Literature*, ed. George Watson, Cambridge 1981, is organised in broad periods, and includes criticism and biography. There are bibliographies in the third revision of *The New Pelican Guides to English Literature*, ed. Boris Ford, now in progress; and reading lists for students in the new edition of *The Short Oxford History of English Literature*, by Andrew Sanders, Oxford 1996*. The two volumes of *The Norton Anthology of English Literature*, 6th edn, 1993*, have annotated bibliographies both of periods and of individual authors. There are separate bibliographies of virtually every major author, but some of them may be hard to find outside university libraries; modern edited texts of classic literature, such as Penguin Classics*, Oxford World's Classics*, Everyman Classics*, and New Mermaid* plays usually include an author bibliography.

4. Authors: Fiction

Look out for the cut-price but well-edited classic novels in the Penguin Classics* and Oxford World's Classics* series. Useful collections of critical essays (not mentioned separately below) on general themes, authors and individual works are to be found in Macmillan's extensive *Casebooks* and *New Casebooks* series. Contemporary (and later) criticism is reprinted for most major authors in the splendid *Critical Heritage* series.

a. Cervantes

There is no major biography in English, but see William Byron, *Cervantes: A Biography*, London 1979. *Don Quixote*, translated and introduced by J. M. Cohen, Penguin Classics 1950*, is the handiest version; *Don Quixote* is included in *The Portable Cervantes*, tr. and ed. Samuel Putnam, Penguin 1980*.

b. Richardson

The best critical biography is T. C. D. Eaves and B. D. Kimpel, *Samuel Richardson: A Biography*, Oxford 1971, but it is out of print and may be difficult to find; in which case see Jocelyn Harris, *Samuel Richardson*, Cambridge 1987*. The 1740 text of *Pamela*, volumes 1 and 2, edited by T .C. D. Eaves and B. D. Kimpel, is available as a Riverside edition, Boston 1971*; and the 1801 text of the same volumes, edited by Peter Sabor, is a Penguin Classic, 1980*.

c. Jane Austen

David Cecil, *A Portrait of Jane Austen*, London 1978, and Mary Lascelles, *Jane Austen: Her Mind and Art*, Oxford 1939, are both recommended; see also Jan Fergus, *Jane Austen: A Literary Life*, London 1991*. The Oxford World's Classics edition of *Pride and Prejudice** has a valuable introduction and apparatus by James Kinsley, Isobel Armstrong, and Frank W. Bradbrook; the Penguin Classics version is edited by Tony Tanner*.

d. Dickens

Edgar Johnson, *Charles Dickens: His Tragedy and Triumph*, revised and abridged, London 1977, and Peter Ackroyd, *Dickens*, London 1990 (also abridged 1994*), are both excellent; see also Grahame Smith, *Charles Dickens: A Literary Life*, London 1995*. *David Copperfield* is well edited with an introduction by Trevor Blount, Penguin Classics 1966*; about half of Phiz's illustrations are included.

e. George Eliot

The best life is Gordon S. Haight, *George Eliot: A Biography*, Oxford 1968*; see also Kerry McSweeney, *George Eliot (Marian Evans): A Literary Life*, London 1991*. The Oxford World's Classics *Middlemarch** is edited and introduced by David Carroll, and has good explanatory notes; the Penguin Classics text is edited by W. J. Harvey*.

f. Conrad

John Batchelor, *The Life of Joseph Conrad: A Critical Biography*, Oxford 1994*, is an excellent guide to the whole of Conrad's *œuvre*; see also Jacques Berthoud, *Joseph Conrad: The Major Phase*, Cambridge 1993*, and Cedric Watts, *Joseph Conrad: A Literary Life*, London 1989*. Professor Batchelor is the editor of the Oxford World's Classics *Lord Jim**.

g. Joyce

The essential biography is Richard Ellmann, *James Joyce*, revised edn, Oxford 1982*; also excellent is C. H. Peake, *James Joyce: The Citizen and the Artist*, London 1977*. See also Morris Beja, *James Joyce: A Literary Life*, London 1992*, and *The Cambridge Companion to James Joyce*, ed. Derek Attridge, 1990*. Several adequate texts of *Ulysses* are available, but none that is well edited with introduction and notes; for the first reading, therefore, it is best to use Harry Blamires's crib, *The New Bloomsday Book*, 1988*. For further analysis, episode by episode, see *James Joyce's Ulysses: Critical Essays*, ed. Clive Hart and David Hayman, London 1977*.

5. Authors: Poetry

Well-annotated selections from the works of major poets are to be found in series such as Penguin Classics*, Everyman Classics*, and Oxford Authors*; and, for biography, see Macmillan Literary Lives*.

a. Chaucer

D. S. Brewer, *Chaucer and His World*, London 1978, is a well-illustrated introduction; see also *The Cambridge Chaucer Companion*, ed. Piero Boitani and Jill Mann, 1986*. Most twentieth-century texts of *The Canterbury Tales* are good enough, the standard one being in Chaucer, *Works*, ed. L. D. Benson, Boston 1987 (known as "The Riverside Chaucer", Oxford*); the annotated *Canterbury Tales*, ed. A. C. Cawley, rev. edn, Everyman 1975*, is based on the standard text.

b. Spenser

Gary F. Waller, *Edmund Spenser: A Literary Life*, London 1994; see also

The Spenser Encyclopedia, ed. A. C. Hamilton, London 1992*. Spenser's *Poetical Works*, ed. A. C. Hamilton, are included in Longman's Annotated English Poets*; and there is an annotated edition of *The Faerie Queene*, ed. T. S. Roche Jr, Harmondsworth 1978*.

c. Donne

John Carey's *John Donne: Life, Mind, and Art*, London 1981*, is a vigorous critical biography; see also George Parfitt, *John Donne: A Literary Life*, London 1989*. A well-annotated edition of Donne's verse is C. A. Patrides, *The Complete English Poems of John Donne*, Everyman 1985*; and the Oxford Authors *Donne*, edited by John Carey, 1990*, includes a good selection of Donne's prose.

d. Milton

Start with A. N. Wilson, *The Life of John Milton*, Oxford 1983; and see Cedric J. Brown, *John Milton: A Literary Life*, London 1994*, and *The Cambridge Companion to Milton*, ed. Dennis Danielson, 1989*. *Paradise Lost* in Penguin Classics* is edited by Christopher Ricks, 1989. The Oxford Authors *Milton*, edited by S. Orgel and J. Goldberg, 1991*, contains both verse and prose.

e. Dryden

Paul Hammond, *John Dryden: A Literary Life*, London 1991*; and the Oxford Authors *Dryden*, ed. Keith Walker, Oxford 1994*, are both recommended. See also J. A. Winn, *John Dryden and his World*, New Haven 1987*.

f. Pope

There is no major biography of Pope, but Felicity Rosslyn, *Alexander Pope: A Literary Life*, Basingstoke 1990*, is a good starting point; see also Maynard Mack, *Pope, a Life*, New Haven 1985. For the *Poems* (not including the translations of Homer), there is the excellent annotated one-volume Twickenham edition, ed. John Butt, London 1961*. See also the Oxford Authors *Pope*, edited by Pat Rogers, 1993*.

g. Johnson

Boswell's unsurpassable *Life* (which is available in Oxford World's Classics*) is supplemented by James L. Clifford, *Young Sam Johnson*, London 1955, and *Dictionary Johnson*, London 1980, for the sage's earlier years before Boswell knew him. The Oxford Authors *Johnson*, edited by Donald Greene, Oxford 1984*, is an excellent collection of writings from the whole of Johnson's career; and there is a useful Penguin *Selected Writings*, ed. Patrick Cruttwell*.

h. Blake

Peter Ackroyd's *Blake*, London 1995*, is an excellent modern biography. For annotated poems and selected prose, see the Oxford Authors *Blake*, ed. Michael Mason, Oxford 1988*; and for a brief survey of his art, poetry, and thought, see Kathleen Raine, *William Blake*, Thames and Hudson World of Art*.

i. Wordsworth

Stephen Gill, *William Wordsworth: A Life*, Oxford 1990, is a satisfactory recent biography; see also John Williams, *William Wordsworth: A Literary Life*, London 1996*. *William Wordsworth: Selected Poems*, ed. J. O. Hayden, Penguin Classics 1994*, is a convenient annotated edition; and the Oxford Authors *Wordsworth*, edited by Stephen Gill, 1984*, includes the Preface to *Lyrical Ballads* and other prose. *Lyrical Ballads, 1798 and 1800* is reprinted with both Prefaces, ed. R. L. Brett and A. R. Jones, 2nd edn, 1991*.

j. Byron

For biography, see Leslie A. Marchand, *Byron: A Portrait*, London 1976. For selected poems, including the whole of "Don Juan", the Oxford Authors *Byron*, ed. J. J. McGann, Oxford 1986*, is outstanding. The Penguin Classics *Don Juan* is edited by T. G. and E. Steffan and W. W. Pratt*.

k. Tennyson

The best biography is Robert Martin, *Tennyson: The Unquiet Heart*, London 1983; see also Leonée Ormond, *Alfred Tennyson: A Literary Life*, London 1993*. The standard *Poems* is edited by Christopher Ricks (2nd edn, 3 vols, Longman Annotated English Poets), who also edited *Tennyson: A Selected Edition*, Harlow 1989*. Another very good annotated selection is *In Memoriam, Maud, and Other Poems*, ed. J. D. Jump, Everyman Classics, 1974*.

l. T. S. Eliot

For critical biography, Peter Ackroyd's *T. S. Eliot*, London 1984*, is outstanding, though many of Eliot's papers are not yet available to biographers. See also Lyndall Gordon, *Eliot's Early Years*, Oxford 1977*, and *Eliot's New Life*, Oxford 1988*; Tony Sharpe, *T. S. Eliot: A Literary*

Life, London 1991*; and *The Cambridge Companion to T. S. Eliot*, ed. A. D. Moody, 1994*. For the verse, Eliot's *Collected Poems 1909–1962*, London 1963*, or *The Complete Poems and Plays*, London 1969*.

6. Authors: Drama

For annotated editions of individual classic plays, the New Mermaid series (published by A. and C. Black*) is recommended. See also the Revels Series*.

a. Sophocles

The Penguin Classics *Sophocles: The Three Theban Plays*, 1982*, ed. Bernard Knox and tr. Robert Fagles, includes biographical and critical materials, and a fluent English verse translation of *Oedipus the King*.

b. Mystery and morality plays

See *York Mystery Plays: A Selection in Modern Spelling*, ed. R. Beadle and P. M. King, Oxford World's Classics 1984*; and *Everyman and Medieval Miracle Plays*, ed. A. C. Cawley, Everyman 1993*. E. K. Chambers, *The Medieval Stage*, Oxford 1905, is still unsurpassed; but see *The Revels History of Drama in English, 1: Medieval Drama*, ed. A. C. Cawley et al., London 1983.

c. Marlowe

The best critical biography is still F. S. Boas, *Christopher Marlowe: A Biographical and Critical Study*, Oxford 1940. The Penguin Classics *Complete Plays*, 1969*, has a good introduction and notes by J. B. Steane. The New Mermaid text of *Dr Faustus* is edited by Roma Gill, 2nd edn, 1989*. The Revels *Dr Faustus*, ed. David Bevington and Eric Rasmussen, Manchester 1993*, has both the 1604 and 1616 texts.

d. Shakespeare

An authoritative and digestible biography is S. Schoenbaum, *William Shakespeare: A Compact Documentary Life*, rev. edn, Oxford 1987* (documents being all that we have). See also Richard Dutton, *William Shakespeare: A Literary Life*, London 1989*; *The Cambridge Companion to Shakespeare Studies*, ed. Stanley Wells, 1986*; and Kiernan Ryan, *Shakespeare*, Harvester New Readings, 1989*. The latest, and best, collected edition of the *Works* is edited by Stanley Wells and Gary Taylor, compact edition, Oxford 1988*; but individual plays are best read in such annotated series as the New (and "New New") Arden Shakespeare*, the revised Oxford Shakespeare (also in Oxford World's Classics*), and the New Cambridge Shakespeare*.

e. *Jonson*

For biography, see Rosalind Miles, *Ben Jonson: His Life and Work*, London 1986, and Anne Barton, *Ben Jonson, Dramatist*, Cambridge 1984*; see also W. David Kay, *Ben Jonson: A Literary Life*, London 1994*. The New Mermaid text of *Volpone* is edited by Philip Brockbank, London 1968*. See also the Oxford Authors *Jonson*, edited by Ian Donaldson, 1984*, which includes Jonson's poetry.

f. *Webster*

So little is known about the lives of Webster and Ford that they are adequately covered by the introductions to the New Mermaid texts; that for *The Duchess of Malfi* is edited by E. M. Brennan, 2nd edn, London 1983*. *The Selected Plays of John Webster* is edited by Jonathan Dollimore and Alan Sinfield, Cambridge 1982*.

g. *Ford*

See the note on Webster. The New Mermaid text of *'Tis Pity She's a Whore* is edited by Brian Morris, 1968*. *The Selected Plays of John Ford* is edited by Colin Gibson, Cambridge 1986*.

h. *Dryden*

See Authors: Poetry, *e*, above. The New Mermaid text of *All For Love* is edited by N. J. Andrew, 1975*.

i. *Vanbrugh*

Kerry Downes, *Sir John Vanbrugh: A Biography*, London 1987, is a substantial modern life. The New Mermaid text of *The Relapse* is edited by Bernard Harris, 1971*.

j. *Goldsmith*

The standard life is Ralph M. Wardle, *Oliver Goldsmith*, London 1957. The New Mermaid text of *She Stoops to Conquer* is edited by Tom Davis, 1979*. See also Katharine Worth, *Sheridan and Goldsmith*, London 1992*.

k. *Sheridan*

A recent critical biography is James Morwood, *The Life and Works of Richard Brinsley Sheridan*, Edinburgh 1985. The New Mermaid text of *The School for Scandal* is edited by F. W. Bateson, 1979*. See also Katharine Worth, *Sheridan and Goldsmith*, London 1992*.

l. Ibsen

The abridged version of Michael Meyer, *Ibsen*, London 1992*, is a superb critical biography; see also the *Cambridge Companion to Ibsen*, ed. James McFarlane, Cambridge 1994*. Translations (none of them bad) of all of Ibsen's plays from *Brand* onwards are variously available in Penguin Classics*, Oxford World's Classics*, and Methuen's plays*.

m. Shaw

Michael Holroyd, *Bernard Shaw*, 5 vols, London 1988–92, covers the ground very thoroughly. Louis Crompton, *Shaw the Dramatist*, London 1969, examines twelve major plays. There are Penguin plain texts* of most of the plays.

III. Creative Writing

1. Guides

Of the many guides available, Michael Legat, *Writing for Pleasure and Profit*, London 1986*, is sensibly down to earth; as is Barry Turner's *The Writer's Companion*, London 1996*, which takes us ten years further on, and covers writing for films, TV, radio, and multimedia, as well as fiction and poetry; Turner includes useful sections on PLR, contracts, and copyright (now in a state of some confusion). For reference, see the annual *Writers' and Artists' Year Book*.

2. Language and Usage

See Section I, above. Most writers will also need a good *Thesaurus* (or word-finder, often referred to as "Roget"); the Penguin version* is recommended.

3. Publication

Libraries will have up-to-date directories of publishing houses. See also Michael Legat, *An Author's Guide to Publishing*, London 1982*. Evangeline Paterson, *What To Do With Your Poems*, Newcastle 1991*, is a useful short guide, despite its title.

Index

Main entries are given in **bold type**.

actors and acting, 109, 113, 116, 138
  women played by men, 116, 117, 117n
Addison, Joseph, 93–4
Aeschylus, 110
allegory
  in fiction, 42
  in poetry, 80
alliteration, in poetry, 79
Altman, Robert, *The Player*, 43
Amis, Martin, 68
antithesis, in poetry, 80
Aristophanes, 110
Aristotle, on tragedy, 108, 110
Arnold, Matthew, 9, **26**
  Culture and Anarchy, 26
  "Dover Beach", 26
assonance, in poetry, 79
Auden, W. H., 79, 103
Augustan age, 17, 17n
Austen, Jane, 3, 9, **21**, 50–2
  Emma, 21, 50
  First Impressions, 50
  Mansfield Park, 21, 50
  Northanger Abbey, 21, 50, 51n
  Persuasion, 21, 50
  Pride and Prejudice, 21, **50–2**
  Sense and Sensibility, 21, 50
author and narrator, in fiction, 37
authors, canonical, 1, 3, 8–10

Ballantyne, R. M., *The Coral Island*, 43
Barker, Pat, 68
  Regeneration and Union Street, 149
Beadnell, Maria, 53
"Beat" poetry, 103n
Beckett, Samuel, 3, 131n
  Waiting for Godot, 140

Beethoven, Ludwig van, 13, 19
Belloc, Hilaire, 76
Beowulf, 13n
Betjeman, John, 103
  Summoned by Bells, 76
Blackfriars theatre, 117
Blackwood's Magazine, 60
Blake, William, 3, 9, 15, 19, **20**, 74
  Songs of Innocence and Experience, 20
Blamires, Harry, *New Bloomsday Book, The*,
  29
blank verse, 76, 91, 97
Bloom, Harold, *The Western Canon*, 1n, 3,
  3n, 13
Bloomsbury group, 29n
Borges, Jorge Luis, 3
Boswell, James, *Life of Samuel Johnson*, 18
Brecht, Bertolt, *Threepenny Opera, The*, 140
Brontë, Charlotte, 25
  Jane Eyre, 25, 32–41; narrator of, 37; and
    symbolism, 42–3
  Villette, 25, 35n
Brontë, Emily, 9, **24–5**
  poems, 25
  Wuthering Heights, 24–5
Brooke, Rupert, 30n
Browne, Hablôt K. ("Phiz"), 53, 55
Browning, Elizabeth Barrett, *Aurora Leigh*,
  23n, 35n
Browning, Robert, 9, **23–4**, 74
  "Home Thoughts from Abroad", 24
  "My Last Duchess", 24
  Ring and the Book, The, 23, 76
Bunyan, John, *Pilgrim's Progress*, 42, 115
Burbage, James, 117
Burns, Robert, 9, **20**
  Poems, Chiefly in the Scottish Dialect, 20

"Tam o' Shanter", 20
Butler, Samuel, *Erewhon*, 42
Byron, George Gordon, Lord, 3, 9, 13, **22**, 72, 74
  Childe Harold, 22
  Don Juan, 22, 22n, 73, 78
  "Dying Gladiator, The", 22
  "Eve of Waterloo, The", 22
  Manfred, 22
  Prometheus, 22
  "She Walks in Beauty", 22
  "So We'll Go No More A-Roving", 22
Byronic hero, 22, 35, 38

canon, the literary, 1–30
  and critical theory, 9–10, 10n
  and "Dead White Males", 10
  instability of, 10
  lists of canonical authors, 1, 3, 8–10
Cervantes Saavedra, Miguel de, 3, 44–6
  Don Quixote, **44–6**, 49n
  La Galatea, 44
  Persiles y Sigismunda, 44
characters
  in drama, 108–9, 128–9
  in fiction, 38–9
charts, chronological, 2, 4–7
Chatterton, Thomas, "Rowley" poems, 19
Chaucer, Geoffrey, 8, **11**, 14, 81–5
  Canterbury Tales, The, 11, **81–5**; Coghill's translation of, 83–4; Skeat's text of, 81–2
  Troilus and Criseyde, 11, 13n, 77
Cibber, Colley, *Love's Last Shift*, 130
Cinderella, 32–41
  glass slipper, 33n, 42
  many versions of, 32n
  Perrault and, 32, 32n, 37
cinema films, 105
  metafiction in, 43
clichés, avoidance of in creative writing, 147–8
closet plays, 105
Coghill, Nevill, 11, 83–4
Coleridge, Samuel Taylor, 9, 19, 20, **21**
  "Dejection: an Ode", 21
  "Frost at Midnight", 21
  "Kubla Khan", 21
  Lyrical Ballads, 19, 20, 20n, 21
  "Rime of the Ancient Mariner, The", 20n, 21, 75–6
comedy, nature of, 108

Shaw and, 138
Congreve, William, *Way of the World, The*, 131
Conrad, Joseph, 3, 9, **27–8**, 60–3
  Almayer's Folly, 60
  Chance, 60, 61n
  and Dostoievsky, 28n
  Heart of Darkness, 28
  Lord Jim, 28, **60–3**; narrators of, 62; part-publication of, 60–1, 61n
  Nigger of the "Narcissus", The, 28
  Nostromo, 28
  "Secret Sharer, The", 28
  Shadow Line, The, 28
  Suspense, 60
  Typhoon, 28
  Under Western Eyes, 28
  "Youth", 28
"copy text", editor's, 58, 58n
copyright, law of, 153, 153n
Corneille, Pierre, 128
Coward, Noël, 140
Cowley, Abraham, 19
creative writing, 141–53
  clichés, avoidance of in, 147–8
  copyright, law of, 153, 153n
  dialogue, setting out, 147
  equipment for, 151
  foreign languages in, 149
  forms of address, 148
  grammar, 144–5
  language, 141–9
  planning and research, 149–50
  publication, 151–3
  publishers, approaching, 152–3
  punctuation, 145–6
  qualities of a writer, 141
  reading a requirement for, 141
  revision of, 150–1
  spelling, 143–4
  vocabulary, 143
  typescript or printout, 151–2
  usage, 147–9
critical theory, 9–10, 10n, 43n
Cukor, George, *What Price Hollywood?*, 43

Dante Alighieri, 3, 10
Davies, W. H., 30n
"Dead White Males", 10
Defoe, Daniel, 8, **17**
  Captain Singleton, 17

Colonel Jack, 17
Journal of the Plague Year, A, 17
Moll Flanders, 17
Robinson Crusoe, 17
Roxana, 17
Dekker, Thomas, 124, 125
dialogue
in drama, 106–7
in fiction, 39–42; setting out, 147
and monologue, 39–42
Dickens, Charles, 3, 9, **24**, 25–6, 29, 52–7
Christmas Carol, A, 24
David Copperfield, 24, **52–7**; illustrations
in, 53, 55; part-publication of, 53, 61n
Dombey and Son, 24
Hard Times, 24
Little Dorrit, 24
Martin Chuzzlewit, 24
Oliver Twist, 24
Our Mutual Friend, 24, 52
Pickwick Papers, The, 24, 52
popularity and influence of, 24, 52
rejected children in, 53, 53n
Dickinson, Emily, 3, 75
Diderot, Denis, 46
Donne, John, 3, 8, **14–15**, 85–8, 123
Holy Sonnets, 15
"Nocturnall upon S. Lucie's Day, A", **85–8**
Poems, 86
Satire III, 15
Songs and Sonnets, 15
Dostoievsky, Fyodor Mikhailovich, and
Conrad, 28n
Drabble, Margaret, *Realms of Gold, The*,
44n
drama, 104–40
actors and acting, 113, 116, 138; women
played by men, 116, 117, 177n
characters in, 108–9, 128–9
cinema films, 43, 105
closet plays, 105
comedy, nature of, 108; Shaw's, 138
in decline, 135
dialogue in, 106–7
Elizabethan and Jacobean, 116–27;
imaginary Italian setting of, 121n, 124,
126
Everyman, **114–15**
farce, 131
Greek, ancient, 110–13
Ibsen's revolution, **135–8**

liturgical, 110, 113
medieval, 113–16
miracle plays, 114
modern, 140
morality plays, 114, 115–16; *Everyman*,
114–15
mystery plays, 113–15, 114n; *Second
Shepherd's Play*, **114–15**; *York Play of the
Crucifixion*, 114
nature of, 104–6
neoclassical, 127–35; patent holders, 127
origins and early development, 110–16
production, techniques of, 109; realism in,
137–8
radio plays, 106
ritual, 110
Roman, ancient, 113
saints' plays, 114
staging, 109; ancient, 113; medieval, 116;
open and indoor, 117; single-focus and
multiple, 116, 117
structure of, 107–8
television plays, 105–6
texts, dramatic, three stages of, 104
theatres, 109; ancient, 113; Elizabethan
and Jacobean, 117; Globe, 117; closing of
117, 127; later, 109, 128, 137–8
tragedy, nature of, 108; Aristotle on, 108;
revenge, 123–4
unities, the three, 107–8, 129
Drayton, Michael, 78
Drury Lane, 133
Dryden, John, 3, 8, 14, **16–17**, 42, 128–30
Absalom and Architophel, 16
Alexander's Feast, 17
All for Love, **128–30**
Essay of Dramatic Poesie, An, 128
Hind and the Panther, The, 17
Mac Flecknoe, 16
Medal, The, 17

editorial method, 58, 58n
Eliot, George (Evans, Mary Ann, later
Marian), 3, 9, 15, 24, **25–6**, 57–60
Daniel Deronda, 57
Middlemarch, 26, **57–60**; part-publication
of, 58, 58n, 61n
Mill on the Floss, The, 26
"Miss Brooke", 57
Scenes of Clerical Life, 57
Silas Marner, 26

and Tolstoy, 26, 26n
Eliot, Thomas Stearns, 3, 9, 14, 15, 21, 23,
    30, 80n, 100–3
  Ash Wednesday, 30
  Four Quartets, 30
  "Gerontion", 30
  Hollow Men, The, 30
  "The Love Song of J. Alfred Prufrock",
    30, 30n, 100–3
  Murder in the Cathedral, 30
  Prufrock and Other Observations, 30, 101
  and Symbolism, 30, 42n, 102
  on Tennyson, 23
  Waste Land, The, 30, 102n
Elizabethan and Jacobean drama, 116–27
  imaginary Italian setting of, 121n, 124, 126
Engels, Friedrich, *Condition of the Working
    Classes in England*, 25
English language
  early Modern, 12
  Old and Middle, 11, 82–3
episodic fiction, 17, 45
epistolary novel, 49
equipment for writing, 151
Euripides, 110
Evans, Mary Ann, later Marian *see* Eliot,
    George
Everyman, **114–15**
evolution, cultural, 2–3

farce, 131
Farquhar, George, *Beaux' Stratagem, The*,
    128
Faulkner, William, and interior monologue,
    41
fiction, 31–69
  allegory, 42
  author and narrator, 37
  characters in, 38–9
  definition of, 31, 133–4
  dialogue and monologue, 39–42
  episodic, 17, 45
  epistolary, 49
  "house style", publishers', 57–8, 57n, 152
  interior monologue, 29, 41–2, 41n, 65–8
  intertextuality, 43
  length, 69
  manuscripts and proofs, 53, 57–8
  metafiction, 43–4, 51, 51n
  narrator, 37, 45, 62, 65–7
  nature of, 31–2

picaresque, 17
plots, frequently used, 35–6; and suspense,
    25–6
point of view, 37–8, 51
proof correction, 53n
publication in parts, 53, 58, 58n, 60–1, 61n
reliable and unreliable narrators, 37
revision, 46–9, 53n, 150–1
setting, 38
stream of consciousness, 41–2, 41n
structure and plot, 32–5, 64–5; three-part,
    32–3, 58
symbolism in, 42–3
Fielding, Henry, 8, **18**, 46
  Joseph Andrews, 18
  Tom Jones, 18
films *see* cinema films
Fitzgerald, Edward, 77
foot, in poetry, 71–2; Greek names of feet,
    71–2, 71n
Ford, John, 125–7
  'Tis Pity She's a Whore, **126–7**
forms of address, 148
Forster, Edward Morgan, 9, **29**
  Howard's End, 29
  Longest Journey, The, 29
  Passage to India, A, 29
Fowles, John, *French Lieutenant's Woman,
    The*, 44n
free verse, 74–5
Freud, Sigmund, 3
Friedrich, Caspar David, 19

Gabler, H. W., 64
Gardner, Helen *see NOBEI*
Gaskell, Elizabeth, 9, 24, 25, 59n
  Cranford, 25
  Mary Barton, 25
  North and South, 25
  Sylvia's Lovers, 25
  Wives and Daughters, 25, 59n
Gay, John, *Beggar's Opera, The*, 128
Georgian poets, 30, 30n
Globe theatre, 117
Godwin, William, 22
Goethe, J. W. von, 3
  Faust, 77
Golding, William, *Lord of the Flies, The*, 43
Goldsmith, Oliver, 8, 19, 131–3
  Deserted Village, The, 19, 132
  She Stoops to Conquer, 132–3

Traveller, The, 19, 132
Goya, Francisco, 19
grammar, in creative writing, 144–5
Graves, Robert, 12
Gray, Thomas, 8, **19**, 72
   "Elegy Written in a Country Churchyard",
      19, 72
Greek drama, ancient, 110–13

Hallam, Arthur, 98
Hardy, Thomas, 9, **26–7**
   Jude the Obscure, 26–7
   poems, 27
Heaney, Seamus, 103
Herbert, George, 8, **15**
heroic couplet, 16, 16n, 17
Hervey of Ickworth, John, Lord, 93–5
Homer, 3, 17, 43, 64, 92, 98–9
Hopkins, Gerard Manley, 9, 26, **27**, 30
   poems, 27
   "sprung rhythm", 27
Horace, 3n, 17n
"house style", publishers', 57–8, 57n, 152
Hughes, Ted, 74, 103
hyperbole, in poetry, 80

Ibsen, Henrik, 3, 29, 105, **135–8**
   Catiline, 135
   Doll's House, A, influence of, 136
   the twelve social dramas, **136–7**
   verse dramas (*Brand, Peer Gynt*), 77, 105,
      136
   When We Dead Awaken, 135
   Wild Duck, The, 137
images, in poetry, 80
interior monologue, in fiction, 29, 41–2,
   41n, 65–8
intertextuality in fiction, 43
Intertextuality in critical theory, 43n
irony, in poetry, 80
Italian setting of Elizabethan and Jacobean
   drama, 121n, 124, 126

James, Henry, on *Middlemarch*, 59
James, William, 41n
Johnson, Samuel, 3, 8, **18–19**
   Dictionary, 19
   Idler, The, 19
   Irene, 18
   Lives of the Poets, 19
   Rambler, The, 19

Rasselas, 18
   Shakespeare, edition of, 18–19
   Vanity of Human Wishes, The, 18
Jonson, Ben, 8, 14, 121–3
   Alchemist, The, 121
   Volpone, **121–3**
Joyce, James, 3, 9, **29**, 41, 63–8, 137n
   "Anna Livia Plurabelle", 29
   Dubliners, 29, 63
   Finnegans Wake, 29, 63
   Portrait of the Artist, A, 29, 63, 65
   Stephen Hero, 63n
   and Symbolism, 29, 42n
   Ulysses, 29, 30, 43, **63–8**; interior
      monologue in, 41, 65–8; texts of, 64,
      64n

Kafka, Franz, 3
Keats, John, 9, 13, **22–3**
   the five great "Odes", 23
   "La Belle Dame Sans Merci", 23
   "On First Looking into Chapman's
      Homer", 23
Kipling, Rudyard, 9, **28**
   "Danny Deever", 28
   Diversity of Creatures, A, 28
   Kim, 28
   Plain Tales from the Hills, 28
   "Way through the Woods, The", 28
Kotzebue, August von, 135

Langland, William, 8, 11, **12**, 79
   Piers Ploughman, 11, 12
language
   in creative writing, 141–9
   grammar, 144–5
   in poetry, 80–1
   usage, 147–9
   vocabulary, 143
   see also English language
Larkin, Philip, 13n, 103
Lawrence, David Herbert, 9, **30**, 74
   Rainbow, The, 30
   "Snake", 30
   Sons and Lovers, 30
   Women in Love, 30
length of novels, 69
Lewes, G. H., 58, 58n
line, in poetry, 74
   end-stopped and run-on, 74
liturgical drama, 110, 113

Lodge, David, 68
  Changing Places, 44n

Macpherson, James, "Ossian" poems, 19
Mallarmé, Stéphane, 42n
manuscripts and proofs, in fiction, 53, 57–8
Marlowe, Christopher, 8, 14, 118–19
  Doctor Faustus, 91n, **118–19**
  Edward II, 118
  Tamburlaine, 118
Marvell, Andrew, 8, **16**
  "To His Coy Mistress", 16, 76
Masefield, John, 30n, 79
medieval drama, 113–16
  miracle plays, 114
  morality plays, 114, 115–16
  mystery plays, 113–15, 114n
  saints' plays, 114
Medieval period, 11–12
metafiction
  in cinema films, 43
  in fiction, 43–4, 51, 51n
  in twentieth-century novels, 44, 44n
metaphors, in poetry, 80
"metaphysical" poets and imagery, 14, 14n,
  15, 87
metonymy, in poetry, 80
metre, in poetry, 70–5
Milton, John, 3, 8, 13, **15**, 19, 23, 89–92, 96,
  137n
  Comus, 15
  "Hymn on the Morning of Christ's
    Nativity", 15
  Lycidas, 15
  Paradise Lost, 15, 94, 94n, **89–92**; blank
    verse of, 76, 91–2
  Paradise Regained, 15
  Samson Agonistes, 15
miracle plays, 114
Modernist period, 27–30
  drama, 140
  modernist developments, other than
    literary, 27
  pre-Modernists, 26–7
  values of, 27
Molière, 3
Montaigne, Michel de, 3
morality plays, 114, 115–16
  Everyman, **114–15**
movement, in poetry, 79
Murdoch, Iris, 68

music and poetry, 71
mystery plays, 113–15, 114n
  Second Shepherds' Play, **114–15**

narrators, in fiction, 37, 45, 62, 65–7
nature of poetry, 70
Neoclassical period, 16–19
  drama, 127–35
  values of, 16
Neruda, Pablo, 3
Nietzsche, Friedrich Wilhelm, and the
  Byronic hero, 22
NOBEV (*New Oxford Book of English Verse*,
  ed. Helen Gardner), 11

onomatopoeia, in poetry, 79
Orwell, George, *Animal Farm*, 42
Osborne, John, *Look Back in Anger*, 140
Ottava Rima, 77–8
Ovid, 3n
Owen, Wilfred, 75

para-rhyme, 75, 75n
part-publication, 53, 58, 58n, 60–1, 61n
patent holders, theatrical, 127
Penguin Books, poetry published by, 103
Perrault, Charles, *Cinderella*, 32, 32n
Pessoa, Fernando, 3
Petrarch, 12
"Phiz" (Hablôt K. Browne), 53, 55
picaresque fiction, 17
Pirandello, Luigi, *Six Characters in Search
  of an Author*, 140
planning and research, in creative writing,
  149–50
Plautus, 113
plots in fiction
  frequently used, 35–6
  and suspense, 35–6
poetic licence, 80
poetry, 70–103
  allegory, 80
  alliteration, 79
  antithesis, 80
  assonance, 79
  "Beat", 103n
  blank verse, 76, 91, 97
  foot, 71–2; Greek names of feet, 71–2, 71n
  free verse, 74–5
  hyperbole, 80
  images, 80

irony, 80
languages of, 80–1
line, 74; end-stopped and run-on, 74
masculine and feminine endings, of lines
    74; of rhymes, 75
metaphors, 80
"metaphysical" poets and imagery, 14,
    14n, 15, 87
metonymy, 80
metre in, 70–5
movement, 79
music and, 71
nature of, 70
onomatopoeia, 79
poetic licence, 80
puns and double meanings, 80–1
"quantity", 70
rhyme in, 75–9; para-rhyme, 75
similes, 80
sound in, 75–9
spirituality in, 15, 15n
stanzas, 76–9; Ottava Rima, 77–8; Rime
    royal, 77; sonnet, English and Italian,
    12–13, 77, 78–9; Spenserian, 78, 99
stress, 71; variation of, 72
syllables, 70, 72
synecdoche, 80
verses, 76n
point of view, in fiction, 37–8, 51
Pope, Alexander, 3, 8, **17–18**, 19, 76, 79,
    92–5, 97
    Dunciad, The, 18
    "Elegy to the Memory of an Unfortunate
        Lady", 18
    Epistle to Arbuthnot, 17–18, **92–5**
    Essay on Criticism, An, 17, 73
    Rape of the Lock, The, 18
Pound, Ezra, 101, 102
Powell, Anthony, 68
production, dramatic, techniques of, 109
    realism in, 137–8
proof correction, 53n
Proust, Marcel, 3
publication, 151–3
    in parts, 53, 58, 58n, 60–1, 61n
publishers, approaching, 152–3
punctuation, 145–6
puns and double meanings in poetry,
    80–1
Pushkin, Alexander Sergeyvich, *Eugene
    Onegin*, 77

qualities of a writer, 141
"quantity", in poetry, 70

Racine, Jean, 128
radio plays, 106
reading, and creative writing, 104, 141
Renaissance period, 12–16
revision
    of creative writing, 150–1
    of fiction, 46–9, 53n
rhyme, 75–9
    para-rhyme, 75, 75n
Richardson, Samuel, 8, 18, 46–9
    Clarissa, 46
    Pamela, **46–9**
    Sir Charles Grandison, 46
Rime royal, 77
ritual, 110
Roman drama, ancient, 113
Romantic period, 19–27
    values of, 19
Rousseau, Jean-Jacques, 46
Rushdie, Salman, 68

saints' plays, 114
Savage, Richard, 19
Scott, Sir Walter, 9, 10, **21–2**
    Heart of Midlothian, The, 22
    Marmion, 22
    Waverley Novels, 22
    "Young Lochinvar", 22
Second Shepherds' Play, **114–15**
Seneca, 113
setting, in fiction, 38
Shadwell, Thomas, 17
Shakespeare, William, 3, 8, **13–14**, 15, 17,
    79, 80–1, 118, 118n, 120, 121, 128–9,
    137n
    Antony and Cleopatra, 117, 128–9
    As You Like It, 117n
    Hamlet, 73, 109, 117, 124n
    how to read, 14
    influence of, 3, 120
    Love's Labour's Lost, 106
    Midsummer Night's Dream, A, 132
    "Phoenix and the Turtle, The", 14
    publication neglected, 121n
    Richard III, 118n
    Sonnets, 14, 81
    ten best plays hazarded, 14
    text of, 13–14, 19

Troilus and Cressida, **120**
Winter's Tale, A, 108
Shaw, George Bernard, 9, 27, 131, 138–40
  Androcles and the Lion, 107, 140
  Buoyant Billions, 138
  and Ibsen, 137–8
  Major Barbara, 140
  Pygmalion, 140
  Quintessence of Ibsenism, The, 137, 138
  Saint Joan, **138–40**
  Widowers' Houses, 138
Shelley, Percy Bysshe, 9, 13, **22**, 79
  "Odes", 22
  "Ozymandias", 22
  Prometheus Unbound, 22
Sheridan, Richard Brinsley, 131, 133–5
  School for Scandal, The, **133–5**
  Trip to Scarborough, A, 133n
similes, in poetry, 80
situation/action/resolution, 32–3, 58
Skelton, John, 8, **12**
sonnet, English and Italian, 12–13, 78–9
Sophocles, 110
  Oedipus the King, **110–13**
sound, in poetry, 75–9
spelling, need for good, 143–4
Spenser, Edmund, 3, 8, **13**, 15
  Epithalamion, 13
  Faerie Queene, The, 13, 13n, 42, 78
Spenserian stanza, 78, 99
spirituality in poetry, 15, 15n
staging
  ancient, 113
  medieval, 116
  open and indoor, 117
  single-focus and multiple, 116, 117
stanzas, 76–9
Steele, Sir Richard, *Conscious Lovers, The*, 128
Sterne, Laurence, 8, **18**
  Sentimental Journey, A, 18
  Tristram Shandy, 18; metafiction in, 43
Stoppard, Tom, *Rosencrantz and Guildenstern Are Dead*, 106–7
stream of consciousness
  in fiction, 41–2, 41n
  named by William James, 41n
stress, in poetry, 71
  variation of, 72
structure and plot
  of drama, 107–8

of fiction, 32–5, 64–5
  three-part, 32–3, 58
Surrey, Henry Howard, Earl of, 8, **12–13**
Swift, Jonathan, 8, **17**, 42
  Gulliver's Travels, 17, 42
  Modest Proposal, A, 17
  Tale of a Tub, The, 17
  "Verses on the Death of Doctor Swift", 17
syllables, in poetry, 72
symbolism, in fiction, 42–3
Symbolists, the, 28, 29, 30, 42n, 102
synecdoche, in poetry, 80
Synge, John Millington, 131n

television plays, 105–6
Tennyson, Alfred, Lord, 3, 9, 13, 17, **23**, 79, 97–100, 103
  "Crossing the Bar", 23
  Idylls of the King, 23, 76
  In Memoriam, 23
  "Lady of Shalott, The", 23
  "Lotos-Eaters, The", 23, **97–100**
  "Mariana", 23
  "Now Sleeps the Crimson Petal", 23
  "Oenone", 23
  "Passing of Arthur, The", 23
  Poems (1833, 1842), 23, 98
  "Tears, Idle Tears", 23
  "Tithonus", 23
  "Ulysses", 23
Terence, 113
texts, dramatic, 104
Thackeray, William Makepeace, 9, 10, **24**
  Henry Esmond, 24
  Newcomes, The, 24
  Pendennis, 24
  Vanity Fair, 24
theatres, 109
  ancient, 113
  Elizabethan and Jacobean, 117; Globe, 117; closing of, 117, 127; later, 109, 128, 137–8
Tolstoy, Count Leo Nikolayevich, 3, 137n
  Anna Karenina, 42
  and George Eliot, 26, 26n, 58
  War and Peace, 58
tragedy
  Aristotle on, 108
  nature of, 108
  revenge, 123–4
Trollope, Anthony, 9, 24, **25**

Barsetshire novels, 25
part-publication of, 61n
political novels, 25
Warden, The, 25
Truffaut, François, *Day for Night*, 43
typescript or printout, for publication,
151–2

unities, the three, 107–8, 129

Vanbrugh, Sir John, 130–1
as architect, 130
Provok'd Wife, The, 130
Relapse, The, **130–1**, 133n
Virgil, 3n, 17n, 92
vocabulary, 143
Vonnegut, Kurt, *Slaughterhouse Five*, 44n

Waugh, Evelyn, 68
Webster, John, 8, 14, 123–5
Duchess of Malfi, The, **123–5**
White Devil, The, 123
Whitman, Walt, 3, 74
Wilde, Oscar, 9, 26, 27, 131
Ballad of Reading Gaol, The, 27
Importance of Being Earnest, The, 27, 132

Picture of Dorian Gray, The, 27
Wilson, A. N., 68
Woolf, Virginia, 3, 9, **29–30**
Between the Acts, 29–30
and interior monologue, 41
and Symbolism, 42n
Voyage Out, The, 29
Wordsworth, William, 3, 9, 14, 15, 19, **20–1**,
78–9, 95–7
Excursion, The, 96
"Intimations of Immortality", 21
Lyrical Ballads, 19, 20, 20n; "Preface" to,
21, 80
"Michael", 21, 97
"Old Cumberland Beggar, The", 21, 97
Prelude, The, 21, 21n, 73, 76, 97
"Resolution and Independence", 21
"Ruined Cottage, The", **95–7**
"Tintern Abbey", 21, 97
Writers' and Artists' Yearbook, The, 152
Wyatt, Sit Thomas, 8, **12–13**

Yeats, William Butler, 9, **28**
from Symbolists to Celtic mysticism, 28
poems, 28
York Play of the Crucifixion, 114